Terrorism

Inside a World Phenomenon

Terrorism
Inside a World Phenomenon

Barry Davies BEM

For my son, Lee

First published in Great Britain in 2003 by
Virgin Books Ltd
Thames Wharf Studios
Rainville Road
London
W6 9HA

ISBN 1 85227 964 8

Plate sections designed by Eric Drewery
Typeset by Phoenix Photosetting, Chatham, Kent
Printed and bound in Great Britain by CPD, Wales

CONTENTS

INTRODUCTION

Perhaps because the term is used so often nowadays, you could be forgiven for thinking of terrorism as a modern phenomenon. In fact, it could be argued that there has always been terrorism. One man's terrorist, after all, is another man's freedom fighter. Any sort of resistance movement is going to be viewed by those against whom they are fighting as a terrorist organisation. Bible stories tell of the Jews struggling for their freedom and, when it became known that a new and powerful leader had arrived, many expected him to be a warrior – a terrorist. What they got, of course, was a man of peace.

Sadly, the shadow of terrorism has never left the biblical lands. The path of modern terrorism can be traced back to the aftermath of World War II and the founding of the state of Israel. Since that time small but decisive actions, executed all over the world in the name of freedom, have dominated the media. Almost all of them have been bloody; all of them have been terrifying. Terrorism has blossomed unabated, reaching its zenith on 11 September with the bombing of mainland America.

For some reason I write the date 11 September with a certain amount of unease. To me the terms used to 'name' this atrocity – 'September the Eleventh', '9/11', call it what you will – do not convey the full horror and deeply disturbing nature of what actually happened. In a single action the world's number one superpower was dealt a devastating blow by a handful of suicidal terrorists. Many argue that there are a variety of reasons why America was caught unawares, with few giving credence to the fact that this was a well-planned military assault. Not only was it brilliantly conceived but it was carried out with precision by dedicated men. The sooner we recognise this fact the better prepared will be our defences against the next one.

Many of us listen to the news and believe that we are winning the war on terrorism – we are not. On 12 October 2002, bombs placed in a car and a van killed 180 people on the holiday island of Bali. Terrorists plan and commit atrocities at will . . . and then we respond. At best our anti-terrorist forces are simply fire-fighting; dealing with the problem after the event. Despite the military power available and money spent by governments, terrorism is here to stay. It is part of life in the twenty-first century.

While this book seeks to provide an overall understanding of world terrorism, when it comes to specific examples there is a strong leaning towards the Palestinian/Israeli conflict. Without doubt, this conflict spawned modern day terrorism and, to a large degree, it remains the focal point of world terrorism. In describing this conflict, as with others, I have tried to show both sides of the problem, offering no allegiance or favouritism to either side.

I hope to show that acts of terrorism, and subsequent state retaliation, only multiply the core problem. Whether violence is used in a terrorist action, or in governmental retaliation, it is the common people who always suffer. Violence only serves to perpetuate a conflict. Innocent victims die; the perpetrators of the violence die; yet their deaths bring no compromise and provide no final solution other than oblivion.

Throughout this carefully researched history, I wish to examine the true nature of modern terrorism from its origins to the predicament we find ourselves in today. I will do this by providing examples whenever possible – true stories that affected the lives of real people. Terrorism, once perceived as nothing more than a few hijackers seizing an aircraft to highlight their grievance, has come of age in the twenty-first century. The terrorists, we are told, are now our most feared enemies. Yet who are these terrorists? Who are these people? What does it mean to you? Who funds the IRA? Why does ETA want its independence? How does HAMAS recruit its endless supply of suicide bombers?

This book also looks at the individual lives of terrorists and the reason terrorist organisations are formed. In simple terms, this book examines where we stand at this moment with regard to world terrorism and how we face this menace in the future.

1: THE HISTORY OF MODERN WORLD TERRORISM

In today's world, no one is innocent, no one is neutral. A man is either with the oppressed or he is with the oppressor. He who takes no interest in politics gives his blessing to the prevailing order, that of the ruling classes and exploiting forces.

George Habash,
Leader of the Popular Front for
the Liberation of Palestine

The battlefields of time are littered with suffering and human debris. Nevertheless, man has learned little from the devastation he brings upon himself. Over the centuries, however, power has passed from one regime or one country to another and slowly the world has become a more settled place. World Wars, like those at the start of the twentieth century, were all but halted by the deployment of nuclear weapons. Yet, while conventional wars diminish, the threat of world terrorism increases. Man still kills and maims to the cry of countless causes and motivations and the scourge of modern terrorism is now upon us. Unlike conventional warfare, terrorist wars cannot be fought out on battlefields. Instead, terrorism is on our streets, in our homes; it therefore poses a much greater threat than anything we have faced in the past. Terrorists now use aircraft as smart bombs to destroy buildings and human suicide bombers to kill and mutilate the innocent. Moreover, terrorists have acquired an intimate knowledge of sophisticated modern weaponry, making the threat of a nuclear, chemical or biological attack on a major population centre almost inevitable.

So what is a terrorist? What does a radical terrorist organisation want? Do we use the word 'terrorist' to describe every act of sadistic intimidation? If so, do we include those same acts carried out by repressive governments? And what distinguishes those who are oppressed and struggling for social or political change from those who perform what we term 'criminal terrorist acts'? Although all acts of terrorism are evil, who determines whether a violent act should be branded 'terrorist'?

All terrorist groups start and exist for a reason. In many cases this reason is strong enough to cross several generations. While most acts of terrorism adopt a similar form of violence, not all forms of terrorism are the same. To understand terrorism we must examine the fundamental mechanics of terrorism, and how terror itself is applied. When faced with dictatorship and oppression, we must all appreciate the justifiable right of every individual to exercise their political will. One could argue that terrorism is man's ultimate resort when all other avenues in the quest for self-determination have failed.

While an act of terrorist violence results in brutal killing and carnage, the motivation that drove the terrorist to commit the atrocity may well have been a deep-seated devotion to a noble cause. In the Bible, when the Israelites fled Egypt they were pursued into and through the waters of the Red Sea which then swallowed up the Egyptian soldiers. To the Israelites this was a miracle, while to the Egyptians this was an atrocity – an act committed by the very deity who preached, 'Thou shalt not kill.' Using God as an example may sound a little extreme but one of the problems we mortals have is assessing the true nature and dangers of terrorism. Terrorism feeds on people's fear and anger. Terrorists acquire ever greater power and influence by nurturing and developing that fear and anger through the use of violence. It is vital, therefore, that we all understand not only the nature of terrorism, but also the profile of a terrorist. Only then can we make a concerted effort to control the violence, quell the fear and anger and neutralise the terrorist threat.

Author's Note: I have spent most of my life fighting terrorism, but I have always found it difficult to define it let alone understand it. Like the rest of us, I have made comments and judgements while ignorant of some very basic facts. The problem for most people is understanding the layered history of each terrorist group as it is defined by its individual struggle. For example, in the conflict between the Israelis and the Palestinians, awareness of their past history prior to 1948 influences comprehension of the situation created by the establishment of modern Israel. I make no apologies for my simplistic version of events, nor do I swear to the dates, but it does clarify and set the scene of how a terrorist conflict can be created.

'Next year in Jerusalem' would end many a Jewish prayer – a mystic dream sustained by religious teachings through the years in the wilderness of dispersion; spoken in the ghettos; silenced by Nazi gas chambers. God's Word had endured for 2000 years. Zion had been promised, and the promise lived on in the hearts of the world's Jews.

Occupying the south-west corner of the ancient Fertile Crescent, the modern state of Israel encompasses a sizeable proportion of what was once called Palestine, named after earlier coastal settlers called the Philistines. The names Israel and Palestine stem from the different peoples who entered the region roughly around the twelfth century BC. The Jews, or the tribe of Israel, believed that the land had been given to them by their god. The Philistines, a people of Greek origin, were also settlers searching for a new homeland. Before the region was Israel or Palestine, it was known as Canaan and was populated by a cultured people. It was the Canaanites who developed a linear alphabet, later converted by the Greeks, which became the basis of western writing symbols.

Around 1000 BC, the Jews wrested control of the land from the Philistines and took over Jerusalem, making it the centre of their religion by building the first temple to their god. The country expanded until around 900 BC when it was divided into two kingdoms; Israel in the north and Judah in the south. From then on various conquering armies occupied both kingdoms. After the conquest by the Babylonians, Persians, and Greeks, an independent Jewish Kingdom was revived. Then came the Romans. Around this time Christianity was born, a religion that was adopted by most of the eastern Roman Empire, and thus Palestine became equally as important for the Christians as it was for the Jews. Indeed, the oldest Christian map in the world, the *mappi a mondi,* which is housed in the English town of Hereford, clearly shows Jerusalem at the centre of the known world.

Around AD 132 the Jews rose up against the Romans in a revolt known as Bar Kokhba. The Jews were crushed in the most brutal fashion, with the Romans slaughtering over half a million of them. The Emperor Hadrian determined to wipe out Judea forever, before scattering the rest of the race to the four corners of the earth. The city where David had sat upon his throne was devastated in a destruction of all that was Jewish. Judea was renamed Syria Palaestina, derived from Israel's ancient enemy, the Philistines. This in turn became anglicised to Palestine. Then, to complicate matters, the Arabs took over the region, bringing with them a new religion, Islam.

Muhammad was born around AD 570 in Mecca, a prosperous trading community that lay on the caravan routes. One of Mecca's great attractions was a large black meteorite, which became the focal point of Islamic religion. Muhammad was a member of the Quraish tribe, which had taken the trading town of Mecca about a century earlier. As an adult, Muhammad preferred his own company and was often found sitting in the surrounding hills meditating. It was here that the Angel Jibril (Gabriel) appeared before him, instructing Muhammad to pass on his words. When he first started to preach the word of God (Allah) he was driven out of Mecca and forced to flee to a nearby oasis which came to be known as Medina. The word Islam means 'submitting to the word of Allah', while those that believe in Allah are called Muslims. It is important to know that Muhammad was a human being who was selected by God (Allah) as his messenger. Before Muhammad died, he stopped briefly in Jerusalem on his way to heaven, tying his horse to the wall and setting foot on a rock on Temple Mount. This act makes the city the third most holy city, equally as sacred to the Muslim faith as it is to the Jews and Christians.

Further turmoil was to engulf the region with the coming of the Crusades, then subjugation by the Turks as part of the Ottoman Empire. Turkish rule lasted for four centuries until eventually, in 1917, the British took the land. Shortly afterwards, following the Balfour Declaration, the state of Israel and a Jewish homeland began to emerge.

So at last the prayers were answered. But the Jewish dream was flawed. In their long absence, the land had been occupied. This was no longer a land without people for a people without land. The Palestinians were still there. Yet the Jews persisted. Ererr Yisrael (land of Israel), the land God granted to them alone, would be re-born under the nation's religion. Yet all the faith in the world is of little consequence if you lack the political clout to turn your dreams into reality. This clout was forthcoming, not just from the British Government, but also from the Americans. It would seem that the Jews had gained political experience in many lands under a great variety of governmental systems during their long exile. In the early 1930s, the Israelis acquired more land in Palestine, purchased with monies provided by American and British Jews. These Arab land sales and Jewish land purchases contributed greatly to the evolution of an Arab landless class. As a result, many peasants had to leave the land and look for work in the cities, or with the Jewish owners of the citrus groves. Consequently, the number of land sales to Jews by smaller Arab landowners, who needed the capital and were willing to sell portions of their land to try to survive the adverse times, increased. The Jewish intention was, clearly, to establish themselves both numerically and territorially within Palestine and, despite actions to stop immigration, they came in vast numbers from Russia and from the tyranny of Nazi Europe.

From the time the Nazis rose to power in Germany in the early 1930s, their relentless persecution of the Jews drove many to migrate to Israel. This mass influx brought bloody protest from the Palestinians, who carried out raids on Jewish settlements. To protect themselves, the Jews raised an army called the Hagana which armed itself and carried out nocturnal counter-attacks on Palestinian bases. The Hagana were joined in 1937 by a revolutionary group known as the Irgun, which also began its own operations. The Irgun advocated terrorist tactics equal to those used by the Arabs, who attacked individual Jews. In three weeks in 1937, Irgun bombs planted in Arab market places killed 77 Arabs. At around the same time, British forces dished out some pretty harsh treatment to the Arabs, with over 100 hanged between 1937 and 1939 and many more killed by British troops. Homes of Palestinian families suspected of harbouring guerrillas were dynamited, a practice established by the Hagana and continued by the Israeli Government to this day. Even when the British Government tried to curb Irgun acts by hanging one of its members for attacking an Arab bus, it seemed to the Jews to be discriminatory – a cynical attempt by the British to try to show the Arabs they were taking an even-handed approach to the conflict. This act, in turn, appears to have encouraged both the Hagana and Irgun to undertake more intensive actions against Arabs.

It was then that events in European politics began to exert even more influence over events in the Middle East. Hitler invaded Czechoslovakia and Nazi and fascist propaganda encouraged Arabs of the Middle East to revolt against the British, thus endangering their strategic position in Egypt and the Suez Canal. The British quickly realised that containing any such rebellion would entail a large number of troops being tied down in the Middle East when they would be desperately needed in Europe. Such considerations led to the issuing of a 1939 white paper which, in a stunning reversal of the British policy, called for restrictions on the Jewish immigration and seemed to guarantee the achievement of an Arab Palestine within 10 years. This was a typical British ploy to use Palestine for its own political ends. What would happen today if all the oil producing countries in the Middle East suddenly turned round and refused to give oil to the West unless they recognised Palestine? Would we then go to war – would we take the oil by force of arms?

An understandable reason for proposing a state of Israel evolved after the Second World War ended. We all felt guilty. Emerging from the extermination camps of the Holocaust came the surviving, displaced Jews of Europe. Israel became the haven for these peoples of many different nationalities, bonded by their race and religious faith. Yet they were different from the Jews who had lived in Palestine prior to the state of Israel. These were not peasant farmers; most had been educated, and collectively possessed a wide range of sophisticated skills, among which were many highly trained soldiers.

So, who granted the Jews their wish and why? Was there no other place on the earth that they would have accepted, some vast tract of empty land in America, Canada, or even Russia? The Jewish leaders pushing the dream so hard both in America and Britain must have at least contemplated the risks of setting up a new state of Israel. In hindsight, was it worth the cost in human lives? Did those rich Jews and friendly politicians wittingly sacrifice hundreds of thousands of people to establish a Western foothold in the

Middle East? History, religion, politics, even feeling sorry for the Jews made sense. Conversely, the creation of Israel meant dispersing another people, the Palestinian Arabs, a people who have as much legal and moral right to Palestine as any Jew. The creation of an independent state of Israel, with a conflicting religion, just had to be asking for trouble. In November 1947 the United Nations divided Palestine, then under British mandate, into Jewish and Arab states. Six months later the British withdrew and, on 14 May 1948, the state of Israel was proclaimed.

So, at the moment of its birth, Israel was fighting for its life. The neighbouring Arab states tried to annihilate the Israelis who, with no other place to go, other than into the sea, fought like savages. But they were not alone; the state of Israel had many friends in the West and many advantages for the Western governments, thus the moral and material backing for Israel was provided. So the terrifying carnage began. Eager to establish firm defensive lines and rid themselves of Palestinians within their midst, terror tactics were used. The first came a month before the declaration of the new Israeli state. On the night of 8 April 1948, a combined Irgun/Stern (Stern was an organisation of Israeli freedom fighters which utilised terrorist tactics) unit killed more than a hundred Palestinian Arabs in the village of Deir Yassin, close to the Jerusalem road. The Israelis lost their heads and in a blood lust killed many non-combatants. Many mainstream Jewish leaders called it utterly repugnant. Yet a similar incident was to happen a few years later.

At 9.30 p.m. on Wednesday 14 October 1953, Israeli troops attacked the Jordanian border village of Qibya, north-west of Jerusalem. Seven hundred regular Israeli troops participated in the attack in which mortars, machine guns, rifles and explosives were used. More than forty houses as well as the school and the village mosque were destroyed. Every man, woman and child found by the Israelis was killed, a total of 75 innocent villagers were murdered in cold blood.

The neighbouring Arab states of Lebanon, Syria, Jordan, Egypt and Iraq rejected both the partition of Palestine and the existence of the new nation. In the war that followed (1948–49), Israel emerged victorious and with its territory increased by one half. Arab opposition continued, however, and full-scale fighting broke out again in 1956 (the Sinai campaign), when Israel, joined by France and Great Britain, attacked Egypt after that country had nationalised the Suez Canal. Intervention by the UN, supported by the United States and the Soviet Union, forced a ceasefire.

In 1964, Egypt's President Nasser helped set up the PLO (Palestine Liberation Organisation). From its shaky start, it was to become the main voice of a homeless people. Most of the Arab nations backed the organisation, funding and equipping its soldiers, known as Al-Fatah. Yasser Arafat was elected overall leader in 1969. The problem was that Arab disunity led to each state constantly bickering with its neighbour. Consequently, fringe and rival groups within the PLO, received separate sponsorship from different Arab countries. On one hand, Egypt would back George Habash's PFLP (Popular Front for the Liberation of Palestine), while Syria supported the Ahmed Jabril group. At times they were friends, and at times they clashed, fighting each other. Yet through all this Yasser Arafat and the PLO have survived. In 1967, in the Six-Day War, Israel responded to Egyptian provocation with air attacks and ground victories. The result was a humiliating defeat for Egypt; and more territorial gains for the Israelis, including the West Bank, from where the PLO continued to launch punitive attacks. The Israelis, as always, responded with lightning raids, this time directed against the PLO leaders.

In 1968 the Israelis found themselves embarking on a new policy, after an Israeli passenger was killed on 26 December in a grenade attack on an El Al airliner at Athens airport. In Israel, the mood was one of frustration. The public seemed to believe that the Israeli security forces did not have any adequate response to the export of Palestinian terrorism from the Middle East to Europe. Israeli Special Forces were landed by helicopter at the International airport just south of the Lebanese capital, Beirut, on 28 December at 9.15 p.m. Undeterred by a gun battle with Lebanese troops, the Israelis blew up thirteen empty civilian aircraft belonging to the

Lebanese Middle East Airlines and other Arab countries. The world was shocked by the audacity of the move and condemned Israel as engaging in what was referred to as 'state terrorism'.

Despite this condemnation, the state of Israel continued to counter all forms of aggression. One such development was the gathering of intelligence on terrorist organisations operating on foreign soil. This was done in conjunction with various Western intelligence agencies working closely with Mossad (the Israeli Intelligence Agency) agents. In 1973, Mossad received excellent information about a plan to fire rockets at an El Al jet at Fiumicino airport in Rome. The information included precise details of the modus operandi, the exact date and the names of the attackers. Mossad issued a warning to the Italian security services, who set an ambush for the terrorists and captured five.

The joy felt by the Israeli intelligence did not last long. Italy, under economic and diplomatic pressure from Libya's Colonel Gaddafi, used the first pretext that came its way to release the five Arabs. They were flown to Tripoli in a low-key operation using an old Italian Air Force C-47 Dakota. On 23 November 1973, barely two weeks after returning from Libya, the same aircraft crashed near Venice. Four Italian military officers, the same men who had flown the terrorists to their Tripoli refuge, were killed. Sabotage was immediately suspected, but could never be proved. Thirteen years later, the former head of Hitler's counter-intelligence service, General Viviani, charged that Mossad had caused the crash. The Italian press said that the Israelis were out to punish the government in Rome for being soft on terrorism.

In the Yom Kippur War of 1973–74, Egypt, Syria and Iraq attacked Israel on the Jewish holy Day of Atonement, catching the Israelis off guard. Israel recouped quickly and forced the Arab troops back from their initial gains, but at great cost to both sides. Again, a ceasefire was imposed. Israel emerged from these conflicts with large tracts of its neighbours' territories, which it refused to surrender without a firm peace settlement. The first real move towards permanent peace came in 1978, when Israeli Prime Minister, Menachem Begin, and Egyptian President, Anwar al-Sadat met at Camp David in America. A peace treaty between

Egypt and Israel was signed in 1979 in Washington DC, and Israel began a phased withdrawal from Sinai, completed in 1982. However, little progress was made in negotiations on autonomy for the Gaza Strip and the West Bank of Jordan. Devoid of any further overt help from the Arab nations, the Palestinians were left to continue the struggle alone.

In 1982 came a massive Israeli attack, aimed at destroying all military bases of the PLO in South Lebanon. Afterwards, a ten-week siege of the Muslim sector of West Beirut, a PLO stronghold, forced the Palestinians to accept a US-sponsored plan whereby the PLO guerrillas would evacuate Beirut and go to several Arab countries which had agreed to accept them. Israeli forces withdrew from Lebanon in 1986. Since then, unrest has continued in the occupied territories with frequent clashes between Arab demonstrators and troops. In the squalid refugee camps of the Arab states the Palestinian refugees waited for vengeance and multiplied so that by the 1980s there were more refugees than there had been forty years earlier. The Arab population of the West Bank, Gaza and East Jerusalem totalled more than a million and a half. Still, most of us in the West were only aware of the struggling Israelis constantly trying to build their new state and defend it at the same time. What we did not see was the plight of the Palestinians and the atrocities committed against them. A state, peopled by those who had escaped oppression, had in turn become the oppressor. The only headlines in the Western press devoted to the Palestinians had been in 1972, when the Palestinians turned their ire upon the world. This fury came in the form of black-hooded murderers, who vented their anger on Israeli athletes during the Munich Olympics, before hijacking a plane to Entebbe. With these events, modern international terrorism had truly begun.

The brief history of the Israeli/Palestinian situation outlined above is intended to demonstrate that the seeds of modern terrorism were sown in Israel during the late 1940s. Some twenty years later these seeds had produced their first blossom. The

THE HISTORY OF MODERN WORLD TERRORISM

1960s saw the start of mass revolution. For the most part the revolutionary fervour belonged to the young. They had found a voice, expressing themselves through a new type of music. Their songs decried the war in Vietnam and the nuclear threat that had hung over America and Europe through the Cold War years. It was an age when individual freedom became more important than the organised authority it challenged. At one end of the scale there was flower power and the peace movement; at the other a hard-core revolution was being established. Organisations such as the Palestinian Liberation Organisation, Germany's Baader-Meinhof, and the Irish Republican Army (IRA) were finding their feet.

Around this time, a new phenomenon surfaced – the arrival of satellite communications, giving the media a global platform. In the past, individual terrorist incidents and atrocities have been isolated, unheard of by much of the world's population. Today, those same incidents are pumped live into millions of homes around the world. Terrorism is news and news is television and both elements have grown in stature. Many of us watch terrorist atrocities as we eat our breakfast; eight people killed by a bomb detonated on a bus; four aid workers slaughtered by unknown African dissidents; twelve hostages taken while touring on a jungle holiday. Sitting in the safety of your home, do you ever wonder who these people are?

While the late 1970s saw a response to terrorism, with many countries forming specialist anti-terrorist teams, the same period also saw the terrorist organisations mature. Although the number of international terrorist attacks decreased, the effectiveness of the attacks increased dramatically. Terrorists were receiving better training and were better organised. This was compounded by the Soviet withdrawal from Afghanistan in 1989, which created a vacuum and provided a new terrorist training ground. Many of the radical Islamic religious groups had sent followers to fight with the Mujaheddin against the Soviets; with the war over, there was a plentiful supply of well-trained fighters. The situation in Afghanistan also helps to explain the dramatic growth in Islamic militancy and its spread throughout the world. As we enter the year

2003 more than 50 per cent of all terrorist acts are carried out by Islamic extremists.

Definitions of Terrorism

Many people have tried to establish a definition of terrorism and while all are (to an extent) correct, none actually expresses how terrorist acts develop. America, in particular, is keen on establishing a firm definition for terrorism. This may be because they wish to find a legal definition to justify retaliation. World terrorism is so diverse that to try and pin a single label on it is dangerous, although many have tried. The following quotes are from four of the world's leading authorities on terrorism.

Terrorism constitutes the illegitimate use of force to achieve a political objective when innocent people are targeted.

Walter Laqueur

Terrorism . . . any type of political violence that lacks an adequate moral or legal justification, regardless of whether the actor is a revolutionary group or a government.

Richard A. Falk

Terrorism can be briefly defined as the systematic use of murder, injury, and destruction or threat of same, to create a climate of terror, to publicize a cause, and to intimidate a wider target into conceding to the terrorists' aims . . .

Paul Wilkinson

Terrorism is the use or threatened use of force designed to bring about political change.

Brian Jenkins

Paul Pillar, former deputy chief of the CIA Counterterrorist Center, defined the four key elements of terrorism.

- It is premeditated – planned in advance, rather than an impulsive act of rage.
- It is political – not criminal, like the violence that groups such as the mafia use to get money, but designed to change the existing political order.
- It is aimed at civilians – not at military targets or combat-ready troops.
- It is carried out by sub-national groups – not by the army of a country.

Again much of this is correct but most of the above points also apply to the Allied effort in World War II. Pillar's definition also begs a number of questions. Why is terrorism premeditated? Why is it political? Why do innocent civilians suffer more than the military?

In the end, we must all arrive at our own definition of terrorism. We cannot impose our own definition on others of differing territorial, social and religious backgrounds. Different nationalities and different cultures will view what is and what is not a terrorist act in different ways. As previously stated, one man's terrorist is another man's freedom fighter.

All the wars of history have shown us that this divergence of ethnic groups provides the human race with untold permutations for conflict. We could argue, therefore, that world terrorism stems from the differing political, social and religious beliefs of which we are all part. From the moment we are born we become involved; it is simply the order of things.

Terrorism only exists within the human social framework and individuals within that framework define and execute terrorist acts. In order to prevent terrorism we must first understand the human element. People do not just become terrorists or anti-hijack experts; there is always a basic cornerstone on which all lives turn.

George Habash and Wadi Haddad

As the British left Palestine and the bitter internal war started, many Palestinian families were forced to flee their homeland. At the height of the initial fighting, the Israelis drove out many innocent non-Jewish families, often at the point of a gun, while those that would not leave were murdered. Forced to live in refugee camps where conditions fell to one of daily survival, many wished to return to Palestine. Among these were two young men, George Habash and Wadi Haddad.

> Author's Note: I mention these two men for good reason. They were both responsible for the emergence of modern-day terrorism, not just its concept but also its evolvement. They conceived the idea of hijacking. They sought out and co-ordinated the various terrorist factions around the world. They built specialist training schools where terrorist tactics could be refined. They may not have defined terrorism, but they certainly refined it.

Born in Lydda, Palestine, in 1925, George Habash was the son of a wealthy grain merchant whose family were practising Christians. Towards the end of the 1940s, George Habash, like so many young hopefuls of the area, was attending class at the American University in Beirut. He was studying to be a doctor of medicine and was an intelligent man working hard at his studies. In May 1948, aged 23, he was nearly ready to leave the university and continue his dream to start up a clinic on his own. In that same month of May, however, the British Army withdrew from Palestine and, almost immediately, the fighting started. Within months, his family were driven into exile. The Israelis had taken over completely, even to the point of changing the name of the place where he was born. It had been renamed Lod and one day it would boast a major international airport.

The memories of what George Habash saw and heard at those traumatic times were to affect him deeply. Finally, he graduated in the early 1950s and, almost at once, started a clinic for the poor in Amman. One of the other co-founders of the clinic was another doctor like himself, also a Greek Orthodox Palestinian, Dr Wadi Haddad. Wadi Haddad was the son of a teacher and was born in Safad, in Galilee, just before World War II. By the age of nine, he too had become a refugee and was forced with his family to lead a peripatetic life. The difference between the two men lay in their intellect; Habash was a brilliant student, whereas Haddad had struggled and qualified with difficulty. By profession and from their training, both men were committed to the preservation of life but the great trauma of their young lives haunted and embittered them.

Ultimately they would both completely reverse their strongly held beliefs of putting the sanctity of life before death, and put death before life.

At the start of the PFLP George Habash is quoted as saying, 'I speak here with the authority of someone who really knows his society and the world it is living in. We have to train a totally new kind of militant.' He went on to say, 'As regards the hijackings, we have always done everything to ensure the safety of the passengers. No Westerner has been harmed in any way. In other words our operations have been carried out flawlessly, and as a whole they provide evidence that our organisation is honourable. Of course, we have violated international law – but what of international law in 1949, when Israel absolutely refused to return the Palestinian refugees to their homes? Though the West may have been shocked by it, the hijacking of planes was popular among Palestinians and the Arab masses in general – and to us that matters a lot. The struggle is far from being a purely military one; it is psychological too, and we have to raise the morale of the masses while at the same time harass the Israelis.' (Quoted from *The Palestinian Resistance*)

The 1960s were to become a decade when revolutionary rhetoric was in plentiful supply throughout the world. This was an era of extremes and dreams. Terrorism, death and disruption at one end of the spectrum and hippies, flower power, peace and freedom of speech at the other. In the melting pot of the Middle East, Habash and Haddad dreamed of rebellion. Both were educated, middle-class men who had been displaced from the land of their birth and together they threw down the gauntlet. In the years to follow, Habash became so embittered that he discarded his religious beliefs and replaced his religion with Marxist concepts. His medical equipment he exchanged for an arsenal of guns and he created the Popular Front for the Liberation of Palestine. Although Habash continued to run his clinic for the poor, he was forced to move it from Amman to Damascus. Then, due to a change in political philosophy in the area, coupled with his own belligerence towards the local authorities, he was forced to move back to Beirut. In 1968 he was arrested and imprisoned by the Syrians for plotting to overthrow the current regime.

During his imprisonment, Dr Wadi Haddad, Habash's co-conspirator, organised a daring escape plan to rescue his friend from a high security prison. The rescue plan succeeded and the attendant drama reflected well on the newly formed PFLP. With the example of such brave deeds, the ranks of the PFLP swelled from five hundred militants to three and a half thousand active members and won the support of many ordinary Palestinians. George Habash spelt out the PFLP policy in very simple terms. They were against the Jews and their re-establishing a Jewish state in Palestine; they were against Israel, and they were against imperialism. Habash warned that his battleground would ignore the borders and frontiers of the world and his soldiers would go forth and create death and destruction without limitations. 'Our enemy is not Israel, full stop,' said Habash, 'Israel is backed by imperialist forces.'

George Habash became the thinker and philosopher behind the PFLP and his message was the driving force behind the PFLP. He was the intellectual whose reasoned arguments convinced others to follow him and take up the cry of 'Free Palestine!' Haddad, on the other hand, was the tool, the powerful, revolutionary, active partner; the doer of Habash's dreams. His terrorist activities gave Habash the platform to publicise his beliefs, aimed at focusing world and, in particular, Israeli attention on the grievances of the people of Palestine.

After members of the PFLP had firebombed a Marks and Spencer's store in London on 18 July 1969, George Habash is quoted as having said, 'When we set fire to a store in London, those few flames are worth the burning down of two kibbutz.' Although he made these provocative statements, George Habash was less of an extremist than Wadi Haddad. Habash preferred to carry the verbal message of the Palestinians' disruption around the world.

Both George Habash and Wadi Haddad between them were responsible for the creation of the international alliance that carried the first campaigns of terror into Europe in the early 1970s. Because of the publicity generated by their violence, the PFLP created a growing awareness of the situation concerning Palestine So effective was the propaganda that Habash found himself under the scrutiny of Mossad, the Israeli intelligence agency, who tried several times to kill both Haddad and Habash.

On one occasion, in the summer of 1973, the Israeli secret service were given a tip-off from a field operative working in the Lebanon that George Habash would be flying from Beirut to Baghdad on board a Middle East Airlines (MEA) Caravel, flight 006. In order to settle a lot of old scores, the Israeli Prime Minister, Golda Meir, authorised the air force to intercept the aircraft. Minutes after taking off, MEA flight 006 was confronted by two unmarked Mirage fighters which, on approaching the airliner, ordered it to follow them or be shot down. The MEA captain complied with these terse instructions. The planes flew south and were eventually forced to land at Ben-Gurion airport in Israel. As it slowed to a stop, Israeli soldiers leaped aboard the aircraft and searched it. It soon became apparent that George Habash was not on board, so the passengers were allowed to continue their dramatically interrupted flight to Baghdad, Iraq. The Mossad agent, a woman, who had proffered the information was later caught by the Beirut security services and handed over to the PLO, where she spent six years of hell in the hands of her captors until she was exchanged for two PLO members.

George Habash was also instrumental in setting up guerrilla training organisations. The camps where the young fighters were taught the tactics of terrorism and guerrilla warfare provided the forum for the conception and creation of transnational terrorism. One of the new tactics to emerge was the hijacking of international commercial aircraft. The mechanics were simple. A few hijackers with a small amount of weapons held to ransom the lives of hundreds of people. The aircraft also gave them freedom of movement to almost any country on the planet. More importantly, win or lose, it captured the attention of the world's media.

The first of the Palestinian hijacks occurred during the summer of 1968, when an El Al Boeing 707 flying from Rome to Tel Aviv was hijacked to Algiers. The Israeli passengers and crew were imprisoned for two months. Then, in December of that year, another El Al Boeing 707 was attacked. As the plane took off from Athens airport, the sound of grenades and sub-machine-gun fire was heard by the passengers. As a result of this assault, one of the passengers was killed, but the attackers were arrested. In February 1969 another El Al 707 was machine-gunned when it was preparing to take off from Zurich for Tel Aviv. The co-pilot was killed and five of the passengers were wounded. One of the attackers was killed on the plane by an Israeli guard; the surviving three terrorists were sentenced to prison. In both these incidents the terrorists who were imprisoned were released when further action was taken by the PFLP in future hijacks.

By now, airline passengers were becoming nervous and avoiding flights whenever possible. In August 1969 the PFLP, led by an armed female terrorist, again hijacked a plane, this time a TWA flight from Rome to Tel Aviv. The plane was taken to Damascus where all the 213 passengers were released except for two Israelis. These men lived in fear of being assassinated until they were exchanged for two Syrian pilots. The flight deck was then rigged with explosives and the plane was destroyed.

The above story describes two men born of Palestinian parents in a social environment that was, at the very least, chaotic. Both where intelligent and politically motivated, both possessed the ability to lead and direct others. Neither was Muslim and the motivation for their terrorist actions persists to this day and will continue for many years to come.

Paul Taylor (pseudonym)

By comparison to the lives of Haddad and Habash the social surroundings of Paul Taylor differed greatly. Paul Taylor was born just as the Second World War was coming to an end. The place of his birth was Wem in the beautiful English countryside of north Shropshire. He was raised by a poor but very loving family; all his early memories were happy ones. The family was large, swelling to four brothers and two sisters. This was not uncommon among the farming community of which he was a part. School came and went and, at the unworldly age of 15, he left without achieving a single certificate in any subject and went to work in a butcher's shop.

The proprietor's name was Joseph Coleman. Together with his wife and Paul, the new apprentice, they ran a keen little business.

Normally, as Mrs Coleman served in the shop, Mr Coleman would instruct Paul on the finer points of dissection and disembodiment of butchery and, as he worked, Mr Coleman would relate thrilling stories of his army days. As with all his stories they told of wonderful adventures full of daring deeds. These stories were the seeds that germinated in Paul Taylor's mind and led him to become a soldier. Despite the objections of his family, he ran away and joined the army. Paul's first regiment was the Welsh Guards. After basic training he was posted first to Germany and then to Aden.

Aden was a shipping port of some importance and had been under British control since 1839. In 1962, the Soviet Union supported internal strife in neighbouring Yemen, which led to the overthrow of the ruling Imam. Britain covertly supported the Imam, who was now operating out of Aden. The problem was that the Yemen laid territorial claims to Aden. Such a situation leads to what governments like to call 'a confrontation'. To soldiers, confrontation is loosely translated as action.

Paul Taylor's first taste of action came when the 'recce' platoon, of which he was a part, was stationed up country close to a small Arab village called Al-Mella. The platoon's assignment was to safeguard the Royal Engineers who were constructing a road. Several times the camp at Al-Mella came under 'Adoo' (the Arabic word for enemy) fire, but most of it was stand-off stuff. That is to say, they would sneak up on the British, mostly at night, and from a range of three hundred metres blast away for all they were worth; the British in turn would happily respond.

One day, while enjoying a rest day, Paul and other members of the platoon were playing volleyball on the concrete pitch which also served as a helicopter landing pad. The game was interrupted by the arrival of an unexpected incoming helicopter. That helicopter was to change his life. He stood watching idly as the chopper came to rest and two soldiers leaped down from the doorway. But these soldiers were different. They were irregularly dressed but looked intensely professional. Above all, they operated with an air of supreme confidence. Both soldiers reached into the chopper and between them pulled out the body of a dead enemy. Then they unceremoniously dragged it to the nearby medical tent.

They did the same with a second body. After a few moments, they re-entered the helicopter and departed. That is when Paul Taylor first heard those magic letters, SAS. He just had to join.

The Special Air Service (SAS) was formed during World War II. Today it stands as the premier military unit in the world. To join the SAS a professional soldier must endure what is known as SAS selection. This course is not just hard – it's very nearly impossible! Selection takes place mostly in the Brecon Beacons of South Wales and, although not high mountains, they are treacherous. Exposed and battered by constant weather changes, the threat of hypothermia is seldom far away for the soldiers, and many have suffered this slow death. There is no way to explain the full impact of the six-month course, but suffice to say that only a handful ever pass. For those who do make it, there is untold adventure. There is also a high risk of premature death. Paul Taylor's military life was full of minor skirmishes from the jungles of South America to the deserts of the Middle East. The SAS were also chosen to form Britain's first anti-terrorist unit, of which Paul became a part. To this day he is proud of his 18 years with the SAS.

Comparing the life of Paul Taylor, raised in peaceful surroundings in rural England and choosing to become a dedicated, highly trained soldier, with those of Haddad and Habash, who suffered hardship and deprivation on their way to becoming terrorists, serves to illustrate the difference between those on either side of a terrorist situation. It is not simply a matter of good versus evil. While Paul Taylor is motivated by the defence of liberty and the way of life he enjoyed as a boy, the terrorists inevitably fight for their own version of Paul's idyll. The British army, like all volunteer armies, relies upon those like Paul, whose background and upbringing make them ideal material to be shaped into professional soldiers. A terrorist organisation relies upon those like Haddad and Habash.

As well as the lifestyles into which we are born, there are many other factors that exert a serious influence on our chosen way of life. One of those factors is the type of government in our country or the nature of the ruler who holds power in our country. Throughout history there have been those in power who have used their position to cause suffering and death to others. The principle applies equally to individual and state alike – the abuse of power in any form creates fear, and fear is the lifeblood of terrorism.

Fear is the main weapon in the terrorist arsenal. Terrorists use fear to control and discipline their own followers and supporters almost as much as they do to achieve their goals. In the words of Chairman Mao Tse-tung, 'Kill one, frighten a thousand.' Fear can be many things; pain, fatigue, boredom, loneliness, cold, thirst or hunger can all generate fear. Fear of death or injury is the terrorist's stock in trade. Spreading fear among their enemies means trading on the fear of the unknown that affects most ordinary people. Where will the next bomb go off? Will I receive a letter containing anthrax in the post? Dispensing fear makes the terrorist successful; it is the main consideration when planning an attack, as fear guarantees the attention of the media.

In war, targets are selected for their strategic and economic importance. While terrorists may also target these, their main strategy is to perpetrate acts with a high shock value and to spread fear and alarm among the general populace of their enemy. The deaths of innocent people, especially children, or the destruction of a hospital, will all create terror.

Yet fear itself is not our enemy. Fear is a normal and necessary emotion which prepares the body for flight or fight during times of danger. Fear releases high levels of the hormone adrenaline into the system to help it cope with the greater demands about to be put upon it. Admitting to your fear helps you face the problem and the adrenaline released provides the body with greater strength and stamina, reduced pain sensation and the ability to think more clearly and act in a co-ordinated manner. The best defence against terrorist-created fear is to reject its influence on our own behaviour. Neither must we forget that all terrorists are human; fear affects them in the same way it does the rest of us.

Author's Note: I have faced death on several occasions. No matter how committed, at the final moment fear of death is a very real emotion. Yet often there is nowhere else to go; nothing else we can do. At that moment fear actually has no meaning. Ask any soldier

> who has been tried and tested in combat, any fireman or policeman who has walked away from certain death – they will tell you. Sometimes you simply have to make a stand. Fear has its own borders; at the point of death fear ceases to exist.

One of the major influences on any society or culture is religious belief. Different religions have formed into blocks around the world. Some of these blocks share many common elements of everyday life and it is within these social groups that we can study the root causes of terrorism.

Ask me what I believe in and I will tell you it is my fellow man. I have lived for 57 years and fought in many wars where the background hatred has been religiously motivated. I am not a Muslim, Hindu, Buddhist or Catholic, therefore I cannot say how the people of those religions feel towards their fellow man. Neither am I a real Christian. True, I grew up in a Christian society and attend such Christian ceremonies as weddings and funerals, but in my heart I have seen the stupidity of blind obedience to religious dogma and the deaths it can cause. Yet, despite all this death and pain I have seen so much good come out of the human race. The struggle of one human to save the life of another, for example, knows no bounds and I believe that most humans are basically good. Where humans fail, they fail through fear and the generation of fear.

Territorial blocks work in much the same way as the religious blocks and are also a factor at the root of terrorism. Tribes, states, countries and continents have fought each other since man has walked the earth. Terrorist struggles over territory rarely relate to entire continents. In the main, terrorist organisations act only to regain something which has been denied them or taken from them through the imposition of unjust laws or under force of arms.

For example, the IRA seeks to reunite the whole of Ireland, while ETA wishes to have a homeland separate from that of Spain or France. Some terrorist organisations simply wish to remove a government that they see as corrupt and unjust. Many of these organisations harvest real sympathy for their cause both at home and abroad. Some also receive direct or indirect help from foreign governments who are also opposed to the established regime.

Media and its Effect on Terrorism

The problem with terrorism is that, although global in profile, the incidents are isolated and do not always directly affect the mass. Terrorist actions, however, do add to the overall fear felt by the mass. Modern communications have done more than anything else to promote terrorism as an effective way of waging war. Without television or radio, it would have been months, even years before some countries heard about the attacks on America on 11 September. In reality, the satellites enabled most of the planet to watch live as the horror unfolded. By the same token, the media are also a siren, a warning that such acts are taking place.

Most terrorist acts are extremely violent and violence is exceedingly newsworthy. While we do not condemn the media for their transmission of world events it is true to say that they are unwittingly partly responsible for the escalation of terrorism.

Pictures of the bombing of a bus on the streets of Tel Aviv evoke a variety of feelings. Jewish people around the world will feel great sympathy for what has happened to their fellow Jews and hatred for the perpetrators of the atrocity, while the same pictures received in Baghdad will cause some of the viewers to rejoice. The rest of us will watch and think, 'Thank God it's not us.' Hearing the news may well trigger subconscious thoughts about religion or social values. For example, does seeing a traditionally dressed Muslim on the street lead to an association of that man's presence in your country with the threat you have just seen on television? Does the manner of his dress annoy you? The point is, what feelings has the media deposited in your mind? Is their broadcast responsible for generating fear and hatred? Equally, are the news media showing any degree of responsibility in their general description of the terrorist threat? Should they be more considerate of the fact that they have the power to spread great fear and alarm? The media may well promote a public understanding and acceptance of what individual governments consider to be terrorism, but the fear and alarm created by sensationalist reporting gives governments the excuse, perhaps even the public mandate, for extreme retaliation against acts of terrorism. Do we then support this retaliation out of fear or hatred based on reported 'facts' (not always unbiased or objective) presented by some ambitious TV journalist?

The flip side of the mass media coin is, of course, that the rapid expansion of all forms of media since the end of World War II has given previously isolated communities that did not have access to radio, cinema or television, a window on the rest of the world. Can you imagine the effect on the poor and starving as they listen to, and watch the rich Westerners who live in nice homes and send their children to school while mother strolls slowly around the packed shelves of the local supermarket? These social and economic inequalities are the embers that create and drive the fire of terrorism.

Terrorists and the Government

Since 11 September, America might see itself as the victim of terrorism, yet this same nation is equally guilty of terrorism and vicious, heartless violence. There are, as we have seen, many definitions of terrorism and many reasons why terrorism exists and the closer you look, the harder it is to differentiate between the 'legitimate' activities of the state and the criminal atrocities of the terrorist organisation. How do the actions of FARC (the Armed Revolutionary Forces of Colombia) differ from those of the American CIA? You can't just say we are good and they are evil. Is the pilot of a bomber dispensing his payload over Afghanistan any different from the HAMAS suicide bomber? They both kill innocent people. The difference is one of intention. But what happens when the 'good guys' deliberately commit acts of terrorism? We return again to the definition of terrorism. How can we define that which is terrorism when the execution of military actions taken by governments is, in the expression of violence, equal to or greater than that of any terrorist act?

War is an act undertaken by two or more factions. A state of war can be declared and various 'rules of war', many of which are defined by the famous Geneva Convention, come into effect. It is a recognisable act in as much as we are clear about its definition. Although most people can recognise an act of terrorism when they see it, its definition is not universally clear to everyone. Some will view a bomb blast as terrorism, while others will see it as rebellion or resistance. The American State Department defines terrorism as 'premeditated, politically motivated violence perpetrated against non-combatant targets by sub-national groups or clandestine agents, usually intended to influence an audience.' Yet that very definition could be used against the American Government for it, too, has carried out operations that fall perfectly within such a definition. While America might claim these as legitimate military covert operations, others, especially those on the receiving end would see their actions as state-sponsored terrorism.

One example. In 1997, the CIA released 1,400 pages of secret files on their first covert operation in Latin America. This operation has been such a success that it became the blueprint for similar CIA operations and many of the techniques are still used today. Today, in an atmosphere of openness, everyone is free to examine these documents and they should for they expose the horrific details of what we would now call 'acts of terrorism'.

In 1952 Jacobo Arbenz Guzman became the second legally elected president of Guatemala. His first task was to change the rules under which a minority elite had previously governed. These changes included the recognition of the Guatemalan Communist Party and some serious land reforms that threatened US companies, like the powerful United Fruit Co. America did not see the democratically elected President as an ally and therefore set about organising his downfall. This task was given to the CIA and a plan of action was developed that included assassination plots and sabotage. The CIA planned to attack Jacobo Arbenz Guzman from all angles, but mainly the campaign was aimed at undermining his support from the Guatemalan military. Arbenz needed the military in order to control the country. The CIA succeeded and in 1954 Arbenz relinquished power to the military, the latter seen by America as the only power capable of maintaining order. The military regime became nothing more than dictatorship – do as we say or you will be killed. Whenever a small insurgency developed, Guatemala's US-equipped and trained military would let loose a savage wave of repression that left thousands of peasants dead. This oppression has lasted for forty years, totally destroying the fabric of Guatemalan society and causing the death or disappearance of almost a quarter of a million people. This type of story is not new. Ask any Special Forces soldier and he will tell you that they have all participated in something similar.

> *As a CIA operative, I trained Guatemalan exiles in Honduras to invade their own country and unseat the elected president . . . The coup I helped engineer in 1954 inaugurated an unprecedented era of intransigent military rule in Central America. Generals and colonels acted with impunity to wipe out dissent and garner wealth for themselves and their cronies . . . Later I realized we weren't fighting communism at all, we were fighting the people.*

> Philip Roettinger,
> retired US Marine Corps colonel and CIA operative

Types of Terrorism

Terrorism is not new. In seventh century India, many a passer-by would be grabbed and strangled by the Thuggee (hence the word Thug) in full view of the public. Centuries before that, many a Roman citizen would find themselves prisoner of the Jewish zealots, who had a terrible habit of cutting the throats of their victims, again in public. During the eleventh century the 'assassins', a drug-crazed Shiite sect would hide along the routes frequently used by their enemy, prior to ambush and murder. Similar acts can be traced to all continents throughout history, most of which were carried out to instil a sense of fear within the local community.

Terrorists' aims are as diverse as the terrorist groups. In the main, the groups can be identified as left wing, right wing, nationalist, state-sponsored, anarchist and religious. In many cases individual terrorist groups can fall into several of these categories.

Nationalist terrorism seeks either to reunite a divided land, or liberate the people of a subjugated country. These groups are the most successful of the terrorist organisations. While the government in power may refer to them as terrorists, many, especially their own countrymen, see them as freedom fighters. The acts carried out by such groups are in general, quite calculated, taking into account the consequences and response from their supporters. Any violence will be designed to grab world media attention without alienating too much of the support either at home or abroad. Many nationalist terrorist groups have caused sufficient impact to have eventually defeated the opposing regime. The Palestine Liberation Organisation, Irish Republican Army and the Tamil Tigers all fall under the banner of nationalist terrorism. Many groups do not seek to impose their rule on the whole country but merely a part of it, as with the Basque Separatists of Spain. Other nationalist groups have conspired to rid themselves of colonial nations – the Irgun fighting the British (1940s) in Palestine is a good example.

There are about fifty international terrorist groups currently active around the world; of these almost half are religiously motivated. That is to say, they wish to impose their religious beliefs upon virtually anyone who opposes or fails to submit to them. The type of religion they represent can vary from almost any of the major religions to small, unknown cults. All are extremely dangerous. The danger lies in their fanaticism. Nationalist terrorism is a basic struggle over land and the right to rule that land and its people. By comparison, the religious terrorists often pursue a vision of divine will. They seek total submission to a specific code of religious beliefs. To achieve this impossible aim, religious terror groups will resort to attacking just about any target using horrendous violence against anyone who is not an associate of their order.

Osama bin Laden's Al-Qaida network is a prime example of religious terrorism. Prior to the war in Afghanistan, the religious fervour that had been stirred up there was largely contained within the Afghan borders and it was the ordinary Afghani who was forced to endure its excesses. Women in particular suffered under the archaic religious laws. Just as terrorists use fear to control their own supporters, so too do they use religion. HAMAS, the Palestinian Sunni Muslim organisation, uses religion in a most sinister way.

State-sponsored terrorism normally involves organisations

which have allowed themselves to be manipulated either by a foreign government that supports their cause, or by their own government. These terrorist groups can be covertly trained and equipped in order to fight the enemies of the country without the government appearing to get its hands dirty. At one stage, the Chinese Red Guard under Mao operated in this way – the state could distance itself from the terrorist acts the group committed. Another example was the Iranian Government's use of allegedly autonomous young militants in 1979.

On 4 November 1979 militant Islamic students stormed the US Embassy in Tehran, taking 52 American citizens as hostages. The Iranian Government did nothing to stop the students and even condoned their actions. Relations between the American and Iranian Governments declined as President Jimmy Carter ordered a complete embargo of Iranian oil together with other economic sanctions. As the standoff continued and negotiations for the hostages' release failed, the US severed diplomatic relations with Iran. Later that month, Carter authorised a top-secret mission, a military operation aimed at freeing the hostages. Both diplomatic and military endeavours floundered in the continuing state of chaos in Iran. The military option had been under constant consideration since the embassy had been attacked. One of the main problems was the remoteness of Tehran from any available US bases. The plan finally centred on a surprise raid by Delta Force. The rescue attempt failed (see Chapter 5).

Terrorism in Perspective

While we might understand the reasons for terrorism or individual terrorist acts, we must also view terrorism in perspective. Terrorism, and international terrorism, has now become part of our everyday lives. It appears on every continent and in almost every country. But so do many other causes of death. Some forty thousand Americans die each year as a result of gun-related violence, while a similar number are killed on American roads. Efforts by the US Government to reduce these figures have been largely ineffective. The politically powerful 'gun lobby' vigorously defends Americans' constitutional right to bear arms – and the right to drive freely on the public highway is defended just as vehemently. Most states in America have, in fact, increased the speed limit for traffic over the years, adding an additional four hundred deaths each year to the toll. While they are viewed as unfortunate, society seems somehow willing to accept these deaths.

If these deaths are to be viewed differently from those caused by terrorism, perhaps we should ask ourselves why? Is the death of a shop clerk, shot in a grocery store robbery in a poor area of America, considered a local hazard? Does the fact that a drunk driver kills your son or daughter simply rank as a terrible mishap? It could be that society is willing to accept these deaths because they are seen as individual acts of misfortune, and the misfortune of the few is acceptable in order to preserve the civil liberties of the masses.

Acts of terrorism, on the other hand, are not committed with the intention of simply causing misfortune to individuals; they are committed to instil fear and threaten the civil liberties of the masses. The death toll from terrorism in America may be less than that from firearms offences, but it is not the number of deaths that matter – it is the act of terrorism itself. The 40,000 who die on America's roads each year do not deter motorists from taking to the highway. The atrocity on 11 September, however, made millions of people decide that air travel was too dangerous. Several international airlines dependent on US business went bust. The holiday and travel industry on both sides of the Atlantic suffered a major recession. The fear generated by the destruction of the World Trade Centre had social and economic consequences of which the terrorists could only have dreamed. Because the consequences can be so far-reaching, the more audacious terrorist acts become, the harder established society will fight to prevent them.

This does not mean to say that terrorism will not reach the stage where the death count itself is significant. We once envisaged terrorist groups using nuclear and biological weapons, killing not thousands, but hundreds of thousands. That vision has never been closer to becoming reality.

Casualties of Terrorism

Terrorists target the innocent, the unsuspecting – soft targets. For many it is simply a matter of being in the wrong place at the wrong time, as with the victims of the Bali bombing. The following two examples provide a brief insight into how the innocent become the victims of terrorism.

In July 1973, it was believed that Ali Hassan, a Black September leader and organiser of the Munich Olympics massacre, had been tracked down to the small town of Lillehammer in Norway. The Israelis immediately assembled and dispatched a hit team to Norway. Using an old photograph they were convinced that they had located Ali Hassan, also known as the Red Prince. Two days later, on a Saturday evening, they shadowed their victim as, together with a blonde Norwegian girl, he left the local cinema. The couple proceeded to catch a local bus which took them to their flat on the outskirts of Lillehammer.

Author's Note: I interviewed Torill Bouchiki about the assassination of her husband, Ahmed, and this is the story in her own words. She was seven months pregnant at the time.

We left the cinema and walked down to the bus stop. At this stage the only thing I can recall is that Ahmed spoke of his brief conversation with another Arab he had met in the town; neither of us thought any more about it. The bus drove out of town, to the wooded outskirts, where we got off at the stop opposite our block of flats. As the bus continued up the hill we crossed the road, heading for the small gravel drive that led to the ground floor doors. We had gone no more than twenty metres when, from behind us, there was a loud bang. We both stopped, turning to see what had caused the noise. We had not noticed the car that had rolled down the hill towards us, braking almost parallel; but the slamming of the door made us look. A man climbed out of the near side while, at the same time, a woman got out of the other side. I thought, maybe they are looking for directions, but then Ahmed stepped away from me, crying out, 'No! No!'

Then I saw the bright flashes coming from both the man and the woman. They were so close, but I couldn't hear any noise. Shocked, I watch as Ahmed's body twitched, before falling to the ground. I dropped to the ground, hugging my arms around my swollen belly, waiting for death to come. The man stopped firing, but the woman walked up to Ahmed, who by this time had rolled over onto his belly and was trying to crawl away, she deliberately fired two bullets into the back of his neck. Then they were gone. To this day, if I close my eyes, I see it as if it was happening all over again.

Listening to Torill, and watching her expressions, I felt sad. It was her sadness that I felt. She had suffered so much with the loss of Ahmed, but the sadness did not come from that, it came from the loss of love, stolen from her. Two weeks after his death, very pregnant, she was forced to return to work in order to support herself. I wonder if the Mossad assassins would like to go and see the damage they have caused to an innocent family.

The hit team returned to Oslo and reported their success to Israel. The Mossad members who had actually pulled the triggers left the country that night, while the rest of the team planned to leave next morning. Next morning, however, six of them were caught. Although they were held for questioning and admitted to having made a mistake in murdering the wrong man, their prison sentences were only two years – because they were Mossad. While admitting their mistake, they never paid a penny in compensation.

In June 1978, intelligence indicated that an IRA team was to firebomb the post office depot in Belfast. An SAS team was inserted, comprising of a reaction group in a parked van and an OP (Observation Post) in a nearby house. The OP had a clear view of the small alley that ran to the side of the post office compound where vehicles and utilities were housed. The compound was protected by a high fence and it was thought that the IRA might try to climb this in order to gain access.

After several days, the reaction group were moved from the van to a small thicket of shrubs close by the alley, with several cut-off groups secreted around the compound. On the night of 21 June the SAS soldier in the OP, together with a member of Special Branch, observed several men enter the alley and stop. Almost immediately one of the men threw a small satchel over the compound fence, at which time the ambush was sprung in front of them. Two of the IRA members were about to throw more satchel bombs over the compound fence, whereupon the SAS opened fire. Two were killed instantly and the third as he tried to run back down the alley. The men were later named as Jacki Mealy, Jim Mulnenna and Dennis Brown.

This sounds like a successful operation, and it was, but at that moment a further two men walked into the alley and again the SAS called out a challenge. One man obeyed and thrust his hands into the air; the other made a run for it. He was shot with a single bullet. As the situation cleared, it turned out that the two men were just returning from the pub and had accidentally walked straight into the firefight between the IRA and the SAS. Had the man, a Protestant by the name of William Hanna, remained still after the challenge he would be alive today. His reason for running was fear. He had been celebrating his recent release from jail and thought the men, who were dressed in civilian clothes and brandishing guns, were members of the IRA out to get him.

The Terrorist Response to Peace

For the past forty years the direct, confrontational approach to terrorism has gone hand in hand with genuine efforts to establish a lasting peace. In recent years, the Clinton administration in America contributed a great deal to the peace process, with the US making great strides to establish peace between two sets of major warring factions, the Israelis and the Palestinians; and the British and the IRA.

The first sign of a possible Israeli/Palestinian peace settlement came in December 1992 when a secret meeting took place at a hotel in central London. Yair Hirschfeld, a Middle East history professor, broke Israeli law by talking to Ahmed Kriah, head of the PLO's economics department. The meeting lasted only a few hours, and little was accomplished other than that they had confirmed their mutual desire for peace. But it did not end there; the meetings went on in secret, until they were to produce the biggest breakthrough in Middle East negotiations since Anwar Sadat made peace with Menachem Begin in 1979.

Both Kriah and Hirschfeld were acquainted with members of the Norwegian Institute for Applied Social Science, which had sociologists and scientists studying living conditions in the West Bank and Gaza Strip. Hirschfeld contacted Terje Roed Larsen, head of the institute, who pressed his government contacts at home and came back with encouraging news. 'If you need our support,' Larsen told Hirschfeld, 'we'll get the Norwegian government to give you all the facilities you need.'

The peacemakers jumped at the chance. Hirschfeld and Kriah, headed for Oslo in January. During the next eight months, they met 14 times in sessions lasting two to three days. Arriving on separate flights and ushered through the airport in secret so they would not be recognised, the delegates were escorted at high speed by the Norwegian police to rendezvous points in and outside the capital.

Although it was clear that neither of the men were acting officially, merely exploring avenues, both kept in constant contact with their respective administrations. The first question asked by the Israelis was whether the PLO figures were speaking for Yasser Arafat. When they believed that they were, Prime Minister Rabin ordered that a close, but still unofficial, eye be kept on what was being called the 'Oslo Channel'. By then, the Knesset had repealed the law prohibiting Israelis from meeting with the PLO.

Eventually, a draft proposal was worked out; a proposal designed to wear down old animosities. It was interesting enough to gain some real credibility, convincing both Arafat, who was in Tunis, and Rabin in Jerusalem that the proposal had been well thought out. Still, countless revisions kept the negotiators haggling for weeks until, drafted and redrafted, the proposal reached an acceptable state for discussion.

The Israelis informed the Americans of the peace initiative via Secretary of State Warren Christopher, who immediately telephoned the President. Although the US had knowledge of several such peace initiatives, they where surprised at how far this one had progressed. The Clinton administration gave its direct support, congratulating both sides for their persistence in pursuing a peaceful settlement.

By 1994, the Oslo Accord between Arafat and Yitzhak Rabin had created a framework through which Israel would trade land for peace and negotiate a final agreement. Oslo envisaged the Israelis' progressively transferring portions of the occupied West Bank and Gaza Strip to the control of an interim body called the Palestinian Authority. For their part in the Oslo peace agreement, Yasser Arafat and Yitzak Rabin of Israel received the Nobel Peace Prize.

After years of conflict and the loss of many lives, the British Government and the IRA finally came to an understanding. In fairness, much of this was brokered by President Clinton with equally as much help coming from the Irish Prime Minister. At last, in April 1998, the Good Friday agreement, as it was known, was signed by all. There was some protest from the Unionist camp, but in the interest of peace this was set aside. The agreement would install an assembly in Stormont consisting of all parties in the conflict, including Sinn Fein. There was a price, and demands were made by all parties. It also called for the IRA and UDA to decommission their weapons and the release of political prisoners, both Republican and Loyalist, over the following two years.

Things went well until a new republican splinter group calling itself the Real Irish Republican Army (rIRA) threw a spanner in the works, declaring its opposition to Sinn Fein participating in the Good Friday agreement. Although the path was still not smooth, the Northern Ireland peace process forged ahead until 24 May, when the people voted with a clear majority to accept the peace process. The rIRA decided to demonstrate its anger with a bombing campaign, culminating in one of the worst atrocities ever committed in the province. On 15 August, a car bomb containing some 500 pounds of high explosive was left in the market town of Omagh, County Tyrone. It was 3 p.m. on a Saturday afternoon when the bomb exploded. To make matters worse, a warning had been given indicating that a bomb had been placed, but the location given was totally wrong. This resulted in the police evacuating the area identified in the warning, confining shoppers to a tightly packed area where, in fact, the car bomb was located. The devastation was horrendous; 29 people died and over three hundred were injured, many seriously. The dead and wounded were mainly women and children. The rIRA admitted to the crime and declared a 'ceasefire'. Three weeks later six men were arrested in connection with the bombing, names and information as to their whereabouts coming from a rIRA member who was sickened by the death toll.

It was not long before Northern Ireland's newly elected, semi-autonomous executive started to show signs of fragmentation. The hoped-for confidence and new beginning between the Protestant Unionist and Catholic Nationalists was not achieved. The Ulster Unionists refused to share power with Sinn Fein until the IRA had disbanded and its weapons were decommissioned. For their part, the IRA wanted dramatic restructuring of the Royal Ulster Constabulary, and the removal of British troops from the province. It is thought that the IRA still hold over a thousand assault rifles together with a million rounds of ammunition. In addition, they are thought to have about three tons of Semtex high explosive and several ground to air missiles.

While this standoff continues, so does the violence, much of which has reverted to the pattern seen when the troubles first started, i.e. tit-for-tat killings of Catholic and Protestant. Nevertheless, the Good Friday agreement has helped stabilise the province at grass roots level, with both sides seeing the return of some semblance of normality.

These two conflicts demonstrate the benefits of peaceful negotiation as opposed to continued confrontation. How many people have died as a result of the Palestinian/Israeli war? How many people have died as a result the bombings and shootings carried out by the IRA and the British Army in Northern Ireland? How many lives is enough? Terrorism cannot be fought on a battlefield where the victor takes the spoils. The only real answer is a compromise through negotiated peace.

2: TERRORIST ORGANISATIONS

Many of the world's fifty terrorist groups will be unknown to the average reader purely because some of the groups are unique to a single country, or because their activities are infrequent and low-key. It should be recognised, however, that hardly a day passes without a terrorist act taking place somewhere on the planet. Many of these attacks are extremely violent and almost all involve death of the innocent and the destruction of property. Sometimes these acts make mainstream media, other times they get little more than a small column in a local paper.

Most people would agree that the driving force behind most terrorist acts is fuelled either by repression, ineffective political/legal systems, race, religion, or territorial disputes. But at what point does the frustration of the individual turn him, or her, into a terrorist? How can ordinary people become seemingly heartless terrorist monsters?

It is easy to think that terrorists are a different breed of human being – they are not. Terrorist organisations consist of members, all of whom have families and homes, all of whom are subject to the same range of human emotion as the rest of us. Almost every one of them believes in what they are doing and, on a personal level, most of them are convinced they are acting for the greater good of their society. The killing and violence their organisation has adopted is, in the eyes of the terrorist, necessary to achieve their aims; justified as an act of war. This is really no different from a regular soldier who believes that the order to kill the enemy is a legitimate use of force.

Many of the world's fifty terrorist groups will be unknown to the average reader purely because some of the groups are unique to a single country, or because their activities are infrequent and low-key. It should be recognised, however, that hardly a day passes without a terrorist act taking place somewhere on the planet. Many of these attacks are extremely violent and almost all involve death of the innocent and the destruction of property. Sometimes these acts make mainstream media, other times they get little more than a small column in a local paper.

There is no definitive profile in the make-up of an individual terrorist. They can be doctors or teachers, farmers or shopkeepers. Terrorist organisations, on the other hand, are broadly similar, sharing the same methods of operation. In most cases, they function on their own territory surrounded by their supporters.

They do not, however, walk around with a sign saying, 'I am a terrorist.' They operate in much the same way as those who oppose them – undercover. The need for secrecy and security means that recruitment into a terrorist organisation is never straightforward. To be accepted into a terrorist group, the individual must fulfil certain criteria. Terrorists have strict rules for those joining their organisations; lie or try to trick your way into an organisation and you will most probably end up dead. In general, the rules are designed to maintain the security of the organisations and keep out government agents or enemy infiltrators.

A simple criterion might be that the individual joining must be known to most of those already within the organisation. The political or religious leanings of the individual and the immediate family will also be known to the organisation. New recruits will have been born and raised within the immediate area and will have not left that area for any length of time. Where an individual has been in a foreign country for any length of time, it is possible that they have been enlisted by the CIA or a similar covert security agency and sent back home to spy on their old friends. The world's major security services are constantly on the look out for such recruits.

Higher-ranking terrorists will have worked their way up through the organisation, learning their craft while acting as a lookout, perhaps even from the time they were children. From simply acting as a sentry they will have progressed to more responsible tasks, such as moving weapons or they may have been trained as a driver. Then, when they are deemed ready, young volunteers are sent away to training camps in order to learn the techniques of terrorism.

The training of a terrorist is vast and complicated, varying from organisation to organisation. If a terrorist group is operating in a rural environment they invariably travel armed; the Tamil Tigers are a good example of this. If the terrorists are at large in an urban environment, their weapons or bombs will be concealed and produced just prior to any planned action, a technique demonstrated by the working methods of the IRA. However the terrorists choose to operate, the training available to them in the use of modern weaponry (and terror tactics) is as comprehensive and as sophisticated as the weaponry itself.

In the smaller or closed cell organisations, training is undertaken on a one-to-one basis. An individual might learn how to make a bomb, or use a machine gun. The larger organisations, such as those operating as a rebel force in a rural area, might set up purpose-built training camps where new recruits can be trained in large numbers. In such camps they may also receive political, religious or motivational instruction.

Author's Note: I have seen several Middle Eastern training camps used by terrorists. They are usually located in the middle of the desert, surrounded by high mountains. If not, they are extremely well concealed. The camp itself consists of various flat-roofed buildings, the remnants of an old village. These are normally reserved for training or for instructor accommodation. The recruits are forced to make do with tents. Normally, the recruits eat in a simple cookhouse. This will also serve as a meeting area during any free time. Close by will be a designated area for training, and shooting ranges. These camps are rarely fenced and would have no resemblance to western military barracks, as they are extremely inhospitable places. But training is not about smart barracks with marvellous facilities and spotless parade grounds. It is about knowledgeable, effective and motivated operatives. Vetting and security within the camps is also strict and rigorous, with many recruits dying from barbaric initiation ceremonies. Believe me, these camps are not for the faint-hearted.

The Individual and the Terrorist Organisation

The story that follows is true, as are the names, unless otherwise stated. It illustrates several aspects of the relationship between the individual and the terrorist organisation. To qualify the story, there is attached, at the end, a real intelligence file that was compiled by one of the world's best spies. Both the story and intelligence report form a clear indication of how the individual fits into a terrorist organisation.

Towards the end of 1994, a warrant was issued in Germany for the arrest of a woman called Monika Haas. According to the investigators, Haas was supposed to have smuggled weapons and explosives to Palma de Mallorca and to have handed them over to the Palestinian terrorist commando which, on 13 October 1977, had seized the Lufthansa plane, 'Landshut' (see Chapter 5).

Haas had previously been arrested in the 'Landshut' affair. In the spring of 1992, after unification, federal lawyers had come across remarks in documents of Section 22 (anti-terrorism section) of the former East Berlin Ministry of State Security (Stasi), that maintained that Haas was supposed to have delivered weapons to the Landshut hijackers. After seven weeks of interrogation, however, the Federal Court of Justice dismissed the arrest warrant. Reason: Stasi documents alone did not meet the constitutional requirements for establishing the facts of the case.

The new arrest of Haas came after German investigators apparently located a Palestinian woman, Soraya Ansari, the only member of the hijack commando who survived, critically injured, during the GSG 9 mission in Mogadishu. On 13 October, 17 years to the day after the Landshut hijacking, she was arrested in Oslo. While the Norwegian court was considering her extradition to the Federal Republic, Heidi Bache-Wüg, her Norwegian lawyer, fought to prevent it, arguing that her client, still suffering from the effects of the shooting, should be allowed to remain in Norway on humanitarian grounds. Additionally, Soraya Ansari was now married and her nine-year-old daughter would also be the victim of any extradition.

During a 48-hour, non-stop interrogation, German BKA (Federal Criminal Office) officials questioned Soraya Ansari, who acknowledged her participation in the seizure of the Landshut. She was also supposed to have offered to turn state's evidence in order to achieve mitigation of sentence, by implicating Monika Haas. It is assumed that the two women probably knew each other from the Yemen; whether they also met on the holiday island of Mallorca when the weapons were delivered, is a question the Karlsruhe Attorney-General (GBA – Generalbundesanwalt – Prosecutor's office) had been trying to establish for three years. While the legal wrangles and protracted investigations continued, both women found themselves prisoners: the Palestinian Soraya Ansari, 41, in temporary extradition custody at her home in Oslo, where she had lived since 1991; the German Monika Haas, 46, in a German jail.

The authorities believed that both women belonged to the Palestinian splinter-group PFLP which had its most important base in a desert camp barely two and a half hours drive from Aden, the capital of south Yemen. Like the cadres of other terrorist organisations, the officials of the PFLP also travelled in and out of the former Eastern block, coming to the attention of Stasi agents. The PFLP member, Zaki Helou, for instance, was a regular customer of the notorious weapons factory KINTEX in Sofia, which was controlled by the Bulgarian Secret Police. Zaki Helou was formerly married to Monika Haas but, despite this close connection, Haas denied involvement in any terrorist activity.

The Prosecutor's office now brought forward the results of further inquiries, which, according to GBA press spokesman, Rolf Hannich, furnished 'confirmation of the accuracy of the former conclusion'. On a Stasi list of 'members and sympathisers' of the terrorist group, could be found one after another the names, Zaki Helou, Monika Haas and Soraya Ansari.

Although not mentioned at the time, a thread of suspicion started to appear, running throughout the Stasi documents. The documents contained claims that Monika Haas might also be a West German or French secret agent used as a mole in Palestinian terrorist circles – a view that was not unique to the East German secret service. Several PFLP fighters were also certain that Haas was an agent; so much so that they were believed to have planned her murder. In October 1988 a Stasi official noted in a dry, bureaucratic manner that Abu Hanafi was preparing the 'liquidation of the West German citizen, Monika Haas'. Her murder would be an act of revenge against West Germany. Abu Hanafi sat in an Israeli prison following a failed attempt to take an El Al plane in Nairobi in 1976. To him, it must have seemed obvious that Monika Haas had blabbed about the action.

In 1984, the husband of Haas, Zaki Helou, was shot dead in Madrid in the open street. He was travelling with the Syrian weapons/drugs-dealer, Monzer Al Kassar, considered by Western as well as eastern security services to be the weapons supplier for the PFLP. In November 1993, BKA officials interrogated Al Kassar about Monika Haas. Al Kassar was also to find himself up before a judge in Spain, accused of supplying weapons to the commando which, in October 1985, seized the cruise ship *Achille Lauro* (see Chapter 3).

Author's Note: What you are about to read is a direct translation of a secret service file. Many names and terrorist organisations are mentioned, the only ones you need concentrate on are those of Monika Haas, or 'H' as she is referred to. Likewise, for reference to organisations, such as BDR, BND etc., read Germany and German secret service. For authenticity the original format has been maintained.

1

Department XXII/8   Berlin, 19.February 1981

Confirmed: [Signature illegible]

OPENING REPORT

In the OV "Wolf", the person

HAAS, Monika *
born 2.5.1948 / Frankfurt/Main
29.12.1948 / Stuttgart

shall be handled operationally according to § 98 StGB in connection with § 108 StGB. [StGB - Strafgesetzbuch = penal code]

About the person
The first accounts of H. date from 1970. At this point in time she was in a US Army establishment in Frankfurt/Main, working as a telephonist, and kept up contacts with members of the "RAF" [Red Army Fraction]. She declined at that time active support of this group in a bomb attack on this US establishment. Only in 1975 did she properly join the "RAF", the so-called "Haag group", the main motivation for this decision being the liberation of her imprisoned friend.

* Note: names in bold are in manuscript in the original document, the typescript giving only .... in each case.

2

HOPPE, Werner
(sometime member of the "RAF" sentenced in 1972 to 10 years imprisonment)

Still in the same year she went together with Haag and other members of this group to the VDR Yemen. At that time she arranged for her son to stay with the wife of

GEISSLER, Christian
born on 25.12.1928 / Hamburg living in Hamburg

In Aden she got to know the then second-in-command and today the leader of the base of the former "WADI-HADDAD Group"

SAKKI

and married him about the middle of 1976.
From this marriage have come two children (1973 and 1981) so far. Since September 1980 she has resided again with her children in the Federal Republic of Germany.

Political-operational assessment

- As a member of the "RAF" and "WADI-HADDAD" groupings she completed guerilla training in Aden, and gained knowledge of structures, logistics as well as operational areas and timing of terrorist power.
  As the wife of the present leader of the base in Aden this knowledge was obviously strengthened.

- As a member of the "WADDI-HADDAD Group" she was in January 1976 in Kenya preparing for the action against the EL-AL plane at Nairobi airport.

After the failed action and arrest of - SCHULZ, Brigitte and REUTER, Thomas - she was sent once again with the same passport to Kenya, according to her own account, and is supposed to have been arrested by the Kenyan police on the basis of her passport immediately on entering the country. Allegedly she was interrogated and tortured for three days in order to gain information from her about a Palestinian woman associate. During the interrogation, which was conducted by the Israeli secret service "Mossad", she is supposed to have given information about another woman associate whom she believed to be in safety.

3 (a)

In order to make contact with the latter in the company of the "Mossad" secret service, they went allegedly to Tanzania in order to fly from here to Beirut.

According to her own account she managed to escape from her companions in Tanzania, and to go again to Aden.

Her explanations were doubted by the "RAF" and the "Carlos" grouping, and further collaboration was refused.

- About the middle of 1977 she travelled with a Peruvian passport to the Federal Republic of Germany in order to fetch her child. Even though the whereabouts of the child were known to the opposing side, she travelled out again without difficulties to Aden.

It is significant in this connection that the serial number of the passport was known to the BKA [Bundeskriminalamt]. The "RAF" member, - POHLE, Rolf - was arrested in July 1976 on the basis of a Peruvian passport of the same series.

- In the presence of an unofficial source H. claimed in 1981 that she had handed over the weapons for the Palestinian commando for the hijacking of the Lufthansa plane "Landshut" in October 1977 in Mallorca.

According to other unofficial indications it became known however that she handed over the weapons in Algeria, and therefore had no clue about the actual place and timing.

It is significant in this connection that the Israeli wireless announced, one day before the hijacking, such an action, but could give no information about details.

- Unofficially it was possible to work out that H. was keen to procure comprehensive financial resources. It can be shown that she received in 1979 from the Federal Republic of Germany money transfers to a Kuwaiti bank, and was there several times to do some shopping.

In 1980 it was possible to detect that she appeared unhappy, expressing several times anti-communist and anti-soviet sentiments, and had differences in her married life. At that time she also made contact with the French ambassador in Aden, from whom she bought furniture, that is, is said to have received some.

3 (b)

From the middle of 1980 these indications and information intensified, so that the suspicion that H. was acting for hostile security organs can be inferred.

In connection with the arrest of five members of the "RAF" in May 1980 in Paris, it became known from various sources that the arrest resulted from a tip-off from an agent from Aden.

4

Through unofficial evidence this information has been confirmed.

It is significant that the husband of **HAAS** knew the telephone number of the flat in which the arrest took place.

From this flat two telephone conversations took place with an agent of SAKKI.

Immediately after the second call the 5 "RAF" members were taken into custody.

As has been proved, and contrary to western reports, the member of the "RAF" - HOFMANN, Sieglinde - arrested at the same time in Paris did not travel by plane but by train to Paris.

At the end of November 1980 the Austrian Ambassador

Dr. AMRY

voiced the suspicion in Beirut with regard to the "PLO security" that the arrest in Paris was possible on account of information from a traitor within the ranks of the PFLP.
The information is supposed to have been passed on through the French Embassy in Aden in exchange for financial consideration. (Even today the former "WADDI-HADDAD-Group" is still equated with the PFLP membership).

From corresponding information of Department III it is possible to work out that the BND (Bundesnachrichtendienst - Federal Information Service) demonstrably received information from within the sphere of the PLO which made the arrest in Paris possible. According to Department III we are concerned here with one person, who is controlled, or rather taken advantage of, by a diplomat or BND colleague having diplomatic status, stationed outside of the Federal Republic of Germany.
These indications were confirmed by a complaint by the President of the BND

KLINKEL, Klaus

to the President of the BKA

HEROLD, Horst

concerning the indiscretion of the BKA (Bundeskriminalamt) towards the BRD Press, because in "Die Welt" of 5.6.1980 "Beirut", or rather "Aden" was named and published as initial -indication for the arrests in Paris, and that the 5 "terrorists" travelled from Aden to France.

5

- In the opinion of KLINKEL the source of the BND was as much endangered by this as the diplomat acting as a go-between.

- On 22.5.1980 four members of the "ETA" were arrested on arrival at the"Barajas"/Madrid airport coming from Aden.
Here it was a matter of members of the "ETA", who had undergone training in Aden for "guerilla warfare".

On the basis of the latest activities of **HAAS**, her trip to the BRD, further suspicious elements can be deduced.

- In the middle of September **HAAS** with her children travelled to the BRD with a Lebanese passport in the name of

SAKKI, Helou

and a valid visa for the BRD until 2.11.1980.
In conversations with an unofficial source she claimed that she received the visa for the BRD by mistake, originally however intended to go to the DDR (Deutsche Demokratische Republik).
However, since the DDR keeps an embassy in the VDR Yemen and the BDR only an office, a mistake in this connection is hardly possible.
Check-ups made in the DDR Embassy established that no application to enter the DDR had come in.
The anti-socialist attitude of H. also confirms this.

- The trip itself was made via Prague, at a time when several leading members of the "RAF" were staying in the capital of the CSSR.
  When they left the CSSR **HAAS** too continued her travel to the BRD.

- In the BRD she took up contact with a certain

  BAETZ, Regina
  residing: Frankfurt/Main,
  Mauerweg 3

  lived at the beginning with her and tried from there to make contact with members of the "RAF" scene known to her. From such a contact the leading personnel of the "RAF" also learnt of the stay of **HAAS** in the BRD.

6

- In Frankfurt/Main she established contact with a legal supporter of the "RAF". Her behaviour and attitude were intended to show that taking up this contact happened totally accidentally.
  Investigations established that **HAAS** contacted this person in a targeted and well-prepared manner.

- It is also significant that she is supposed to have looked up her mother living in an old people's home. According to her own account she had been observed after the visit by state security officials.
  It is unrealistic in this connection that a wanted "terrorist" in the BRD was only observed.

- Equally implausible and suspicious are her remarks concerning the inquiry and information via a lawyer at the Federal Prosecutor's Office [Bundesanwalt-schaft].
  Although her co-combatant HAAG was condemned to 15 years imprisonment on account of forming a "criminal association", it is supposed that nothing significant exists against **HAAS**, and that proceedings were discontinued on account of the person not being traceable.

Because the membership of **HAAS** in the so-called "Haag group" was known to the opposing security organs, a proceeding according to § 129 a (membership of a "criminal association") should at least have been available.

On 18.10.1977, in connection with the hijacking of the "Landshut", it was made known that **HAAS** was trained as a "terrorist" in South Yemen and had taken part in this action. It is significant too that no search measures whatever in the BRD against **HAAS** were started by the opposing security organs.

- It is interesting that **HAAS** took up contact, first by telephone, then personally, from Frankfurt/Main with

GEISSLER

in Hamburg.
GEISSLER played an important role in the "freedom struggle" of her former friend

HOPPE

from custody, and presently maintains personal contacts with imprisoned "RAF" members.

7
- Through assistance from **GEISSLER** and the former "terrorist" **BERSTER, Christina**, **HAAS** acquired a flat in Hamburg in the

Eimsbüttler Str. 75

There she lived legally under her name of birth. The necessary BRD passport for this she obtained without difficulty from the appropriate authorities in Hamburg.
After the birth of her third child in February 1981 she moved into a new flat, which was renovated by the Senate for about DM.-6,000. She also without difficulty received relatively quickly social welfare.

The whole behaviour and attitude of **HAAS**, her
remarks as well as the contacts taken up,
point towards her being used to look for, to
establish and to build up contact
purposefully in the anarchist terrorist group
on behalf of opposing security organs.
In this connection it has to be said that
information is available, according to which
she envisages possibilities of a meeting with
her husband **SAKKI** in the capital of the DDR,
Berlin, but at the moment no interest seems
to exist for this.
In connection with her husband, it is
significant that he has been called an Israeli
or Jordanian agent.
On the strength of circumstances there are
indications suggesting concerted action with
her husband.

Criminal assessment

The information and the proofs so far worked on
allow the suspicion that in

HAAS

we are dealing with an informer or agent of a
French or BRD secret service.
In connection with the VDR Yemen and in
connection with possible activities on the
territory of the DDR the suspicion exists that
HAAS offends against penal laws of the DDR in the
sense of § 98 StGB in connection with § 108 StGB.

Orzschig
First Lieutenant

Despite having been arrested several times, Monika Haas has never
been convicted of being a member of a terrorist group or taking
part in a terrorist action. I believe she is still free and living in
Germany. So was she a terrorist or a French or German agent?
Although she is far from being a typical terrorist, she is
representative of a significant number of people who inhabit the

dangerous, murky world of terrorism and espionage. You will find similar people in just about any terrorist organisation and no doubt the secret service files held by the various agencies would prove equally as interesting. Alongside the committed, highly motivated, dedicated terrorists, there lurk the shady people. People like Haas have obvious uses for both the terrorists and the anti-terrorists. Such people have certainly been known to swap sides when it suits them, and it must often seem to all concerned that no one really knows whose side they are on.

The relationship of the individual with the terrorist organisation can, therefore, be as complex and confusing as the historical, political or religious reasons for the existence of the terrorist group.

Terrorist Organisations

A detailed study of each of the terrorist groups currently active around the world would fill several volumes; consequently, I have tried to select groups which are representative of the world's terrorist organisations (a comprehensive list of terrorist organisations is to be found at the end of this book). My knowledge has come from working directly against some of these organisations, and researching information on the others in the event that we might have become adversaries.

It is interesting to see how each of the groups operates and how they go about achieving their aims through acts of terrorism. It is equally interesting to see that those groups which, it could be said, are pursuing a legitimate grievance, seem to fare better than those bent on general chaos and anarchy.

FARC

FARC (the Revolutionary Armed Forces of Colombia) came into being in 1964 as a response to the violent oppression of a group of angry Colombian peasants by the Colombian army. During a three-week operation, the army, aided by the United States, carried out a programme of bombing, imprisonment, torture and executions in the fertile farming lands of Marquetalia. Forty-eight of the surviving farmers decided to take their struggle further despite the fact that they possessed hardly any weaponry. These were the early days of FARC. Later it was to become the military wing of the Colombian Communist Party.

Almost forty years on, FARC has become the largest and oldest of Colombia's various insurgent groups. It is the best equipped and claims to have around 20,000 members, with at least 12,000 of those being armed combatants. Support comes mainly from rural areas, although of late many indigenous populations have complained of FARC intimidation and violence, or of displacement as a result of the wars between the various Marxist groups and the government.

FARC is run by a secretariat, the head of which is the elderly Manuel Marulanda, also known as 'Tirofijo'. Six others share the leadership, including Jorge Briceno, the senior military commander, and Paul Reyes who is in charge of maintaining FARC's relationships with the international community. FARC is run as a military organisation and is split into seven urban 'fronts', the location of which ebbs and flows with various battles with the state military as well as with right-wing paramilitaries.

Funding comes from various sources, both internally and externally. FARC itself raises funds through kidnapping ransoms, extortion and the control of the production and trafficking of drugs, such as coca and heroin. Outside aid comes from Cuba, which provides some medical care and political guidance. Recently the FARC has also been linked with the IRA, allegedly colluding with the Irish group over technology and tactics.

FARC's continual reign of terror in Colombia has been a big problem for the Colombian Government. Many rural regions have become no-go areas, especially for foreign nationals, who are prime targets for kidnapping. Military operations, such as Operation Exterminate, Operation Destroyer and Operation Claw, some with the covert aid of the US military, have all failed to destroy FARC. And the policy to spray weed killer on all drug crops has done more to harm the health and livelihood of the rural peasants than it has to eliminate a revenue earner for the terrorist group. Trying another method, in 2001 the government of Andrés Pastrano entered into a peace process with FARC, creating a demilitarised zone where the group could operate under a limited autonomy.

The process was not smooth, with great disapproval from certain sections of the general population, as well as businesses and paramilitary groups. In particular, they objected to FARC's insistence that the anti-drugs 'Plan Colombia' be dropped. This scheme, implemented by the government and supported by a concerned United States, set out to combat drug production and transportation. Negotiations became increasingly tense and it seems that both sides lost trust in each other. Feeling that they were getting nowhere, especially in the run up to Colombia's elections, FARC resumed its old tricks in May 2002, kidnapping a candidate and carrying out several bombings. The peace process collapsed and war between the two sides recommenced.

The Tupac Amaru

The Tupac Amaru, also known by the Spanish initials MRTA, is a traditional Marxist-Leninist revolutionary movement that was founded in 1983. Its basic aims are to establish a Marxist regime and to rid Peru of all imperialist elements, principally US and Japanese influence. The organisation consists of no more than 100 members, consisting largely of young fighters who lack leadership skills and experience. Their activities include bombings, kidnappings, ambushes and assassinations. One of the MRTA's greatest causes is ridding its country of what it sees as the detrimental influence of Japan on President Fujimori (who himself is half-Japanese) and the proliferation of Japanese companies operating in Peru. These include Matsushita Electric Industrial; Mitsui Mining and Smelting; Tomen Corp; Nissho Iwai; Kanematsu; Mitsui & Co; Marubeni; Mitsubishi; Ajinomoto; NEC; Toyota; Nissan; Asahi Chemical Industry; Fujita; Japan Water Works; Japan Airlines; NGS Consultants.

MRTA made its last major impact on the world's media when its members took over the Japanese Embassy in Lima. Their attack was timed to coincide with a large party at the embassy, thus ensuring the capture of many foreign VIPs who were held hostage. The situation lasted for several months and attracted massive media attention before the embassy could be assaulted by specialist troops (see Chapter 5), who ended the siege by tunnelling under the embassy building. All those MRTA members who had taken part in the siege were killed during the assault.

The IRA

The root of the 'troubles' in Northern Ireland can be traced back to 1610 and the colonisation of Northern Ireland by Scottish Presbyterian settlers. Some 90 per cent of Londonderry was given to the newcomers while the native population were forced to pay double taxes on the remaining ten per cent. By 1622 around 13,000 settlers, most of whom were anti-Catholic, were in occupation.

The Irish Republican Army can trace its heritage back to the 1790s when the United Irishmen chose to resist the oppression of the British government, first by non-violent protests and then, when this was met with repression, armed struggle. The next hundred years saw various uprisings against British rule, each one ruthlessly put down and its leaders executed. Political tactics aimed at pushing legislation for home rule in Ireland fared no better either. A new organisation – The Irish Volunteers – which was later to become the Irish Republican Army, was established in 1913. During the Easter rising of 1916 the IRA issued the Proclamation of the Republic – a document which declared an independent Republic and 'equal right and equal opportunities' for all Irish people. This proclamation is generally regarded as the founding charter of the IRA. By 1921, the south of Ireland had been granted independence, leaving only the six counties of the north still in British rule. Support for the IRA dwindled and soon the organisation became all but extinct.

The 1960s saw the beginnings of Civil Rights protests in Northern Ireland, where Irish Catholics demanded basic rights on voting, housing and jobs. This unarmed and largely peaceful movement met with violent opposition and by 1969, nationalist districts in Belfast and Derry were being attacked by the RUC and unionist mobs. In response to this, what remained of the IRA became split, as one half wanted to continue peaceful protest and the other insisted that armed struggle was the only way forward. While the political arm of the new organisation, Sinn Fein, tried to find a political solution, the militant arm, now known as the Provisional IRA (PIRA), soon became locked into a violent and bloody struggle with the British Government and various loyalist groups.

Author's Note: My first real introduction to the IRA came when Harold Wilson ordered the SAS into Northern Ireland. I was on a ship heading out to Norway and the Prime Minister's directive made headline news in the morning paper. Several months later, I found myself walking the countryside of South Armagh dressed as a private in the Parachute regiment – this was my covert way of seeing the situation first hand. I knew very little about the IRA then, but after several years in the province, I learned.

Throughout 1970 and 1971, the IRA carried out shootings, bombings and organised riots. Support for their cause was growing within the oppressed Catholic communities. This support only increased when the Government introduced an internment without trial policy, leading to mass arrests of PIRA activists and sympathisers. It was the events of 30 January 1972, however, that brought about the greatest loss of support for British rule within the six counties. On this day British paratroopers fired on a peaceful protest march killing thirteen Catholic civilians. Despite the army's insistence that they were fired upon first, 'Bloody Sunday', as it has become known, is still cited as an example of state brutality.

From 1973 onwards, the frequency of bombings and shootings increased. The British Government fought back with counter-insurgency forces, intelligence units and, controversially, the use of state-sponsored loyalist death squads. Despite this, the PIRA continued to gather support and acquire greater stocks of weaponry and explosives. Their methods became more sophisticated, as did their organisation of operations.

Although the IRA had massive support from the Catholic community in Northern Ireland, it only had about fifty active members at any one time. The active members were those who would carry out the military operations of the group. These members were organised into four-man cells that fell under the command of the General Council. Logistics and the supply of weapons were handled by an individual, local to the cell, known as the Quartermaster. The money needed for these operations was often provided from far afield. Sympathisers in the United States set up a fund, supposedly for the relief of Republican prisoners and their families, although much of the money went towards buying arms and expertise. Sponsorship, including arms and training, was also provided for a while by Libya, while other international terrorist groups, such as ETA, shared their knowledge. The Provisional IRA soon became a force responsible for the death and injury of hundreds of people in a most brutal way, as the events described below show.

On 21 November 1974 a PIRA active service unit, as they liked to be called, bombed two pubs in Birmingham. The devastating explosions resulted in the deaths of 21 people and numerous injuries. Outrage and public pressure following the attacks led to the Prevention of Terrorism Act being passed. Six Irish men were later arrested and convicted. The men, known as the 'Birmingham Six' insisted they were innocent and were freed on appeal 16 years later.

Author's Note: I was in Birmingham training on an SAS medic course on the night of the attacks. Birmingham Accident Hospital, as it was then called, was overrun with casualties. The wounds, many caused by broken glass and splintered wood from the chairs and tables, were an appalling sight.

The British Royal Family also suffered at the hands of the IRA. Earl Mountbatten was murdered on 27 August 1979 as he sailed his motor cruiser out from the small fishing village of Mullaghmore on the Sligo coast of southern Ireland. His twin grandsons, aged 14, his daughter and her husband together with the Dowager Lady Doreen Bradbourne, aged 83, accompanied him. The only crew was a young fifteen-year-old boy from Northern Ireland. Lord Mountbatten had reduced his official protection to the minimum and the two Irish policemen who should have accompanied him were left on the shore where they watched the boat's progress through binoculars. The intention that morning was to lift several lobster pots that had been previously laid. The boat stopped some 200 metres from the shore ready to lift the first lobster pots. Then it exploded. The bomb, estimated to be five pounds of plastic explosive, had been placed in the midsection of the boat where it would do the most damage. It was detonated by an improvised radio-control unit similar to those used for flying model aircraft.

The blast was devastating, instantly killing Earl Mountbatten, one of the twins, Nicholas Bradbourne, and the crew boy Paul Maxwell. The Dowager died soon after due to her injuries. The three others survived despite serious wounds.

Later that same day the PIRA ambushed a truckload of British soldiers at Warrenpoint, County Down in Northern Ireland, detonating a bomb which killed 18. The ambush area was rigged with a second device that detonated as help arrived on the scene, killing several more soldiers. As six of the soldiers belonged to the Parachute Regiment, the regiment responsible for Bloody Sunday, this was seen as a great victory in Republican circles.

The IRA continued its bombing and shooting campaign with great ferocity during the 1980s targeting not only British soldiers in Northern Ireland but civilian targets in Great Britain and Europe (see Chapter 3). The late 1990s, however, saw the first signs of hope that would eventually lead to a settled peace between the IRA and the British Government (see Chapter 1). Despite several setbacks, that hope still remains.

ETA

ETA is to the Spanish what the IRA is to the British. There are many similarities in their cause and the chosen mode of their offensive operations against the Spanish Government. Unsurprisingly, the IRA and ETA maintain close links, working and sharing strategy and even providing assistance to each other with various operations and training.

Founded in 1958, Euskadi Ta Askatasuna (ETA), meaning Basque Fatherland and Liberty, was formed in response to a growing sense of nationalism in the area. The Basque people have lived in the region that straddles northern Spain and south-west

France for thousands of years. They have their own culture and a language that is different from both French and Spanish. Proud of their heritage, the Basque people have long resented Spanish rule and the oppression it brought. A political party, known as the Basque Nationalist Party was formed to tackle these problems but its actions were seen as inadequate. Therefore, a group of young student activists founded EKIN, aiming to have their voice heard through more robust means.

In 1958, EKIN was renamed ETA and its activists started to acquire arms to help them in their struggle. The first targets for their bombs were the cities of Santander, Bilbao and Vitoria along the northern coastline. By 1961, they had increased the stakes by attempting to derail a train full of veterans on their way to celebrate the twenty-fifth anniversary of the Spanish Civil War in Donostia. The effort failed and the Basque people paid the price as the police responded with roadblocks, arrests and house searches, sometimes using torture to extract information from sympathisers. Fearing this new atmosphere of terror, many Basques fled Spain and went to live in exile in France. Other Basques decided to stay, their determination for freedom from Spanish rule strengthened. Support for ETA grew.

ETA's military wing, ETA-Militar, developed a strategy of mounting attacks against Franco's government and its enforcers, the police. One of their greatest early victories was the assassination of Admiral Luis Carrero Blanco, the Spanish Prime Minister tipped to become Franco's successor. The massive bomb that killed him in a Madrid Street was the beginning of the end of Spanish fascism.

In 1976, Franco died and Spain gained a democratic Government. This Government granted the Basque region a certain amount of autonomy and many exiles, hoping for peace at last, began to return. But, for those in ETA, the reforms did not go far enough; they still did not have an independent homeland as set out in their original demands. The violence continued and even intensified against the state machinery, especially the Guardia, who had heavy-handedly policed the region for so long. The new government tried further concessions to stop the violence –

replacing the Guardia with a locally recruited security force and encouraging Basque culture and language. With these new concessions, many Basque people began to feel that independence could be gained through political negotiations rather than by the bomb. Support for ETA's violent methods began to slip away but ETA continued, regardless.

Spain's frustration with the insurgents soon spilled over into action. The Government of Felipe Gonzalez introduced the use of GAL squads – state-supported anti-terrorist liberation groups. They quickly brought about the deaths of 28 ETA members. This new development prompted ETA to enter into secret talks with Spain in 1992 but to no avail – the two sides still did not trust each other enough. In 1997, ETA kidnapped and murdered Miguel Angel Blanco, a young Basque politician, but instead of bringing the group nearer to their demands, it caused mass public outrage. An estimated six million people took to the streets all over Spain to protest. Recognising the strong public feeling against terrorism, the Government started to hit back once more at ETA, imprisoning 23 members – the whole leadership – of ETA's political wing, Herri Batasuma.

ETA began to realise that military force alone was not going to further their cause. At around the same time, the peace process in Northern Ireland was beginning to make headway, influencing their decision to call a ceasefire and enter into peace talks with the Spanish Government. The Government, however, was not convinced, even though this was ETA's first ceasefire since the start of the conflict. Their intelligence services told them that ETA was still carrying out raids on arms depots and re-arming for a future struggle. Attacks against local politicians still continued, although there were no major outrages during this time. Fourteen months later, in November 1999, after no real progress, ETA called an end to its ceasefire, announcing that the peace process was 'blocked and poisoned'.

ETA has never had a large membership, probably because the majority of Basques are happy with the level of autonomy they now possess. At most, there are only about 20 active members who carry out the attacks, supported by a few hundred members. Of late, they have become unpopular within their own region due to the imposition of a 'Basque Revolutionary Tax' – a form of extortion – on their own people. Other sources of funding, apart from their supporters, include kidnapping ransoms, armed robberies and drug trafficking. They have strong links with other terrorist organisations, particularly the IRA, and have offered assistance to terror groups in Latin America.

ETA has a non-hierarchical structure, which often makes it difficult for the Spanish security forces to infiltrate. The small active cells tend to operate separately from all the others and only have occasional links with the leadership. Although operating mainly from within Spain, ETA also has bases within south-west France and often attacks targets there as well.

Apart from events detailed above, their other notable terrorist activities include their failed assassination attempt on King Juan Carlos in August 1995. That same year there was another failed attack on the leader of the opposition Popular Party, Jose Maria Anzar. Anzar, later to become Prime Minister, survived the car bomb that was meant to kill him. Their third attempt at assassination succeeded when they car-bombed a prominent member of the Popular Party, killing Manuel Zamarreno.

As well as these three incidents, ETA have perpetrated hundreds of less sensational bombings and killings during their bloody history, claiming over 770 victims. They have also been responsible for 46 kidnappings, all for ransom money. At present their terror continues, with bombs planted in areas heavily frequented by tourists.

Baader-Meinhof

The Baader-Meinhof gang, so named after is founders Andreas Baader and Ulrike Meinhof, was a group of terrorists that plagued the German Government during the period from the late 1960s to the mid 1970s. While the IRA could claim to be fighting for the freedom of their country from the British, the Baader-Meinhof never seemed to have any justifiable cause for their terrorist activities other than their dislike of capitalism. The Baader-Meinhof were a group of very misguided young people who had let their ideological convictions carry them further than would normal left-wing student activities. The Baader-Meinhof group were no ordinary terrorists. They operated on a basis of pure destructiveness – terrorism for terrorism's own sake. They had no sound genuine left-wing policies, other than their aim to disrupt capitalism. Yet most members never did without the middle-class luxuries to which they were accustomed. They didn't even want to overthrow the German Government and replace it with a more radical administration. Neither were they a gang of super-criminals operating for pure cash. It seemed that they merely wanted to disrupt the society that they lived in, advocating violence for violence's sake.

Although the Baader-Meinhof gang grew in numbers across the whole of Germany, the majority of their membership seemed to consist of active sympathisers who were willing to help with the supply of funds, safe houses or transport, joining them on protest marches and waving placards. During their most notorious periods they also acquired the services of a number of radical left-wing lawyers. These men were always ready to defend their clients in court, turning the proceedings in to high-profile media events. The laws in Germany were so complicated at the time, that the lawyers frequently had the hard-core members of the gang freed from custody on some technicality. During the seven years of the gang's most aggressive action, twenty people were to die as a result of Baader-Meinhof terrorist activities, with scores more being injured. The group was to hit the public's attention when, on 14 May 1970, Gudrun Ensslin rescued Baader from prison. This involved a dramatic gun battle, resulting in the shooting of an innocent man.

Andreas Baader had been serving a prison sentence for 'arson endangering human life'. He was to serve his sentence in Tegal Prison, Berlin. This was not his first time in custody. But this time he was serving three years because he and Gudrun Ensslin had placed an incendiary bomb in a large department store in Frankfurt. At his trial, he had admitted that he had planted a bag containing a device in a cupboard in the store. He had been sentenced but, while appealing against his sentence, he had been released on bail. He absconded with no intention of going back into prison. During his time on the run he made many underground contacts and increased his followers and supplies of equipment such as firebombs and guns. He was re-arrested following a tip-off from one his contacts, who was actually a member of German counterintelligence. A trap was set for Baader on the pretext of selling him some guns. Counter-intelligence, who had set the trap, caught Baader and he was taken back to Tegal prison.

Ulrike Meinhof had kept in contact with Baader while he was in Tegal. They decided that they should jointly write a book on the welfare of young people and they had a publisher prepared to pay for such an article. Under the pretext of working on this book, Baader requested that the prison authorities allow him to meet Ulrike Meinhof in the Library of the Social Institute in the suburb of Dahlem. The pair were accompanied by two prison officers and also present were two library assistants.

A man called Georg Linke was working in his office across the hall from the reading room. While he was busy working he was disturbed by two women calling on him. He asked them to wait in the hall and returned to his office. The next moment he heard a confusion of unusual sounds. He went out and saw two people wearing balaclava masks, both holding guns. One of the people pointed the gun at him and shot him in the stomach. In the ensuing mayhem of gunfire, further aggravated by the release of tear gas, Andreas Baader made his escape with Ulrike Meinhof, Gudrun Ensslin (who was later identified as one of the people wearing a balaclava mask), and another unidentified male. Georg Linke almost died from his injuries. The Government pulled out all the stops to find the members of the Baader-Meinhof gang, raiding hundreds of suspected safe houses and setting up road blocks all over Germany .

As the heat was turned up, the gang decided that it was time to leave Germany and it was agreed that they should go to the Middle East. Here Haddad's PFLP had promised them aid and military training at one of their camps in Jordan. Around the end of the year, the main players of the Baader-Meinhof gang flew to Beriut from East Berlin. When they eventually reached Amman they were warmly welcomed by the leaders of the PFLP military and taken to their headquarters. Here photographs of them were taken and all personal details recorded – years later, the Israelis captured these headquarters and came into possession of all their files. The Baader-Meinhof then enjoyed the training and hospitality provided by the PFLP before planning their return to Germany.

Once back in Germany, the gang regrouped and prepared for a major onslaught against the Government and capitalism. They had now increased in number and were also increasing their criminal activities. These consisted of firebombing, bank robberies and a nice little sideline in car theft. In the early 1970s they carried out several raids on various banks in their local district in Berlin. They used stolen cars for their getaways and illegal firearms to hold up the bank staff. During these raids some of the bank guards were shot and killed.

At the end of December 1971, the RAF, as they were now known, suffered a considerable misfortune when a parcel addressed to them was discovered by postal officials. The package was coming apart at the post office and inside the postmen found 16 pistols, three automatic rifles, silencers, telescopic sights and a large amount of ammunition. It also contained eight pounds of explosives and walkie-talkie radios. Fearing a new wave of violence and killings, the government brought in three thousand extra police and launched a massive search of all known terrorist-associated addresses. Although they achieved nothing of any significance, they compromised a number of safe house addresses and forced the gang to keep on the move, which curtailed their criminal activities to some degree.

During the next few years the gang continued to participate in bank raids successfully and without being caught, stealing large amounts of money. They continued to carry out firebomb attacks on large German corporations and institutions and they attacked naval and army bases, always with the intention of maiming and killing. The German newspapers wrote provocative articles stating that the gang had declared war on Germany. The group in return wrote to the papers declaring their intentions to disrupt German society. All over the country members of the public were reporting to the police, usually inaccurately, that they knew where members of the gang were hiding.

One day in Frankfurt the police received yet another tip-off. The information was from a man who thought that a garage near him was being used to make bombs. The police started to watch the garage. On 1 June 1972 three men arrived at the garage. They were Andreas Baader, Holger Meins and Jan-Carl Raspe. Immediately, the police approached the garage and were spotted by Raspe who fired his gun at them and ran off. Fortunately, the police managed to capture Raspe.

When the other two looked out from the garage doors they saw the police coming towards them. Gesturing with his machine gun, one of the officers ordered Baader and Meins back into the garage. As they complied, another policeman drove his Audi car against the garage doors to secure them. Baader started to fire at the door but his shots were blind and no one was hit. So they remained trapped until police reinforcements arrived and the garage was totally surrounded by 150 officers all pointing guns at the besieged men.

Despite the futility of the situation, Baader and Meins refused to surrender. They continued to smoke cigarettes and wave their guns at the police through the window. About an hour later the police decided to throw containers of tear gas into the garage through holes in the rear of the building. Thinking that this would finish the two, the police announced through loudspeakers that they should throw out their guns and surrender. Slowly, the two pushed on one of the garage doors trapped by the Audi as if they were going to do as they had been instructed but it appeared that they found it difficult to move the doors because of the vehicle. Eventually, the police shifted the car whereupon the door opened wider and Baader laughingly threw out the tear gas canisters, forcing all the police to back off.

The police then sent for an armoured car with four officers in it. The situation was turning into a complete farce with a huge armed police contingent failing to apprehend two men in a garage. Finally, the two men were given one last chance to sur-render, but refused. The police then stormed the front of the garage using the armoured vehicle as a battering ram. At the same time, they threw more tear gas cylinders at the garage. The armoured vehicle was not able to get through the garage doors. In fact, it just forced them more tightly shut and this meant that the tear gas containers did not go into the garage but gassed the area outside where the police were. They were forced to withdraw. Meanwhile, Baader and Meins continued to fire their rifles from the garage.

While all this chaos was going on, a policeman had gone into the building opposite the garage and entered a flat on the third floor that gave an excellent view of the garage and the surrounding yard. Armed with a rifle with a telescopic sight he watched the farcical situation below and pinpointed Andreas Baader. He took aim and fired at Baader, hitting him in the thigh. Baader fell screaming to the ground in agony. Again the two men were told to throw out their guns and surrender. Holger Meins complied and came out with his hands up. Baader lay where he had fallen, writhing and screaming on the floor of the garage as two police officers dressed in bullet proof jackets approached him. One of the police kicked the gun out of Baader's hand and they dragged him outside. Still ranting and raving, he was taken into an ambulance under heavy escort. They now had several of the most wanted members of the gang in custody.

Two weeks later, acting on yet another tip-off, the police found Ulrike Meinhof hiding in an apartment of a friend. During the previous fifteen days the police managed to apprehend Meins, Ensslin, Baader, Meinhof and Brigitte Monhaupt. At long last the German security departments must have begun to show signs of relief as they appeared to be getting control of the situation.

All the prisoners were now confined to isolation cells in separate prisons. There had been one slight problem. When they detained Ulrike Meinhof they had no previous criminal records by which to identify her. What they did know was that she had had an operation some years earlier for a burst blood vessel in her brain. This had been sealed by using a silver clip. The police doctor examined her head for signs of a scar but could not find any evidence of a surgical operation. Ulrike Meinhof was forcibly anaesthetised so that they could x-ray her head and prove who she was from her medical records.

On the 5 October 1974, nearly two and half years after their arrests, all five were indicted for five murders and taken to Stammheim High Security Prison. The trial would begin the following year. When it did start, it was without Holger Meins who had died during a hunger strike the previous year. The trial was to be held in the grounds of the prison in a specially built reinforced steel and concrete building. So tight was the security that they covered the area with steel netting and all aircraft were banned from flying over the prison. This was an indication of how nervous the German authorities were of these few people and their power.

On Saturday 8 May 1976, Ulrike Meinhof was in her cell on the seventh floor where she could be heard using her typewriter. The next morning, at 7.30 a.m., two officers unlocked her cell door. In front of them, hanging from her cell window grating was Ulrike's body. It seems that Ulrike Meinhof, at the age of 41, had hanged herself using a towel that she had tied through the crossbar of her cell window. The prison officers called the prison doctor who verified that she was dead. They cut her body free at 10.30 a.m. During that time many officers visited her cell and checked for clues and took pictures. From their observations they concluded that she had ripped up one of the prison towels into strips and knotted them together to make a rope. She had pushed this through the rails of her window and jumped off a chair that she had balanced on her mattress. An official post-mortem was carried out and from that the cause of death was determined as suicide by strangulation.

Oddly, there was no suicide note to endorse these findings. Meinhof was well known for her love of the written word and had been typing the previous night. It seems strange that she had nothing to put in writing at this final moment. Many claim she was murdered, after which her brain was removed for examination. Many, at the time, scoffed at this idea as being far fetched. Strangely enough, a small column appeared in several English newspapers in late December 2002, stating that the brain of Ulrike Meinhof had recently been cremated and buried. It would seem a German university had kept the brain for research into terrorism over the past 26 years.

HAMAS

HAMAS is an acronym for Harakat al-Muqawamah al-Islamiyya, translated as the Islamic Resistance Movement. The word also has the meaning, 'courage and bravery'. This terrorist organisation, formed originally as Al-Mujamma Al Islami in 1978, has its roots in the Muslim Brotherhood of the 1920s. It started out as a legitimate organisation dedicated to serving the social needs of the people of Palestine. Providing an extensive social, religious, educational and cultural infrastructure in Gaza and the West Bank, it was upheld as a viable political alternative to the Palestinian Liberation Organisation (PLO). In the twenty years prior to the Intifada, it had a largely peaceful policy, preferring to shun the armed struggle of the PLO and other radical groups in favour of its religious teachings and social work, especially among the poor.

Through its humanitarian actions the group gained much support for its ideology and its aims to create an independent Islamic territory of Palestine that stretched from the Red Sea to the banks of the Jordan. By 1987, however, the organisation's passive approach had somewhat changed and a stronger militant element began to rear its head. The leader of the organisation, Sheik Ahmed Yassin, changed its name to HAMAS in late 1987 and set up in opposition not only to the hated Israeli state, but also to the PLO. Behind the scenes, the organisation was being restructured to give it a military arm and a security section in addition to the existing recruitment facility.

On the street level, HAMAS organises violence in the forms of riots and active dissent. Any youths who show extreme dedication or bravery may be invited to move on a stage further – into the military apparatus of the group, either the Izz al-Din al-Qassam hit squads, or the Jehaz Aman security section. The Izz al-Din al-Qassam is the latest incarnation of the attack groups set up just before and during the Intifada. Sheik Yassin had started to organise such a group, then known as Al-Majahadoun Al-Falestinioun, in 1982 by obtaining arms and laying the groundwork for armed struggle. His activities were discovered in 1984 and he was sentenced to thirteen years in prison. Within a year, however, he was out again, released in a prisoner exchange deal. Continuing his plans, Yassin first purged his own organisation and locality of any persons he thought might be collaborators, or heretics, i.e. anyone not acting in accordance with Islamic law. By 1989, Yassin had turned his terrorist plans upon Israel and HAMAS started their reign of terror in the region by kidnapping and killing two IDF (Israeli Defence Force) soldiers.

Izz al-Din al-Qassam hit squads appeared in 1992, manned by some of the most wanted men from Gaza. They have been responsible for some of the worst outrages committed by HAMAS, including suicide bombings. They have no fear of death, seeing it as martyrdom sanctioned by Allah. In their eyes, those who are killed in action, as many have been, go straight to paradise.

The Security section of HAMAS deals with the surveillance and collection of information on suspected collaborators and those who flout Islamic law. During the formative years of HAMAS, anyone suspected of drug dealing or peddling pornography was singled out for extermination by the Majd hit squads. Some of those former Majd units are now part of the Izz al-Din squads.

HAMAS enjoys many sources of funding, among them patronage from countries such as Iran. Western Muslims channel money into HAMAS-related charity funds in the UK, Germany, France, Holland and Belgium. HAMAS also receives finance from the Muslim Brotherhood as well as some of its own small economic projects. Despite the efforts of Israel, the United States and other Western powers to stop the flow of money into terrorist hands, the organisation still receives enough to sustain itself.

Since 1989, HAMAS has been responsible for many terror attacks and murders, mainly within Israel and the territories. The group has hit at innocent civilians, including children, as well as Israeli military or administrative targets. The increasing use of suicide bombers – men and women prepared to die for their beliefs – has created large-scale fear among Israelis. Bombs are often exploded in busy public places, such as markets, or placed on buses carrying school children.

Author's Note: For most of us it is difficult to come to terms with HAMAS, their use of young teenagers to deliver suicide bombs and the willingness of those young people to go to their deaths. An insight into the tactical use of suicide bombers came in reply to a question asked by a colleague of mine who was interviewing a HAMAS commander. It was simple – they cannot match the Israelis on military hardware as Israel has one of the largest armies in the world. While it is true that the Palestinians have a limited supply of small arms, automatic riles and the odd RPG 7, they are in no position to fight the Israeli army in a conventional war. They are not equipped to fight tanks, or shoot down fighter aircraft or helicopter gunships. They therefore rely on the one special weapon they do have – the suicide bomber. In the same interview, the HAMAS commander also made certain assertions about the young bombers. They are not, as many in the West think, led to believe that they will earn a place in paradise if they commit an act of suicide. They are told they will die, but for a cause they believe in.

On 25 February 1996, a suicide bomber boarded the No. 18 bus in Jerusalem and took a seat near the middle. As the bus neared Jerusalem's Central Station, the bomber detonated the bomb killing seventeen civilians and nine soldiers. A week later, on 3 March, another suicide bomber also boarded the replacement No. 18 bus. As the bus drove along the Jaffa Road in Jerusalem the bomber detonated the bomb, this time killing sixteen civilians and three soldiers. Numerous others were injured.

The suicide bombings continued at the rate of about ten per year with an average death toll of five people per attack. Then, on 1 June 2001, a device exploded outside a night club in Tel Aviv. The entire area in and around the club was crowded with young people enjoying the area's nightlife. The explosion claimed twenty lives and injured another 120. Two months later, on 9 August, young people and families once again became the target for a suicide attack. This time, the bomber struck at a Pizzeria near the centre of Jerusalem. Fifteen people were killed and more than ninety wounded in the explosion. One family lost five people including three children aged fourteen, four and two. In all, six children were killed.

On 18 June 2002, a suicide bomber exploded his device aboard a bus travelling into the centre of Jerusalem. Nineteen people, including several schoolchildren, were killed and 74 were injured. Such news is almost a daily occurrence. The increasing number and ferocity of the suicide attacks has led Israel to carry out limited re-occupation in the territories, ostensibly to flush the terrorists from their homes and safe havens. While the operations have had some success it can also be argued that the heavy-handed methods of the IDF have left a legacy of even greater hatred among the Palestinians. Such feelings can only produce a future increasing spiral of violence with many more, including women, prepared to end their lives as suicide bombers for their cause. HAMAS and Israel are further than ever from reaching a peace agreement.

Palestine Liberation Organisation (PLO)

The (PLO) is one of the better-known terrorist organisations. It was founded in 1964 during the Palestinian Congress, a meeting set up to discuss the plight of thousands of Palestinians living in refugee camps in Lebanon. As various individuals disagreed over the best way of liberating Palestine, a number of splinter organisations arose, such as the Popular Front for the Liberation of Palestine; the Popular Democratic Front for the Liberation of Palestine – General Command; and al-Fatah (translating to The Movement for the National Liberation of Palestine). Despite their disagreements, however, all of these organisations stayed more or less loyal to the PLO and its ultimate aim which, by 1967, had changed to bringing about the end of the state of Israel.

With this new aim in mind, the PLO changed tactics and embarked on a terrorist campaign, bringing death and fear to Israelis as hundreds were killed in the attacks. In return, Israel retaliated by attacking PLO strongholds and Palestinian camps causing just as many casualties. In 1974, with nothing gained from the years of bloodshed, the PLO decided to change its tactics again, adding a political front in the hope of initiating a dialogue, hoping that this might bring them results where force had failed. Not all within the group were happy about this change of direction and another splinter group formed – the Rejectionist Front. It was at this time of unrest that Yasser Arafat, head of al-Fatah, took over the leadership of the PLO.

Arafat was a deft politician as well as a military leader and his abilities as well as charisma began to pay off when the PLO became recognised by the United Nations as an organisation with legitimate claims. It was also recognised by many Arab countries at the Rabat Conference. Israel now found itself out of favour and became determined to destroy the PLO once and for all. Marching into Beirut in Lebanon in 1982, it forced the PLO from its base. Left without any other option, Arafat was forced to negotiate with the Israelis, although no lasting agreement developed. The situation did, however, highlight the increasing tensions among the ranks of the PLO and it wasn't long afterwards that some of the less militant leaders were assassinated.

With the PLO on the edge of crisis, Arafat once more took the initiative and lent his support to a terrorist operation he may have hoped would provide a morale boost to his organisation. The hijacking of the cruise ship *Achille Lauro* in 1985, a PLO operation carried out along with the PLF, turned out to have damaging consequences when members of the team shot and killed a Jewish passenger confined to a wheelchair. Suddenly, the PLO found themselves condemned for their actions by world opinion and once more out in the cold.

The fighting and deaths of Israelis and Palestinians continued unabated, with neither side giving ground. In 1988, Arafat again tried to elevate the status of his organisation by renouncing PLO terrorism and agreeing that the state of Israel had the right to exist. Such a statement convinced Israel to come to the negotiating table and they eventually conceded the right to partial Palestinian self-rule as well as further talks concerning recognition of a Palestinian homeland. By September 1993, Arafat had taken this one stage further and, in a letter to Israeli Prime Minister Rabin and Norwegian Foreign Minister Holst, he promised the end of all PLO-related violence and terrorism. A few days later, the Israelis and

Palestinians signed the Declaration of Principles in Washington DC, setting the seal on the new relationship. Except for a couple of isolated incidents, thought to be individuals acting upon their own initiative, the ceasefire held relatively well.

During the Gulf War in 1990, Arafat publicly supported Saddam Hussein which, although earning him popularity with fellow Palestinians, also caused him to be shunned by the richer Arab states that had been giving him financial support. The PLO now found itself without some of its greatest sources of funding. During the 1990s, tensions once again surfaced between Israel and the PLO as distrust started to corrode the past agreements and PLO-related terrorism was once more killing innocent people. The situation intensified as Israel retaliated against the PLO, and Arafat in particular, by destroying his headquarters in Remallah and keeping him under house arrest. Today, although negotiations still continue behind the scenes, the violence and counter violence continue, although it would be fair to say that the PLO are no longer quite as much of a threat as they used to be.

Liberation Tigers of Tamil Eelam (LTTE).

The Tamil Tigers, or, as they are properly known, the Liberation Tigers of Tamil Eelam (LTTE) came into being in the early 1970s in response to what they saw as Sri Lankan oppression against the Tamil people. The Tamil people had originally been brought from southern India by the British to work on their plantations in what was then called Ceylon. After independence was granted from Britain, the majority Sinhalese people took political control and by 1972 had changed the island's name to Sri Lanka. They also changed the official language to Sinhalese and the official religion to Buddhism, thus isolating the minority Tamils. Further discriminatory actions against the Tamils followed until tensions spilled over, precipitating the creation of the LTTE and also the Tamil United Liberation Front (TULF), which in the elections of 1977 won seats in all Tamil areas.

The Tigers continued to develop a strong militant force, deriving support from the economically deprived Tamil workers whose livelihoods had been taken away during drastic economic reforms of the 1970s. Further support also came from several Indian administrations that trained and armed the LTTE.

Financial support comes mainly from the activities of ex-patriots in the West who gather funds not only from legal commercial activity but also from extortion and other illegal practices. With such funds the LTTE have been able to buy up-to-date weaponry, mostly from the countries of the former Soviet Union. Their home-based actions have also provided them with a large amount of arms and ordinance captured from the security forces. The rebels are known to have surface-to-air missiles and rocket launchers in addition to conventional artillery.

The leader of the Tamil Tigers is Velupillai Prabhakaran, born in a town on the Jaffna peninsula in 1954. Extremely reclusive and dedicated to his cause, he is also said to be ruthless and fearless and has been accused of being responsible for the murder of the mayor of Jaffna in 1975. In the spring of 2002 he made his first public appearance at a press conference as a step on the way to peace negotiations with the Sri Lankan Government.

Like their leader, Tamil rebels are reputed to be fearless and ruthless. Numbering approximately 10,000, including women and children, their military training is hard and thorough and they are expected to avoid capture at all costs, if necessary committing suicide with the cyanide capsule they all carry. This ideological devotion to suicide also carries over into their style of attack as both men and women have turned themselves into human bombs in order to carry out acts of terrorism. The LTTE have the worst reputation of any of the world's terrorist groups for carrying out this kind of attack. In one attack where the LTTE carried out a suicide bombing of Sri Lanka's holiest Buddhist site in Kandy in 1998, sixteen were killed. And in 1996, a suicide bomber drove a truck packed with explosives into the Central Bank, killing 91 and wounding 1,400.

Apart from suicide bombings, the Tigers have been accused of other atrocities. One group of Sinhalese villagers, including women and children, was hacked to death in a pre-dawn attack in late 1999. The LTTE has also been responsible for a campaign of ethnic cleansing in Jaffna, the area they consider to be their 'homeland'.

The LTTE have also been implicated in, or responsible for, high-level assassinations such as that of India's premier Rajiv Gandhi in 1991 and Sri Lanka's president Premadasa in 1993.

Attempts at negotiating a peace were made during the early 1990s under President Kumaratunga, but the talks soon collapsed in an atmosphere of mistrust and fighting soon resumed. Once Kumaratunga's Government resigned in October 2001, a new hope for peace emerged. The new cabinet, led by Ranil Wickramasinghe, had a pro-peace mandate and a determination to succeed where others had failed. After the LTTE declared a unilateral ceasefire, the Government agreed to talks and the ceasefire was made permanent in an agreement between the two sides in February 2002. The talks proceeded throughout 2002 with both sides making concessions and exchanging prisoners. The LTTE dropped its demand for a separate state and the Government lifted its ban on the rebel organisation. By December 2002, during peace talks in Norway, it was agreed that both sides should share power and that the Tamils should have autonomy in the predominantly Tamil north and east.

Japanese Red Army (JRA)

Formed in 1970 as a breakaway group of the Japanese Communist League, the Red Army Faction, or Anti-Imperialist International Brigade (AIIB) as it is also known, is Japan's only international terrorist group. It is small in size, numbering no more than a dozen members, and is believed to be located in Syrian-controlled areas of Lebanon, but also has bases in Asia. The group established itself as 'International' when it made several attacks on behalf of organisations such as the PLO. Its members were mainly left-wing students who followed the blueprint for terrorism flowing from the Middle East.

The group got off to a slow start with petrol bombs and weak demonstrations, most of which were dealt with by the Japanese police. The group was, if nothing else, self-critical and its members underwent severe punishment and bizarre initiation rites. Their first hijack was on 26 March 1970, when a group of nine JRA took control of a Boeing 727, threatening the 130 passengers with pistols and grenades. The aircraft finally finished up in North

Korea, where the hostages were released and the JRA given political asylum. This act drew the attention of George Habash who, it is reported, made contact with the group in order to establish some link and support in the Far East. Whatever the contact, it is clear that some accommodation was reached as the JRA formed an alliance with the PFLP. Shortly after, some of the Japanese found themselves being trained in PLO camps situated in the Lebanon. Over the next two years, the JRA concentrated on re-training most of its membership, while those that remained in Japan set to raising funds through bank robberies and extortion. Leadership of the group also changed with a woman, Fusako Shigenobu, taking command. Her style of control was ruthless, those that disobeyed orders or appeared weak being executed. During a police interrogation of a JRA member it was revealed that several bodies were hidden in shallow graves in the high mountains close to Maebashi. A search revealed the bodies of fourteen ex-JRA members, most of which had been tortured, and some that had been buried while still alive. Shigenobu was said to be dedicated to PFLP leader George Habash as well as a close personal friend of Leila Khaled.

On 30 May 1972, three Japanese Red Army members met with Shigenobu in Rome, where she outlined a simple but horrendous plan. Once briefed, she handed over machine guns and grenades with the express instructions that these were to be hidden in their luggage. Later that night, the three men boarded an Air France flight for Tel Aviv. They sat out the flight and arrived at Lod airport in Tel Aviv on time. The baggage hall was full as several aircraft had landed within a few minutes of each other. Amid this mass of humanity, the three terrorists waited until all three had received their suitcases before removing their weapons and grenades. The three then stood and opened fire indiscriminately on the crowd before throwing several grenades. They murdered 26 innocent people, before one of them accidentally shot an accomplice and another was killed by one of his own grenades. The third was captured and under interrogation highlighted the link between the PFLP and the JRA.

This act of terror horrified not just the Israelis but most of the free world. So great was the backlash that it caused a rift between Wadi Haddad and George Habash, as well as a sharp decline in sympathy for the Palestinians. Despite the criticism, the JRA continued to operate with the PFLP, carrying out further hijacking and other terrorist operations.

One such incident was the hijacking of a Japanese Airlines DC8 with 146 passengers on board. The plane was flying from Paris to Tokyo, with a stopover in Bombay. Shortly after leaving Bombay, the terrorists seized the aircraft and forced the pilot to fly to Dacca, Bangladesh. The demands from the terrorists were issued shortly after landing. They were for the release of nine terrorists currently in Japanese jails and a ransom of six million dollars, to be made up of $100 bills.

The Japanese Government, fearing that some of the hijackers were 'Kamikaze' and had taken part in previous atrocities, agreed to the demands. Unfortunately, when it came down to it, three of the terrorists held in Japan refused to go and, therefore, the demands could only be met in part. The hijackers finally accepted this and gave an extension to the deadline in order to allow the Japanese Government time to collect the money and get the prisoners to Dacca. At this stage a further problem developed: the hijackers had demanded the six million in $100 bills but this quantity of notes could not be found in Japan and four million dollars had to be flown in from America.

Finally, the six jailed terrorists and the ransom money flew to Dacca but, as the aircraft arrived, for some reason the hijacked DC8 began to move down the runway ready for takeoff. At this stage the Bangladesh air vice-marshal in charge of the negotiators ordered jeeps and fire tenders to block the runway. Despite the hijackers firing shots from the aircraft at the vehicles, the aircraft was forced to stop. The Bangladesh negotiator then told the hijackers that they had started the deal and now that the prisoners and ransom money had arrived they would 'damn well finish it'. Strangely enough, the hijackers agreed and returned the aircraft to its original parking area.

The exchange was carried out, but the hijackers retained a number of hostages to ensure their safety as they flew out to their unknown destination. Once en route they were forced to land at Kuwait to take on more fuel. The Kuwaitis only agreed to exchange fuel for hostages and a further seven of the retained hostages were released. On 3 October, the hijacked DC8 touched down in Algiers and the hijackers released the last of the hostages and crew. The Algerian authorities took the five hijackers and released prisoners away to an undisclosed destination – they have not been heard of since.

Thus ended the six-day, 6,000-mile ordeal of the passengers and crew. In Tokyo, Mr Takeo Fukuda, the Japanese Prime Minister, told Parliament, 'The Government decided to comply, in principle, with the hijackers unlawful demands to protect the lives of more than 140 people.' On this occasion, acceding to the terrorists' demands proved to be the correct strategy and, as the Japanese Red Army have proved themselves to be totally ruthless in the past, it was probably the only way to save the lives of the hostages.

The JRA leader, Shigenobu remains at large, although the same can not be said for other members of the organisation, eight of whom have been arrested since 1996. In April 1988 Yu Kikumura, a member of the JRA, was arrested at the New Jersey Turnpike. He was in possession of explosives and was, it seems, planning an attack to coincide with the bombing of a USO club in Naples. Kikumura was convicted of these charges and is serving a lengthy prison sentence in the United States. Ekita Yukiko, another JRA activist, was arrested in Romania in March 1995 and subsequently deported to Japan.

Aum Supreme Truth

Aum Supreme Truth is a religious cult based in Japan. Its aim is to seize power in Japan and then take over the world. The cult is also known as Aum Shinrikyo – Aum is Sanskrit for 'the powers of destruction and creation in the universe', and Shinrikyo is 'the teaching of the supreme truth'. The founder, Shoko Asahara, was born with the name 'Chizuo Matsumoto' in 1955 in the southern island of Kyushu. He had a normal education but, when he moved to Tokyo in 1977, he failed to gain entry to Tokyo University. Somewhat disillusioned, he turned his interest to religion, joining a new order called Agonshu. Agonshu preached deliverance from bad karma through meditation. Asahara transformed this belief, adding to it several forms of suffering to purge the body and mind; this became the basis of the Aum cult. In 1987, after travelling alone to the Himalayan Mountains, he changed his name and started to recruit more followers.

Many of these new recruits were forced to endure extremely painful initiation ceremonies. These include placing members in near-boiling water, extremely painful stress positions and even mutilation. Quite a few Aum members have disappeared over the years and most of these are thought to have been murdered. The current method of execution of a 'failed' member is lynching. News of these initiation rites soon became public and in May 1989 several worried families with children who had been recruited into Aum hired the Yokohama lawyer Tsutsumi Sakamoto to investigate the cult. His main brief was to establish the conditions Aum's followers where forced to endure. As the story became newsworthy, many more worried parents came forward. The cult became offended with this investigation and denied all allegations of cruel or unusual practices. Shortly afterwards, the lawyer, together with his wife and child, disappeared. Despite the police finding an Aum symbol at the scene there was no evidence to link the cult and the disappearance. Six years later, in September 1995, the bodies of all three were discovered in remote mountain locations.

Aum Supreme Truth also entered the political arena when the Supreme Truth Party ran 25 candidates in a Japanese parliamentary election in 1990. Although they had expected to win some seats, all of their candidates lost. This led the cult to be ridiculed and 'Aum bashing' became popular. As a result, the group started to isolate themselves and their activities. There was also a shift in the ideology of the cult whereby they started to consider ways of mass retaliation.

It is estimated that the cult is some 2,000 strong but it claims to have many more supporters worldwide, including an unknown number in Russia. The cult has no problem finding new recruits, most of whom are used to provide free labour for its profitable commercial ventures, and it has bought several properties. Aum generates most of its own funds; this is mainly from membership donations and its computer software business. The latter is by far the most profitable source of income as it has been able to undercut most of its rivals by producing cheaper software.

The cult had secret laboratories where highly qualified devotees experimented with various biological agents with a view to causing mass murder. When these experiments proved to be ineffective, the cult turned to manufacturing nerve agents of which sarin proved particularly effective. Several mysterious incidents involving nerve agents occurred throughout Japan during the summer of 1994 as the cult tested its production of sarin. In June 1994, Asahara ordered an attack on three judges who were sitting in a court case against him – the method of attack was sarin gas. Two refrigerated trucks specially converted to spray the agent were driven around the Kita-Fukahi district of central Japan. This attack was successful in injuring the judges. It was first thought that a local gardener had caused the gassing until several Aum members were reported running, in respirators, away from a building that was billowing gas. The whole area was contaminated and the incident led to the arrest of several cult members.

Aum's first major terrorist attack came on 20 March 1995 when Aum members released their home-made nerve agent upon the unsuspecting people of Tokyo. The attack was aimed at travellers using the Tokyo subway where the cult dispersed the nerve agent in such a manner as to affect several trains. In all, ten members attacked five trains during the peak morning rush. They concealed the sarin inside bags wrapped in newspapers. These were punctured just prior to the members exiting the train. This resulted in the deaths of twelve people and up to six thousand injuries. Aum perpetrated a second attack on trains in the Tokyo-Yokohama area which killed several more and raised the total of those injured to almost 10,000. Two months later, the police, who had suspected that Aum were behind the attack, arrested Asahara.

Apart from the nerve gas incidents, Asahara and other Aum members are also accused of the kidnapping and murder of Tsutsumi Sakamoto, the lawyer representing Aum members' parents, together with his wife and infant son. They were also charged with kidnapping and murdering the Tokyo notary, Kiyoshi Kariya in February 1995.

Al-Qaida

This terrorist group has become the greatest potential threat to the national security of many countries, especially after the Twin Towers atrocity of 11 September 2001 (see Chapter 3). With bases and supporters in many countries, it embraces and supports radical Islamic movements worldwide, urging them to overthrow 'heretic' and pro-Western Muslim Governments and to bring down the United States, which it sees as its prime enemy.

The organisation was formed in 1988 by Osama bin Laden, a radical Islamist from a wealthy Saudi Arabian family. Travelling to Afghanistan in 1979 to support the resistance movement against the Soviet invaders, he saw that the Muslim fighters were ill-equipped to carry out a sustained conflict against a technically superior enemy. Not only were they lacking in numbers and skills, but also the infrastructure necessary to support the fighters. Using his wealth and influence, he brought both workmen and construction plant to Afghanistan and, together with the Palestinian Muslim Brotherhood leader Abdallah Azzam, began to organise an international programme of conscription through a newly formed recruiting office: Maktab al-Khidamet (MAK – Services Office). As new recruits from such countries as Saudi Arabia, Yemen, Algeria and Egypt arrived, their transportation paid for by bin Laden, he began to build training facilities. Specialists were brought in from around the world to coach the men in guerrilla warfare tactics.

At this time, ironically, bin Laden was probably aided by the Western powers in his struggle. NATO, and in particular the United States, saw Russia's invasion as a threat to its own presence in the area. The CIA launched a multi-million dollar operation to train and equip the rebels, or Mujaheddin as they became known, and this may also have included some of bin Laden's men. With up-to-date weaponry, training and discipline, the Mujaheddin eventually proved more than a match for the Soviet troops and the invading army was forced into an ignominious retreat after ten years of occupation.

By the end of the war, bin Laden had around ten thousand well-trained, equipped and war-hardened veterans under his command. Some dispersed back to their former lives and families, deciding that they had done their duty and could now live in peace. Others had become so fanatical about Islamic fundamentalism that they returned to their countries determined to organise their own terror groups and overthrow what they saw as 'secular' governments. Egypt and Algeria both saw the rise of dangerous new extremist groups intent on causing death and injury to those whom they saw as obstacles in their way to a new fundamentalist state. Other countries, which already had a 'Shariah law-based' form of leadership, welcomed the Mujaheddin and also Osama bin Laden. Sudan, in particular, was friendly towards him, providing jobs and training facilities for his men.

The end of the Afghan–Soviet war was, in many ways, a watershed for the many Islamic groups, which had been formed for the purpose of resistance. In 1988, bin Laden split from his MAK co-founder, Abdallah Azzam, in order to form a group that was to carry on his holy way for Islam. That group was called Al-Qaida. The following year Azzam was murdered by a car bomb. Despite there being a number of likely suspects, a rumour still persists that bin Laden was behind it. As with a number of acts of terrorism linked to his name, however, it has never been proven.

Bin Laden's new fight started with his own country of origin. After the Afghan war, he returned to Saudi to raise an insurrection against the government there. This plan, however, was thwarted and bin Laden was thrown out of the country and his citizenship revoked. Undaunted, he moved his centre of operations to Sudan, using his wealth to create farms and factories, supplying jobs for his followers. He also improved the infrastructure of the country – building roads and an airport. His many business interests included a bank, a construction company and an import–export business. More training camps were set up and former Afghan comrades were encouraged to move to Sudan. During the 1990s, bin Laden's name has been connected with several terrorist incidents, but there has been no direct evidence to link him with the bombings. Other planned incidents, such as an attempted assassination on Pope John Paul II during his visit to Manila and the midair bombing of several US airliners were never carried out.

Sudan's friendliness towards its Al-Qaida guests began to crumble when its government started to bow to pressure from the United States. Not wishing to be subjected to sanctions or other methods of persuasion, the Sudanese asked bin Laden to leave. This he did in 1996, returning with his followers to Afghanistan. With a number of business interests and followers still in Sudan, however, he retained an influence there and many Sudanese companies are thought to act as a front for some of his activities.

Pushing forward with his vision of a fundamentalist Islamic world, in February 1998, bin Laden formed an umbrella organisation known as 'The Islamic World Front for the Struggle Against the Jews and the Crusaders' (Al-Jahhah al-Islamiyyah al-'Alamiyyah li-Qital al-Yahud wal-Salibiyyin). Its members were to include the Egyptian terror groups al-Gama'a al-Islamiyya and al-Jihad, as well as some extreme fundamentalist groups in Pakistan. Its purpose was to take the war to Israel and the United States and its allies. Bin Laden justified its existence by arguing that these countries were responsible for the oppression of Muslims everywhere. Therefore, to protect the vulnerable, as well as the faith, these countries needed to be taken on and destroyed. Three 'fatwahs' were declared, calling on all faithful Muslims to take up the holy war, or Jihad, against the 'enemies of Islam'.

Bin Laden is thought to have been behind a whole series of attacks, most of which were directed against American military personnel. The attack on 11 September prompted a declaration by the United States that it would rid the world of terrorism and Al-Qaida. Backed by most countries worldwide it launched a successful attack on Afghanistan, intending to destroy all of Al-Qaida's bases, overthrow Afghanistan's ruling Taliban government and arrest most of the leaders. In the first two it was generally successful. Some believe bin Laden perished under the heavy carpet bombing, but those closest to him, including the Taliban leader Mullah Omar, are said to have escaped. It is thought that many of their followers are also still in hiding waiting for the right time to strike at America and its allies again. Considering that Al-Qaida has many supporters all over the world prepared to die for what they believe in and, considering that the organisation may yet have the knowledge, if not yet the capability, to produce weapons of mass destruction, this is still the most dangerous terrorist organisation in existence.

Since the Afghan war, there have been several reports that Osama bin Laden is still alive, but with little evidence to support the fact. Then, in February 2003, the Americans received a videotape which clearly shows Osama bin Laden fit and well. The tape, intended to promote action among his many followers, calls for the Muslim extremists to take up arms against the American 'devil'.

Chechen Terror Groups

The relationship between the Chechen freedom fighters and international terrorism is anything but clear. Chechnya is a small state within the Russian Federation but the Chechens themselves are a fiercely independent people who have long fought to free themselves from rule by Moscow. The root of the country's current problems lies during World War II when Stalin thought that the Chechen people were siding with the Nazis against him. His response was to deport the whole population by force to Kazakhstan where many thousands died. Those that remained were only able to return to their homes after Stalin's death in 1953.

Resentment against the Soviet state simmered away until the Soviet Union collapsed in 1991. Seizing the moment, Chechnya's President Dzhokhar Dudayev declared independence from Russia, causing President Yeltsin to send in troops and aircraft. The subsequent war lasted until August 1996 when Yeltsin backed down after losing much prestige for a seemingly unsuccessful campaign. Chechnya was now allowed its independence. Massive loss of life and destruction throughout the whole country had been caused and attitudes had hardened further against any possible future involvement with Russia.

The uneasy peace didn't last long, for in 1999 four massive

explosions tore through apartment buildings in Russia, killing nearly 300 people. During the same period, Chechen rebels made military incursions into nearby Dagestan, trying to set up an Islamist state. These incidents were more than enough of an excuse for Russia's new president, Putin, to send troops into the country again, starting a second war and subsequent occupation which continues into the present.

Chechen terror gangs have also been held responsible for a number of other atrocities and attacks. During June 1995, a Chechen rebel group seized a hospital in the southern Russian town of Budyonnovsk and held 2,000 people hostage. The Russians made two unsuccessful rescue attempts but in the end the hostages were released in return for safe passage for the rebels to escape into the mountains. In January 1996, rebel Chechens again seized a hospital, this time in Dagestan. Russian aircraft bombed the village where more than a hundred hostages were being held. During the four-day bombardment many innocent lives were lost. Also in January 1996, Chechen militants hijacked a Turkish ferry bound for Russia, taking 165 passengers and crew hostage.

More recently Chechen militants are alleged to have been behind a plot to assassinate President Putin in Azerbaijan in January 2001.They have also been blamed for the bomb that exploded at a military parade in Kaspiisk in May 2002, killing 41 people, including 17 children. Conversely, the whole world became more aware of the threat caused by Chechen terrorists when 50 of them took over a theatre in Moscow on 23 October 2002 and held 700 people hostage (see Chapter 5). At least 70 people within that audience were citizens of countries other than Russia, therefore attracting wide media interest and coverage. The leader of the rebels on that occasion was 23-year-old Movsar Barayev, the nephew of notorious warlord Arbi Barayev. Arbi Barayev, who was killed by Russian forces in June 2001, was himself responsible for the kidnapping and beheading of three Britons and a New Zealander in 1998.

Today Chechnya remains as one of the most dangerous countries in the world for foreign visitors. Kidnappings, gun-running and slave-trading is all too common as the various warlords act like a local mafia. It must be stressed that most of these warlords are more interested in their own mercenary trading practices than in any altruistic or religious future for their country. Nevertheless, there are those who do wish to see Chechnya become a radical Islamic state and are quite prepared to use terror tactics throughout the region and elsewhere to achieve it. Some of these groups are known to receive funding from various Islamic charities as well as having logistic support from other militant Islamic organisations.

There is an undoubted link between some rebel Chechen leaders and Al-Qaida. The Chechen warlord Khattab, for example, was born in Jordan and appears to have made the acquaintance of Osama bin Laden in Afghanistan during the Soviet Union's occupation of that country between 1979 and 1989. According to several reports, Khattab, who was killed in Chechnya in 2002, maintained close links with bin Laden. Chechen independence was also fiercely supported by the Taliban regime in Afghanistan, another regime with strong links to Al-Qaida. Today, Russian authorities insist that there is a strong Al-Qaida presence within Chechnya, both supporting its cause and also recruiting fighters for its international ambitions.

3: TERRORIST ATTACKS

For the most part, terrorist attacks fall into two main categories: immediate and continuing. An immediate action would be where a HAMAS bomber has made his way onto a bus and at the precise moment detonated the device killing himself and everyone around him – the planned act has transpired. A hijack that lasts for several days would be classed as a continuing act.

In terms of numbers, there are far more people involved in anti-terrorist work around the world than there are involved with terrorist organisations. Government forces outnumber the terrorists thousands to one, but they are not winning the war. Indeed, if you define 'winning' by counting the number of dead on each side, then the security forces are lagging way behind. From the first hijackings of the 1960s to the attacks on America in September 2001, the terrorist organisations have planned and executed thousands of violent acts, creating an accumulation of dead and wounded so vast that it is impossible to accurately quantify it.

At times it seems the only answer to many of these incidents is political rhetoric, with politicians and world leaders condemning all such atrocities. Unfortunately, much of this verbal diarrhoea falls short of any real action. For example, the British Government announced on 1 March 2001 that it intended to ban many foreign organisations under its new anti-terrorist legislation. This new list included 21 terrorist groups such as the Basque separatist organisation, ETA, the Kurdish PKK based in Turkey, and the Tamil Tiger guerrillas in Sri Lanka. Also on the list was the Al-Qaida network of Osama bin Laden. In reality, this has had no effect whatsoever on preventing terrorism or on preventing more people from being killed – ETA still carried out assassinations, HAMAS continues with its suicide bombers and Osama bin Laden ordered the attacks on America. True, the new law makes it illegal to encourage terrorist activities abroad and anyone who openly supports a banned organisation, either verbally or via fund-raising, can be arrested. Realistically, political criticism carries little weight with terrorist organisations.

For the most part, terrorist attacks fall into two main categories: immediate and continuing. An immediate action would be where a

HAMAS bomber has made his way onto a bus and at the precise moment detonated the device killing himself and everyone around him – the planned act has transpired. A hijack that lasts for several days would be classed as a continuing act. It is important to recognise the distinction, as the outcomes can be so completely different. It is almost impossible to prevent either act from taking place, but a continuing act does provide the authorities with time in which to contain and react to the situation. By comparison, immediate acts of terrorism are generally much more violent, while a hijack or the seizing of an embassy normally results in far less casualties.

The media attention gained from a continuing terrorist action is far greater than that of an immediate act. The various terrorist organisations know this and, as a result, determine the type of act they wish to undertake. Although all the suicide bombs of HAMAS are horrific, we have seen so many that it becomes difficult for the rest of the world to tell each incident apart. Therefore, while such a strategy may well have an effect on the people of Tel Aviv, it loses much of its influence on the world's media. By comparison, during the takeover and siege of the Japanese embassy in Peru, the number of foreign diplomats held hostage guaranteed MRTA excellent long-term publicity.

The examples that follow are in date order and it is interesting to note how the different actions ended, especially when it came to the body count. It is also worth noting how the terrorist has changed from one of hostage holder to one of murderer; this is especially true of those incidents carried out by suicide bombers. The examples provide some understanding of what the terrorist organisations hope to achieve. To put these events in context, however, it is important to recognise and define what and who initiates a terrorist attack, as the first example illustrates.

Beirut Airport – 28 December 1968

At 20:37 on 28 December 1968, several helicopters laden with para-troopers took off – their destination was Beirut airport. As Beirut International airport is situated to the south of the city some two miles from the sea, and approximately 90 kilometres (55 miles) north of the Israeli–Lebanon border, flying time was estimated at 45 minutes. In 1968 the airport comprised of two runways crossing scissors-like, in a north–south direction. Between the two lanes lies the passenger terminal and, in front of it, an open area. At the north-eastern and the south-western edges of the runways were hangars, parking and maintenance areas for the planes. South of the terminal was the standby emergency services' pavilion of the airport, where fire and first aid stations were located.

Each of the helicopters carried a team of highly trained explosives experts. Their objective was to destroy as many civilian aircraft as possible.

Security for the airport consisted of around ninety security men armed mainly with handguns. Backup for a real emergency came from a Lebanese Army commando company situated 3 kilometres away. Extra help was also available from the police in Beirut city, although they would take a minimum of 30 minutes to reach the airport.

The plan was for those security officers confronted while on duty to be held while the bulk of the military and police would be prevented from approaching the airport. The latter was accomplished by the helicopters which, once they had deposited the soldiers on the airfield, proceeded to the approach roads and dropped nails and smoke. Several military vehicles ultimately tried to force their way through this barrier only to be fired on by the helicopters.

While any serious resistance was kept at bay the disembarked troops set about fixing explosive devices to the many aircraft parked on the airfield. Intermittent gunfire could be heard throughout the airfield. Most of this was warning shots to frighten away the civilian maintenance workers. A total of 14 planes, mostly belonging to Middle East Airlines (MEA) were destroyed at an estimated cost of 42 million dollars.

Those responsible for this assault (or act of terrorism as it was claimed by many Western governments at the time) were the Israeli military. This was their retaliation for an assault by PFLP on an El Al aircraft at Athens airport earlier in the year. Is this defined as justifiable retaliation or state terrorism?

Dawson's Field – 6 September 1970

There is no doubt that the technique of hijacking heralded a new era of terrorist acts. It was new, innovative, international, and it attracted excellent media coverage. As with the movies, it produced its own stars, whom many young and impressionable teenagers admired. The female Palestinian terrorist Leila Khaled stands as an example.

Khaled was an attractive, dark-haired, intelligent girl in her twenties. Her charisma and her successes had turned the young woman into a folk legend and the Palestinians and Arab youth idolised her. She had been a teacher in Kuwait and, like Habash and Haddad before her, had studied at the American University of Beirut. She was just four years old when her family were driven out of Palestine. When she was interviewed many years later, she said, 'Like all Palestinians, education only helped me to realise what a loss Palestine was.' Khaled was to be part of a group that hijacked an Israeli Boeing 707 en route to New York, flying from Tel Aviv via Amsterdam. She was to play a pivotal role in a major hijack scenario involving many countries and governments.

The original plan appears to have been to send at least five terrorists to hijack the El Al Boeing. Haddad had chosen Khaled as she had become a most accomplished hijacker and for this reason she was keen to tackle the heavily guarded Israeli airliner. Haddad gave Khaled the only copy of the navigation plans for the plane's destination. All five terrorists were to meet at Amsterdam airport.

Unfortunately, at Amsterdam the suspicions of airport staff had been alerted when three of the hijackers, posing as passengers, tried to insist that their first-class seats should be allocated near the front of the plane just by the pilot's cabin. The airport staff became suspicious and refused to let them on the flight. The uneasy terrorists then failed to inform Khaled and her accomplice, Patrick Arguello, who were waiting in another lounge, about their predicament. As the final call for all passengers travelling on El Al Airways was called, Khaled and her co-conspirator made their way to the aircraft, unaware that the other hijackers had been refused permission to board. Khaled and her male companion sat together on the plane but did not speak or appear to recognise one another.

At some stage they must have realised that they were on their own, although they seemed determined to carry on with the operation.

Ten minutes after taking off, while the aircraft flew over the North Sea, Khaled and Arguello leaped from their seats and threatened the 145 passengers and crew. Khaled waved her hands in the air displaying two grenades, while Arguello gestured towards the frightened passengers with a .22 revolver. Arguello then made his way towards the flight deck. As he ordered an air stewardess to open the door, he was intercepted and shot by a sky marshal. As Leila Khaled made her way into the first-class lounge, an unidentified young man, possibly a security guard, disarmed her. He grabbed her by the elbows and pushed her to the floor, before tying her hands and feet together with a man's neck tie.

The plan had failed due to the courage of the crew and the fact that all El Al aircraft carry professional sky marshals. The male terrorist, Patrick Arguello, died of his wounds some 30 minutes after he had been shot. A steward who had earlier attempted to restrain him and had been shot three times in the stomach, went on to make a good recovery. As the gunfight had happened over the North Sea, the pilot radioed a request for an emergency landing at Heathrow airport. While the plane flew over England, a full-scale police alert was put into operation.

The plane had barely landed at Heathrow before a crew member emerged holding a grenade. While everyone froze, he ran across the tarmac and placed it safely out of harm's way. This was not a show of bravado, the pin had been pulled from the grenade during the preceding struggle but for some reason it had failed to go off. Having landed at London's Heathrow airport, the Israelis refused to hand over Khaled because she was wanted for other crimes back in Israel. The police thought otherwise, and reminded the Israelis that they were on British soil. Eventually the situation was resolved with the Israelis being persuaded, somewhat reluctantly, to hand over Leila Khaled. Once in police custody, she was taken to West Drayton police station in Middlesex, where the police questioned her about Patrick Arguello, whose body had been taken from the aircraft. Khaled replied that she did not know who he was; that their first meeting had been on the aircraft just prior to the hijacking.

The authorities in Britain eventually charged her with entering Britain illegally. Leila Khaled, however, showed no particular signs of worry over her confinement, confident in the fact that Wadi Haddad would somehow get her released. If we are to believe the rumours of the time, she spent most of her time lecturing the women police officers, who accompanied her everywhere, about the joys of Marxism. Yet even as this drama unfolded in England, the PFLP were already busy in the skies over Europe.

The first shock came on 6 September 1970, when an American Boeing 707 of TWA, carrying 145 passengers and ten crew, took off from Frankfurt bound for New York. As the aircraft flew over the French coastline, the crew were threatened by several hijackers who forced the pilot to fly to the Middle East. During the flight, the pilot was informed that he would be landing on a desert airstrip in Jordan. Its name was Dawson's Field. This old British airfield had last been used in 1947, and took its name from Air Chief Marshal Sir Walter Dawson. By 1970 it was little more than a flat, uneven dirt strip and landing a commercial airliner would prove extremely dangerous. Dawson's Field, however, was part of Haddad's overall plan and the pilot was given no choice.

Next came a Swissair DC8 flying from Zurich to New York with 140 passengers and a crew of twelve. This was hijacked as it flew over central France and, as with the TWA flight, the pilot was ordered to the Dawson's Field desert airstrip. The Swissair pilot was more cautious and made several passes to assess the condition of the landing site. The strip was in very poor condition and the landing would be risky, with the chances of a serious crash landing very high. Literally at gunpoint, the pilot cautiously attempted a full-flap landing and finally the aircraft jolted and pitched along the rough surface before coming to a stop.

The third aircraft to be hijacked was a Pan American 747 Jumbo Jet again flying to New York. This time the flight had started its journey in Amsterdam and was hijacked by the three PFLP members who had been thrown off the El Al flight that Leila Khaled had tried to hijack. Then it transpired that none of the three could navigate and were unable to direct the pilot to Dawson's Field as it was in such a remote area. In desperation, they ordered the aircraft to Beirut, where it was allowed to re-fuel. The following day, the hijackers forced the aircraft to take off and fly to Cairo, where the 170 passengers and crew were safely released. The moment the aircraft was empty, the hijackers wired it with explosives before blowing it to smithereens. This last action sent dire warnings to just about every airline and passenger in Europe and the Middle East – air travel was becoming unsafe.

Meanwhile, at Dawson's Field the PFLP held over 300 passengers and crew hostage. Without ground power units, the discomfort inside the hijacked aircraft reached appalling levels. During the day the heat became extremely intense while at night the temperature dropped well below freezing. The Jordanian army had sent in fourteen helicopters full of troops but they were of little use, and could do no more than surround Dawson's Field. Any action on behalf of the Jordanian military would have caused the PFLP guerrillas to take aggressive action against their hostages. The PFLP had reinforced its members from camps inside Jordan and made it perfectly clear they would not release any hostages until Leila Khaled and six other imprisoned Palestinians were released. Three were held in Germany and three in Swiss jails, the latter held on twelve-year sentences resulting from an earlier hijack attempt on a 707 plane in 1969 at Zurich.

The Palestinians warned the British Government to consider carefully its treatment of Leila Khaled, stating that reprisals would take place if anything happened to her. To secure maximum publicity for its cause, the PFLP allowed the press to visit Dawson's Field and conduct a press conference. This included talking to some of the passengers. They also renamed the airstrip 'Revolution Field'. Most of the passengers said that they were being well looked after by their captors, with food and water being their biggest problem. Stiffness from lack of exercise and boredom from sitting in their seats all day was also a worry but many stated that they were allowed out at night for short walks.

Back in Britain, Edward Heath, the newly elected Prime Minister, was in a quandary over the treatment of Khaled. This was not helped when a BOAC VC10 airliner flying from Bahrain to Beirut with 115 passengers, 25 of which were children, was hijacked over the Persian Gulf. After refuelling at Beirut the plane joined the other two hijacked aircraft at Dawson's Field. The hijackers renamed the VC10, 'Leila' and sent the passengers a case of whisky to celebrate. Fearing the British would give in to the PFLP demands the Israelis asked Britain for the 'provisional arrest' of Leila Khaled and her deportation. The British Government was caught in a cruel dilemma between the immediate and obviously humanitarian demands of hostage safety and giving in to terrorism. Heath was advised by the Attorney-General and the Solicitor-General that because the crime committed by Khaled had taken place in indefinable airspace and therefore not in British airspace the authorities would have some difficulty bringing a case against her.

As the Heath Government struggled for an answer, the PFLP reinforced the British Government's anxiety by blowing up all three aircraft at Dawson's Field. This was done in front of the assembled media, ensuring that news reports sent shock waves around the world. The hostages were then escorted by PFLP gunmen, together with the Red Cross, to hotels situated between Amman and North Jordan. As the hostages came from a wide variety of countries, diplomatic relations were stretched in every direction. The principal countries involved were America, Israel, West Germany, Switzerland and Great Britain, and each arranged for representatives to meet in Washington in order to discuss their options.

The Swiss capitulated first, giving in to the PFLP demands. After this, Britain was presented with an ultimatum stating that if Leila Khaled was not freed by Thursday 10 September, 3.00 a.m. BST all British hostages would be shot. Edward Heath decided that the safest course of action to protect the British hostages was to release Leila Khaled. She was immediately taken from West Drayton police station and moved to Ealing police station, which had been turned into a four-storey armed fortress for fear that she would be killed by members of the public. The following day, she was put on board an RAF plane and flown to Beirut. On the way to Beirut the plane stopped in Switzerland and Germany to pick up the six other terrorists in order to complete the deal. In the end, the terrorists had achieved everything they had requested, the successful outcome being beyond their wildest expectations. The expert planning of Haddad and the exploits of the PFLP showed the way for other terrorist organisations and hijacking became the terrorist weapon of the day.

Munich – September 1972

As far back as 1968, groups of Palestinian Fatah had attacked the Israelis. They blew up buses and threw bombs indiscriminately, killing, maiming and terrorising the population of Israel. The Israelis hit back hard but, despite several attempts, failed to locate the terrorist leaders, many of whom had escaped to Jordan where King Hussein offered them accommodation and a base from which to fight. This proved to be a mistake by the Jordanian ruler. The Palestinian presence soon grew to become a major force in the land, making themselves unpopular with their host. The Fatah took no notice of Jordanian requests to desist, to the point where the King himself came under pressure from his own army to take action. With his authority threatened, King Hussein at last agreed to send his Bedouin fighters to control the Palestinians; it was a bloodbath. During the month of September 1970, over two thousand Palestinians died at the hands of their Arab brothers. So barbaric was the fighting that many Palestinians fled to the borders of Israel, seeking asylum and imprisonment, rather than face the Jordanians.

When Syria saw the plight of the Palestinians, she came to their aid; tanks massed on Jordan's border and war looked inevitable. At the last minute, America stepped in, urging Israel to shift its heavy armour against Syria. Slowly, an uneasy peace returned and King Hussein was saved. The Palestinians, however, demanded their revenge and so a new terrorist group called Black September was born.

Black September assassinated and bombed many Jordanian targets before turning its attention to the Israelis. In September 1972, the perfect opportunity arrived when Germany staged the

Olympic Games in Munich. As a direct result of Germany's conscience over the holocaust, and the Nazi Olympic Games held in 1936, the Germans bent over backwards to please and accommodate the Israeli athletic team. Perhaps to avoid any confrontation with the Israelis, when Yasser Arafat applied to field a Palestinian team, the German Olympic committee totally ignored his request. That the games coincided with the second anniversary of Black September, encouraged Black September's leader, Ali Hassan, to carry out his most daring plan yet.

The Olympic village had been deliberately planned with the minimum of security, reducing the unpleasant memories of the past. The Israeli team was billeted in Connollystrasse 31, separated from the public by a wire fence and the odd patrolling guard. A little before 4.30 a.m. on the morning of 5 September, a group of young men were seen climbing the fence. This was not an uncommon sight. Many of the athletes stayed out late in the beer halls of Munich – but these were no athletes. They were Black September and they were there to kill Israelis and barter their lives for the release of jailed Palestinians.

Bursting into the Israeli accommodation, the seven terrorists opened fire, killing many and capturing nine as hostages. The Israeli Government, true to its firm policy, declined to negotiate with the terrorists and refused to free any Palestinian prisoners. Germany refused the offer of Israeli troops to counter the problem and decided to attempt a rescue plan of its own. By 10.00 p.m. that same night, a grey army bus transferred both terrorists and hostages to the edge of the Olympic village, where they climbed into two helicopters. Next they flew to Fürstenfeldbruck, around fifteen miles to the west, where they landed in a well-illuminated area. A requested Lufthansa 727 sat on the tarmac a little over one hundred yards away and two of the terrorists left the helicopter to check it out. At 10.44 p.m. the first sniper bullet was fired and a fierce firefight ensued. The bolt action rifles of the German police were no match for the automatic fire of the terrorists' AK47's. A police sergeant who stepped out from the control tower took a bullet through the head. More police arrived in armoured vehicles and several terrorists died.

Meanwhile, Israeli diplomats watched helplessly from the control tower as inexperienced and ill-equipped German sharpshooters failed to kill all the terrorists in the first volley. Three were still alive, and they fired their guns and detonated their grenades to kill the handcuffed hostages who were slaughtered as they sat in the helicopters. In the end, the three were overpowered and captured, but not before they had murdered all nine hostages. Waves of shock reverberated around the world, with the massacre seen as both a human tragedy and a warning that terrorism was getting out of hand.

Carlos the Jackal – 1975

Many individuals have achieved infamy, though, as modern terrorism has developed, none more so than Ilyich Ramirez Sanchez, alias 'the Jackal'. Born in Caracas, Venezuela, he was the son of an affluent lawyer who believed in Marxist principles. Ilyich joined the communist student movement and soon came to the attention of the local police. When it seemed his son might be in real danger of falling foul of the law, Ilyich's father sent him to London to continue his education. There, his studies soon took second place to drinking, chasing women and high living. If he had any redeeming quality it may have been his ability to speak several languages. Although not an activist himself, Ilyich was surrounded by radicals during his university days. There were also rumours that he had been approached by the KGB around this time, but this was never proved. He finally left Europe for Jordan and the rigours of a Palestinian guerrilla training school.

Around 1972, Ilyich Ramirez Sanchez returned to London and the reputation of the Jackal was born. This was a ruthless murderer; a loan predator, smiling as he tortured and killed his captives. He has been quoted as saying, 'To get anywhere, you have to walk over the corpses.' In London he became an assassin for Wadi Haddad and the PFLP. His first target was Joseph Edward Sieff then head of Marks & Spencer's stores. He attacked Sieff while in the bathroom pointing his gun just inches from the man's face – for some reason the gun failed. The Jackal turned to using hand grenades, tossing two into an Israeli bank.

Despite all his bravado, the Jackal never quite lived up to the image portrayed by the media. That is not to say he was innocent, far from it. He himself claims the credit for over fifty deaths. This is most probably accurate as the French alone charged him with the deaths of fifteen people. His brand of violence was felt all over Europe and the Middle East, yet the intelligence agencies failed to locate the Jackal. Although this elusive mastermind of terrorism failed in many of his early exploits where assassination attempts went wrong, his luck improved when the PFLP ordered him to Paris, again as an assassin. He placed several successful bombs in the city and even fired a rocket at an El Al aircraft sitting on the tarmac at Orly airport in January 1975. His reputation swelled somewhat after this incident, not only because of the audacity of the attack but also through his reaction afterwards.

Carlos had a Lebanese adjutant called Michel Moukharbel who was caught by the French police. They believed him to have been involved in the rocket attack. Under interrogation, Moukharbel offered to lead the police to Carlos's hideout. The armed police entered the building only to find a party in full swing. Carlos excused himself and went into the bathroom, returning a few seconds later with a machine gun. He shot two of the policemen and seriously wounded a third. Then, for good measure, he shot and killed Moukharbel for setting him up. Carlos the Jackal left Paris for Algeria that same night.

Carlos reappeared later that year in Vienna during a high-powered meeting of the Organisation of Petroleum Exporting Countries (OPEC) in Vienna on 21 December. An armed gang of terrorists burst into the room, taking those inside as hostages. The cell of six was led by the infamous Jackal. His five accomplices included Gabrielle Kröcher-Tiedemann, a member of the 2 June Movement, and Hans-Joachim Klein, a member of a small German terrorist group known as the Revolutionary Cells with links to the Baader-Meinhof gang.

The gang managed to take hostage eleven oil ministers, including the powerful minister of oil for Saudi Arabia, Sheik Yermani, as well as sixty others. In the chaos of the attack, shots were fired. Two men were killed by Kröcher-Tiedemann; an

Austrian policeman named Anton Tichler and an Iraqi guard called Khafali. Carlos also shot and killed a Libyan civil servant, Yousef Ismirli. But the hostage-takers did not escape without casualties either – Klein was shot in the stomach but was treated at the scene and survived despite his serious injury. Carlos demanded a ransom of five million dollars in return for the hostages' lives, an amount readily paid. Indeed, it has been alleged that maybe as much as fifty million dollars changed hands, with most of the money coming from Iran and Saudi Arabia. The money was supposed to go towards funding Palestinian causes.

Having secured the money, the gang escaped by flying to Algiers with their hostages as security. Once there, they disappeared into the melting pot of the Middle East with more than one of them seeking refuge in Libya. It seemed as if the trail had gone cold.

Then, 22 years later, in 1988, Klein was arrested in a little village in Normandy, France, where he had been living under a false identity. He was tried on three counts of murder, three of attempted murder and for taking hostages. Klein, however, denied having killed anyone and his actions since the incident were indeed more in line with a man whose conscience had got the better of him rather than a dyed-in-the-wool terrorist. It transpired that two years after the attack, Klein turned his back on the violent world of terrorism and even provided the German security forces with important information that prevented an attack on two prominent German Jewish community leaders. In a very public gesture, he sent his pistol and ammunition to the German magazine *Der Spiegel* along with a statement not only denouncing terrorism, but also including details of assassinations planned by Carlos' group. In 1979 he went on to publish a book denouncing Carlos as a megalomaniac and warning young people away from involvement with such causes.

With such evidence presented at the trial, as well as other allegations that Libya's leader, Colonel Gaddafi, had given his full support to the hostage plot, the prosecution accepted that Klein had played only a small role in comparison to some of the other gang members, none of whom had been brought to justice. Instead of the fourteen years he was expected to receive, he was sentenced to serve nine years in prison, reduced to seven and a half years due to the amount of time he had already spent in French custody.

Carlos was eventually caught by the French Secret Service in 1994 and in 1997 was jailed for life for the murder of two French secret agents in Paris.

Northern Ireland – 2 May 1980

The British 'troubles', as they were generally known, were at their height during the late 1970s. To combat IRA terrorism, a huge intelligence network emerged. In the vanguard of this were such units as E4, an undercover unit of the UDR Special Branch. Other British undercover organisations were also operating in the province, including both the SAS and 14 Intelligence and Surveillance. Overall command and allocation of tasks fell to the TCG (Tactical Command Group) which supervised the flow and collation of all information, including the running of undercover agents among the IRA.

This, however, was a time when nothing seemed to go right in Northern Ireland. April 1980 was a perfect example. The SAS, 14 Int and E4 were all tasked with several different operations in South Armagh. Manpower was stretched to the limit.

The first was to set up an observation point watching the home of two RUC men, whose lives had been threatened. The second was to keep watch on a public house the IRA intended to firebomb. Finally, a well-known IRA terrorist intended to shoot a man at a Saturday night dance. The man was suspected of being an informer; our task was to keep tabs on both the gunman and his intended target. These three operations called for more SAS men to be drafted in to South Armagh. Four men went into the first OP (Observation Post) watching the two RUC officers. Four more went into the OP at the pub, but due to shortage of numbers, this OP was pulled out during the operation against the would-be IRA assassin and his target. This operation required at least twenty vehicles with two operators in each and several men in the dance hall or pub working on foot. In addition to all this, men were needed for drop-offs, re-supply and to act as a QRF (Quick Reaction Force).

Things started going wrong when, after a week, the OP watching the RUC officers was compromised by a farmer. The SAS team asked to be extracted. Special Branch were informed of this and pleaded with the SAS to stay put. The commander of the OP made a decision and, as in all SAS operations it is the man in the field that calls the shots – they were withdrawn. Next morning as the two RUC men returned home from work, their car was shot up – spent cartridge cases were found just a few metres from the OP which had been manned by the SAS hours earlier. Luckily, the two RUC men were unharmed.

A week later, as the OP on the public house was withdrawn to help with the surveillance on the assassin, another disaster happened. By 2.00 a.m. on Sunday morning, both the IRA gunman and his target had been successfully followed to their respective homes without any incident taking place. The operation was again called off until the following weekend. The SAS soldiers were working non-stop but they made ready to reinsert and maintain their vigilance on the public house that was under threat. As the cars drove back to their base in the town of Portadown, their route took them past the public house in question – it was burning. By this time, Special Branch was not very pleased with the SAS, but there was nothing to be done other than continue with operations.

In Belfast, it was discovered that a cache of weapons under observation had been moved. Unfortunately, their new home was a bit of a mystery. The nearest location that could be found was a block of three houses in a terraced row on the Antrim Road. After a check with intelligence, it turned out that one of the three houses had previously been used by the IRA, so this house was targeted. Units of the SAS were tasked with assaulting the house and recovering the weapons.

On the afternoon of 2 May 1980, two cars headed down the Antrim road and screeched to a stop outside number 369. Another vehicle with three SAS men secured the rear. To maintain security, there had been no cordon or military activity prior to the raid, and the men charged straight in. The lead groups were already in the house and up the stairs, when a burst of machine-gun fire filled the air. Unknown to the SAS assault team, the IRA had mounted an

American M60 in the upstairs window of the adjoining house. The men had moved in fast, but the commander, Captain Westmacott, had been sitting in the middle of the rear seat of the front assault vehicle and so had the furthest to move. He was shot dead by a burst from the M60. When it was realised what was happening, the whole assault was quickly switched, but by this time the IRA man had surrendered. The sound of gunfire brought both the army and RUC to the scene. It had also drawn the attention of a Catholic priest who appeared on the scene to see that the IRA man was allowed to surrender. Other suspects, who were armed, were arrested leaving by the back door. The missing weapons were all recovered.

The first SAS soldier to be killed in Northern Ireland, Captain Westmacott had joined the SAS from the Grenadier Guards and was an officer in 'G' Squadron. He was not a typical SAS officer, his fair curly hair gave him the look of a schoolboy, and he had a love of poetry, which he had learned as a child sitting on his grandfather's knee. Inwardly, however, he was as tough as they come; he was awarded a posthumous Military Cross. His death ended the run of bad luck that had dogged the SAS in Northern Ireland at that time. Two days later, the SAS stormed the Iranian Embassy (see Chapter 5) in London, killing all but one of the terrorists who had taken over the building and rescuing the hostages the terrorists were holding.

The IRA was unrelenting in its attacks on Northern Ireland security forces and by early 1980 they had resumed activities on mainland Britain. On 10 October 1981, they bombed Chelsea Barracks, killing two British civilians. They also wounded a further 40 people, of whom 23 were soldiers. This was followed by another atrocity nine months later when, on 20 July 1982, two bombs exploded in Hyde Park. This attack was designed to put pressure on the British Government by bringing bloodshed and fear to central London. The first bomb exploded at Rotten Row just as soldiers of the Blues and Royals passed by on horseback. Two soldiers were killed, as were seven of the horses. Seventeen spectators were also injured. The second bomb exploded underneath the bandstand in Hyde Park killing 6 soldiers of the Royal Green Jackets and injuring 24 others.

The following year, as ordinary members of the British public were doing their Christmas shopping, a large bomb went off in Harrods. In all six people – three policemen and three civilians – were killed, with ninety people injured. There was major damage to the famous store and the attack made Christmas shoppers all over London very nervous indeed. The IRA later claimed that it had not authorised the attack and regretted the deaths. Other reports have since come to light, however, indicating that it was indeed sanctioned by the IRA leadership, although civilian deaths were to be avoided. The same report said that a warning was given but it was given too late to clear the area in time.

On 12 October 1984, the PIRA attempted to assassinate the Prime Minister, Margaret Thatcher, and her cabinet as they slept in the Grand Hotel in Brighton during the Conservative Party Conference. The powerful bomb caused massive damage to the hotel and killed four people, including a minister. Their main target, the PM, emerged unscathed. Nevertheless, this attack showed that the PIRA was able to identify and exploit weaknesses in security at such events, ensuring much higher levels of vigilance by the security services in the future.

Considered to be one of the worst outrages committed by the PIRA, in 1987 on Remembrance Day in Enniskillen, a bomb exploded next to innocent Protestants commemorating their war dead. Eleven people died in the carnage and 63 were injured. This act of violence backfired badly on the PIRA and they lost much support, especially when they tried to put some of the blame on the British. At the next local election, four of their eight candidates failed to be elected, leading to a political disaster for their cause.

On 7 Feb 1991, in a daring daytime attack in London, the PIRA launched a second attempt to assassinate the Prime Minister, this time John Major, and his cabinet. While those inside were busy discussing the situation in Kuwait, three home-made mortar bombs were fired at 10 Downing Street from a van in Whitehall. Luckily, the mortars fell short of their target.

The PIRA next struck in Warrington on the 20 March 1993, when two bombs that had been placed in litter bins exploded. They killed two boys aged three and twelve. The explosions also caused 56 injuries in the small English town. The death of the children caused much outrage in both Britain and Eire and brought widespread condemnation of paramilitary violence. By 1994, feeling that military action was becoming self-defeating, the IRA declared a truce and the British Government issued a statement announcing that it wanted to introduce home rule for Northern Ireland. Part of the deal was that the IRA should surrender its weapons. These demands were rejected time and time again. As far as the IRA was concerned, Unionist paramilitaries should also surrender their arms if any peace was to be achieved. Eventually, faith in the proposed deal fell apart on both sides and the IRA ended its ceasefire. The bombings and shootings were renewed, especially on the mainland.

1996 saw the end to the IRA ceasefire when on 9 February they exploded a powerful bomb at Canary Wharf in London. Two people were killed, many were injured and millions of pounds of damage caused. Their attacks on the commercial buildings continued in June when a massive bomb destroyed a large part of the centre of Manchester. There were approximately 200 injuries but deaths were avoided because of the adequate warnings given.

The next couple of years saw some hard negotiating between all parties, as well as an ongoing cycle of violence and truce by both the IRA and the paramilitary Loyalist groups. Some of the hard-line IRA activists could not accept the idea of the talks and split from the IRA to form an organisation called the Real IRA (rIRA). Despite lacking the numbers and armaments of the IRA, it managed to detonate a powerful bomb in the town of Omagh on 15 August 1998. Twenty-nine civilians died as a result, including a pregnant woman. There was mass outrage at this atrocity and the rIRA found any support they had slipping away.

The Lebanon – 1983 onwards

Hizballah, the Lebanese Party of God, also known as Islamic Jihad, was formed in 1983. This is a radical Shi'ite group whose aim is to create an Islamic style republic, similar to that of Iran, in the Lebanon. They receive much of their backing from Iran, having in the past carried out operations under guidance from Tehran. The organisation claims to be several thousand strong with most of its members being trained in Iran or Syria. Hizballah's political views are extremely narrow and they are strongly anti-Israel as well as being opposed to the 'Great Satan' America. There are good relations between Hizballah and various Palestinian organisations.

Hizballah's main area of influence is the Bekaa Valley, southern Lebanon, stretching into the southern suburbs of Beirut, from where they draw the bulk of their manpower. Their operations are aimed mainly at Israel and the West, America in particular. Active Hizballah units have been identified around the globe and their attacks have been perpetrated worldwide.

On 18 April 1983 a pickup truck loaded with explosives rammed into the US Embassy in Beirut, Lebanon. As the vehicle came to a crashing halt, the suicide bomber triggered the massive device. The devastation was unbelievable, with 63 people killed. The final total included seventeen Americans, eight of whom were CIA employees, including Middle East analyst Robert C. Ames and CIA station chief Kenneth Haas. The suicide bomber was reported to be a member of Hizballah.

Six months later on 23 October 1983 there was another suicide attack on the Americans. This time the target was the US Marines who were barracked at Beirut International airport. They were part of a contingent of 1,800 Marines sent to Lebanon as part of a multinational force to help separate the warring Lebanese factions. The suicide bomber drove a truck full of explosives into the base and parked close to a parade ground – 241 Marines were killed and more than 100 others wounded. Although Hizballah were prime suspects, they denied the attack.

Apart from bombing, Hizballah were responsible for the kidnapping and detention of American and other Western hostages in Lebanon. These operations, however, along with the suicide bombings, soon took second place to a new tactic. Hizballah sent around nine hundred men for specialist training at a camp in Hamadan in the south-east of Iran. On completion of their training, they returned to south Lebanon as a fully-fledged fighting unit; in addition, many had become terrorist instructors themselves. This new unit operated as a proper military organisation, with tactics, weapons and strategic planning. When it encountered Israeli forces, this new brigade stood its ground and fought back, taking the Israelis completely by surprise. Only the lack of air cover forced them to retire.

Hizballah's overseas cells, of course, continued to operate with the Israeli Embassy in Argentina being attacked on 17 March 1992. A huge car bomb exploded, killing 29 people and wounding many more. Two years later, on 18 July 1994, the same group detonated another car bomb in the city of Buenos Aires. The blast all but destroyed a seven-storey building belonging to the Israeli community, killing 86 people. The following day, a bomb exploded on board an aircraft flying over Panama, killing a further twenty-one people, most of whom were Jewish. A sub-cell of Hizballah claimed responsibility. They continue to be one of the main terrorist organisations, with strong backing from Iran.

Achille Lauro – 7 October 1985

The hijacking of the cruise liner the *Achille Lauro* on 7 October 1985 captured the attention of the world's media. The Italian vessel, renowned for its luxury cruises, had about one hundred mostly elderly passengers on board when it was taken over by four heavily armed terrorists representing the Palestine Liberation Front (PLF). Ordering the captain to change course for Tartus in Syria, the hijackers contacted the Egyptian authorities and stated their demand that fifty Palestinian prisoners, held by Israel, be released. From the first, their plans were thwarted as Syria refused them permission to dock at Tartus. It was at this point that an elderly wheelchair-bound Jewish American passenger, Leon Klinghoffer, was shot in the head and chest and his body dumped overboard. One of the hijackers later claimed it was because the old man had been stirring up trouble but no one ever accepted that as an excuse for such a cowardly act.

The terrorists, in response to a further radio message, now set sail for Port Said in Egypt where they were offered a safe passage off the ship in return for the release of both the ship and its passengers. The Egyptians were, at that time, unaware that a murder had been committed aboard. Once the fact had been revealed, the US Ambassador to Egypt requested that the Egyptian Government detain the terrorists and prosecute them. The Egyptian authorities insisted that this was impossible as those responsible had already left the country. US intelligence had found out otherwise; the PLF members were, in fact, still on Egyptian soil but were about to be flown to Tunisia on an Egypt Air 737 aircraft.

Determined not to let the perpetrators get away, orders were issued to the US aircraft carrier *Saratoga* which was in the Adriatic Sea heading north after a NATO exercise in the Mediterranean. The commander of the *Saratoga*, Rear Admiral David Jeremiah, reset his course and prepared to launch an air combat patrol consisting of two F-14A Tomcats and an E-2C Hawkeye. Despite the fact that the departure time of the Egyptian plane was not known, the aircraft were in the air in 22 minutes.

Because of the lack of information, the planes were ordered to intercept and identify all aircraft using a particular route – the one that the 737 would have to take. The first three interceptions were of no consequence but the fourth was the plane they were looking for, carrying the PLF terrorists. The US planes closed on their target and forced it to land at the NATO base in Sigonella, Sicily. Then, surrounded by heavily-armed US Delta Force and Navy Seal units, the terrorists had no choice but to surrender and were taken into Italian custody to await trial. Although the Americans wished to try the prisoners in the United States, the Italians refused to extradite them and, inexplicably, allowed the leader, Mohammed Abbas, to escape to Yugoslavia. In his absence he was found guilty and sentenced to life in prison but to this day he remains a free man, and one with great influence in Middle Eastern terrorist politics. Eleven out of the other fifteen hijackers were also found guilty.

Lockerbie – 21 December 1988

At 19.02 on the evening of 21 December 1988, a Pan Am Boeing 747 exploded in the air above the Scottish town of Lockerbie, killing all 259 passengers and crew and also eleven people on the ground. Pan Am Flight 103 had taken off from London Heathrow airport at 18.25 hours, having previously flown in from Malta via Frankfurt airport in Germany. As it approached Lockerbie, it was cleared to ascend to 31,000 feet. Seven minutes later, the aircraft disappeared from the radar screens of Shanwick Ocean Control.

The violent explosion caused the aircraft to break apart in the air, with several large sections smashing into the ground beneath. In fact, the impact was so significant that the British Geological Survey station in the south of Scotland reported that it measured 1.6 on the Richter scale. The centre section of the aircraft plus the primary section of one of the wings landed on the southern edge of Lockerbie, creating a crater 196 feet long and 155 feet wide. Most of the damage and casualties were in one road – Sherwood Crescent – where, as a result of the impact and subsequent fires, 21 buildings were destroyed. The engines also fell onto the town but major amounts of wreckage also fell to the east of Lockerbie, in countryside. The furthest piece of wreckage was found 130 kilometres away.

Amid massive press coverage, investigations into the crash started immediately, with teams from both the UK and the US brought in to determine why the plane had exploded. The report from the Air Accident Investigation Branch (AAIB) finally concluded that the crash had been caused by an explosive device planted by a person or persons unknown in the cargo section of the right forward section of the aircraft. The spectre of terrorism had once more raised its ugly head and there were many suspects in the frame, most of them having something to do with Middle Eastern politics.

It wasn't until 13 November 1991, however, almost three years later, that the UK and US authorities concluded that the perpetrators were probably two alleged Libyan agents who had been working for Libyan Airlines in Malta. The two men, Abdel Baset al Megrahi and Lamine Khalifa Fhimah, were charged in their absence and Libya was called upon to extradite them to face justice.

Many years of wrangling commenced with Libya first insisting that it would try the suspects itself. The UK and US Governments refused and brought in the United Nations who were eventually forced to place an embargo on Libyan air travel and, later, further economic sanctions. Finally, in 1998, after a visit from Jim Swire, the spokesman for the Lockerbie victims, Colonel Gaddafi of Libya agreed to hand over the suspects for a trial on neutral ground. It was confirmed that the men would be tried under Scottish law by Scottish judges, but the location would be at Camp Zeist in the Netherlands. More years of stalling by the Libyans followed and the air embargo and sanctions were beginning to crumble as Arab nations ignored them. By April 1999 all objections were overcome and the two suspects were finally handed over to face justice for their alleged actions.

At the original trial, al-Megrahi was found guilty as charged but his alleged accomplice, Khalifa Fhimah, was acquitted. An appeal followed but was dismissed and al-Megrahi was taken away to serve his life sentence in a Scottish prison.

There has been a great deal of speculation surrounding this case, one theory being that the bomb could easily have been hidden in an attaché case belonging to an American DEA (Drugs Enforcement Agency) sting operation in Wiesbaden, West Germany. The Wiesbaden unit, which was called COREA, shipped regular consignments of drugs, supplied via the CIA, into Germany for onward sale in the Middle East. This covert operation was to procure information and money by supplying drugs. The money and information were used to fund and organise black (covert, deniable and generally unauthorised) operations in the Middle East and elsewhere. The man in receipt of the drugs and responsible for the return package was said to be Monzer al-Kassar.

Charles McKee, a Special Forces major working in Beirut on plans to rescue seven of the nine American hostages being held at the time, discovered the truth about the COREA operation. It is reported that he was on his way back to the USA to complain when, unfortunately, flight 103 was destroyed. Records show that during the first few days of the investigation, several CIA members arrived in Lockerbie and searched for McKee's brief case. Once found, it was taken away, and returned later – empty. This was confirmed by a Scottish policeman on duty at the crash site.

Many believe that McKee had discovered some terrible truth involving American black operations in the arms for hostages debacle. One theory is that the military flight that crashed in

Canada at Gander airport a couple of years previously contained American TOW missile instructors returning from Iran. Their silence about their covert mission in Iran was brought about by placing a bomb on board the aircraft. It has been suggested that the Lockerbie crash was caused in order to ensure McKee's silence.

Goldstein – 25 February 1994

It is easy to be lulled into the false belief that religious terrorism is solely attributable to the Muslim faith. This is not so. Christians, Hindus, Buddhists and Jews have all provided their fair share of fanatics over the years.

Born into a middle-class neighbourhood of Brooklyn, most people who were acquainted with Benjamin Goldstein, or Benjy as he liked to be called, knew him to be a religious boy. The piety of his Orthodox Jewish family set them apart from more secular Jewish neighbours. The young Goldstein, with his traditional side curls and yarmulke, attended school at a yeshiva where his faith seemed to push him into isolation. Yet in his solitude, a flame was lit deep within in his heart, one day to flare up in a passion of fanatical bloodlust. As he grew, Goldstein became consumed by a love of all that is Israel, but it was a love equally matched by hate for Israel's enemies. He was a first-rate student, graduating with honours in 1977 at Yeshiva University in New York City. Around this time he became a devotee of the detestable Rabbi Meir Kahane, whose Jewish Defence League advocated violence against anyone it perceived as a threat to Jews. In a letter to the *New York Times*, Goldstein repeated the rabbi's call for the forcible expulsion of Arabs from Israel and the West Bank. 'The harsh reality is: if Israel is to avert facing the kinds of problems found in Northern Ireland today, it must act decisively to remove the Arab minority from within its borders,' he wrote.

Goldstein went on to gain a medical degree at Albert Einstein College of Medicine, after which he emigrated to Israel in 1983. Soon after, he met and married a fellow Kahane supporter. Rabbi Kahane performed the wedding ceremony. Eventually, he settled in Kiryat Arba, a West Bank settlement just outside the Palestinian city of Hebron.

He worked as an army doctor at the local clinic, but Goldstein was something of an enigma within his profession, as he would not treat Arabs. A colleague who knew him well remembered, 'He would say, "He's an enemy of my people. I didn't come here to treat enemies."' In his mind, there was no such thing as an innocent Arab, thus he developed a fierce reputation among the Palestinians of Hebron. Here was a Jew who bullied and harassed Muslim worshippers at the Tomb of the Patriarchs, a spot sacred to both Judaism and Islam where the faithful of both religions prayed at separate hours. 'Sometimes he hit worshippers,' says Mohammed Suleiman Abu Sarah, one of the unarmed Palestinian guards at the tomb, 'and sometimes he refused to leave when it was time for the Jews to finish their prayers.'

In 1990 when his hero, Rabbi Kahane, was shot dead by an Arab assassin in New York City, Goldstein's hatred deepened. He vowed revenge for Kahane's death. Some years later, when two of his friends were ambushed by Arab attackers near Kiryat Arba, Goldstein was with the emergency medical team that attended the incident. When Mordechai Lapid and his nineteen-year-old son died in his arms, some present said that a change came over him, he became withdrawn and irritable.

On Friday 25 February 1994, an Islamic holy day during Ramadan, the month of fasting and prayer, Goldstein walked to the Tomb of the Patriarchs. It was the Muslims' time to pray and Ramadan guaranteed a wall-to-wall crowd of worshippers. By 5.20 a.m. about seven hundred men, women and children jammed into the mosque for the dawn prayers. A mosque guard saw Goldstein approach and, recognising him as a troublemaker, he forbade him to enter. In reply Goldstein, wearing the olive-green uniform of an army reserve captain, unslung the military-issue Galil assault rifle and swung the butt at the guard, knocking him down before running into the mosque. Inside, Goldstein took up position facing the backs of the worshippers who knelt row upon row, heads bent in prayer. From less than two metres Goldstein opened fire.

The savage bullets tore into the wall of humanity. They were hit in the back and hit in the head. Rhythmically, the heavy Galil automatic dispensed death. Unmoved by the total carnage about him, Goldstein changed clip after clip. Palestinians were running here and there in an effort to escape. Some fled, while the wounded and the dead swam in a sea of blood, making it difficult to distinguish between the living and the dead.

The firing inside the mosque continued for about ten minutes, until at last some of the worshippers managed to hit Goldstein with a fire extinguisher, momentarily disarming him. Three Israeli soldiers who entered the mosque at this time interpreted the scene as an attack by Palestinians on a uniformed Israeli and opened fire, killing several more worshippers. Outside, other Israeli soldiers, who had just arrived on the scene, simply panicked. As hundreds of frantic and bleeding Palestinians fled the slaughter, they too opened fire. The final total of dead and wounded exceeded even the number Goldstein could have wished for. Israeli officials counted 39 people killed at the mosque – the Palestinians figured 52, plus 70 wounded. These figures did not include Goldstein, whose body was beaten to a pulp.

As the news spread throughout the fanatic Jewish precincts in Hebron, settlers danced in the streets and praised Goldstein's martyrdom. Some residents of Kiryat Arba called his act 'a great gift'. One settler, stopped by a soldier as she tried to assault a Palestinian journalist, shrieked, 'We should kill 500, not 50!'

Oklahoma – 19 April 1995

Just before 9.00 a.m. on 19 April 1995, the residents of Oklahoma were preparing for just another working day. Employees were starting work at the Murrah Federal Building in downtown Oklahoma and parents were dropping off their children at the day care centre on the second floor. Meanwhile, a yellow Ryder rental truck, driven by Gulf War veteran and anti-government activist Timothy McVeigh, made its way through the rush hour traffic. It was packed with seven thousand pounds of explosives, a mixture of ammonium nitrate and fuel oil. McVeigh had already lit the five-minute fuse and, as he approached the Federal Building, he lit the two-minute fuse. Calmly pulling up in an unloading bay beneath the childcare centre, he got out, locked the truck and walked away.

At three minutes past nine the bomb exploded, blowing out the entire north end of the building. As the blast wave spread out from its epicentre nearby cars burst into flames and windows blocks away were blown out. Even McVeigh did not escape the blast. As he was walking towards his getaway car, a yellow Mercury Marquis, flying debris injured him on the leg, but he carried on calmly as if nothing had happened. Within minutes he was on his way out of the city.

Meanwhile, fire, paramedic and rescue crews were at the scene searching for any survivors among the rubble. The fact that children were still trapped in the building spurred them on faster and many risked their lives amid falling debris to pull people out. Unfortunately, bodies were also being pulled out of the wreckage and by the final count 168, including nineteen children, had lost their lives in one of the worst acts of terrorism on US soil.

Sixty miles away and over an hour later, a patrolman pulled McVeigh over for having no licence plate on his vehicle. Noticing that McVeigh was carrying a loaded weapon, the patrolman arrested him. Back at the scene of the explosion, investigators were already making headway in discovering what had happened. They found the truck's axle some blocks away and were able to trace its VIN number to the hired Ryder truck. An artist's impression of the truck driver from witnesses at the hire centre was soon being shown around the area. Eventually, staff at a motel on the outskirts of town recognised the sketch and the man was identified from motel records as Timothy McVeigh. He was just about to be released from custody following his arrest by the patrolman when the sheriff received the call that was to lead to his re-arrest, this time on charges of bombing.

The motel records had provided an address in Michigan, which turned out to be a farm owned by the brother of McVeigh's friend and ex-army buddy Terry Nichols. Terry Nichols' home was searched and further evidence against both him and McVeigh was found there, including a receipt for the ammonium nitrate with McVeigh's fingerprints on it.

Nichols was arrested and charged similarly to McVeigh. Nichols' brother was also arrested but later released without charge. A friend of McVeigh's, Michael Fortier, faced lesser charges and pleaded guilty. He was later to testify at the trial. At McVeigh's trial, the evidence against him, although mainly circumstantial, was damning. He was found guilty and given the death penalty. Six months later, Nichols was also found guilty but was sentenced to life imprisonment. McVeigh stayed on death row for three years while legal arguments went back and forth. Eventually, he admitted to his part in the bombing and seemed to accept his fate. He was executed by lethal injection on 11 June 2001. It is believed that McVeigh carried out the attack as a protest against the failed 1993 government raid on the Branch Davidian sect at Waco in which eighty men, women and children were killed. The date of the Oklahoma blast was the second anniversary of the Waco firestorm.

Luxor – 17 November 1997

The tourist industry is extremely important to Egypt not only in terms of revenue but also for the hundreds of thousands of jobs it provides. This has made it an extremely valuable target for anti-government militant groups who have reasoned that if they can hit tourism by creating a climate of fear, they should be able to overthrow the regime that they hate so much. Over the past twenty years there have been several incidents in which foreign tourists have either lost their lives or have been injured in terrorist attacks. The worst one, took place at the Hatshepsut Temple site on 17 November 1997.

On that morning, just before 9.00 a.m., six gunmen dressed as policemen hijacked a taxi and forced its driver to take them to the temple. At the entrance they leaped out and shot and killed two policemen along with two local guards. Moving on into the temple precincts, they shot indiscriminately at anyone who moved in a terrifying ordeal that lasted for an hour. Women and children were not spared as they tried to hide or feign death. It was later reported that some of the wounded were dispatched by having their throats slit.

In all, fifty-eight foreign nationals died, including thirty-five Swiss, six Britons, four Germans, one French national, a Bulgarian and a Colombian. There were twenty-four wounded, some of them critically.

Above Jubilant Palestinians
dance on the wreckage of a
British aircraft destroyed at
Dawson's Field, September
1970. After the release of
the passengers, two other
airliners were blown up.

Right Munich 1972: a
member of 'Black
September' appears on the
terrace of the Israeli
quarters in the Olympic
Village. Many of the Israeli
athletes were killed when
an abortive attempt was
made by German police to
rescue them.

Left Waddi Haddad, co-founder of the Popular Front for the Liberation of Palestine (PFLP), which was the first organisation to use hijacking as a terrorist weapon.

ight George Habbash, co-founder of the PFLP, renounced his calling as a doctor to take up arms against Israel. He made his terror teams international, attacking Jewish targets wherever they were vulnerable.

Left Terrorist groups vary from urban street fighters to rural guerrillas.

Yasser Arafat, leader of the PLO, a position he retains to this day. Despite the many Palestinian factions, he remains the one single voice that represents the Palestinian people

ila Khalid, the first 'celebrity' of terrorism. She became a symbol for the youth of
lestine.

Above Russian Troops in Afghanistan in the 1980s. Their withdrawal from the country left a huge army of well-trained Afghans behind. Many of these fell under the control of Al Qaida and Osama bin Laden, who used them to propagate world terrorism.

Top right The struggle between the British government and the IRA continued unabated for almost thirty years. Regardless of all the killings and murders, both sides finally realised that peace could only be achieved through negotiations.

Bottom right Captain Westmacott, one of the few SAS soldiers to be killed in Northern Ireland. He was shot by a member of the IRA on 2 May 1980 while exiting a car just prior to an assault being made on a house.

The twin towers of New York's World Trade Center prior to 11 September 2001. The impact of two commercial aircraft totally destroyed the buildings, killing thousands. Terrorism had entered a new age.

The bombing of a nightclub in Bali on 12 October 2002 caused the deaths of dozens o young people. The perpetrator was later caught by the authorities and smiled as he confessed to his crime on television.

Taking control of a tour bus, the gunmen fled into the nearby hills where they engaged in a firefight with police. During this, one of them was seriously wounded and it is reported that he was shot dead by his associates. Not willing to surrender, the gunmen continued to fire against the police until they were trapped and all were killed.

The next day, the radical Islamic group Gamaa't al Islamiya issued a statement claiming full responsibility for the attack and warning foreign tourists not to travel to Egypt. They demanded the institution of Shari'a law in Egypt, the severance of diplomatic ties with Israel and the return to Egypt of Sheikh Omar Abd al-Rahman, the group's spiritual leader. He was being held in a US prison for conspiracy to blow up the World Trade Centre in 1993. To confuse matters, a second statement was issued a few days later by a member of the Consultative Council of the political wing living in western Europe. This statement apologised for the killings and promised that there would be no further attacks on tourists. A third statement, however, was issued on 9 December repudiating the second one, saying that it had not been published by Gamaa't al Islamiya.

After the attack, security around the tourist sites was increased, with Luxor being virtually sealed off. President Hosni Mubarak sent out a plea to the international community for help in combating terrorism, one that was met with great sympathy from many countries. This did not stop many travel companies from bringing back their customers early or cancelling future holidays to the region.

Sri Lanka – 1990 onwards
The Liberation Tigers of Tamil Eelam (LTTE), or Tamil Tigers as they are generally referred to in the media, are not your normal, run-of-the-mill terrorist organisation. The LTTE is extremely well structured, equipped and trained. The organisation has used just about every means of terrorism in the book, from individual suicide bombings to full-scale military attacks. Furthermore, it enjoys support and financial backing from other Tamils all over the world. While most of the money is freely donated, the LTTE is not above employing hard-line tactics when collecting money. Above

all, the LTTE provides excellent training facilities for its recruits as well as maintaining good external communications and transport facilities to support its weapons supply line. The Tigers actions are, in the main, confined to attacks on the Sri Lankan Government and pursuing their claimed territorial rights and ambitions for a Tamil Free State.

The war between the Tamil Tigers and the Sri Lankan Government, which started in the 1980s (see Chapter 2), took a new turn when, on 21 May 1991, a Tiger suicide bomber assassinated the Indian Prime Minister Rajiv Gandhi. Gandhi was addressing a public rally near Madras, the capital of Tamil Nadu, an Indian province. Up until this point, Tamil Nadu had provided extensive support for the LTTE. Many of its soldiers were trained in camps around the district before being committed to operations in Sri Lanka. India had previously sent a peacekeeping force into Sri Lanka but, although initially welcomed, it soon became embroiled in a bitter conflict with the LTTE and was forced to withdraw. It is widely believed that Prime Minister Gandhi was assassinated to prevent any further Indian involvement in Sri Lanka. Seventeen other people died in the blast. Gandhi's death was to have an adverse effect on the LTTE, which was forced to shut down its training and support facilities in India.

Two years later, the LTTE carried out an identical suicide bombing, killing the Sri Lankan President Ranasinghe Premadasa. This led to the election of Mrs Kumaratunga, a woman determined to end the poverty of her country and bring an end to the war with the LTTE. Her message was simple – let's negotiate. This strategy worked and a truce was signed in early 1995. It lasted no more than two weeks. Claiming that the Sri Lankan Government had not kept its word, the LTTE opened up a war against the government forces. The Tigers' war was fought not with terrorist tactics, although the LTTE has always been called terrorist, but as a full-scale guerrilla campaign.

The LTTE opening offensive involved attacking a naval base where patrol boats where blown up. At the same time, two transporters of the Sri Lankan Air Force were shot down with Russian-built Sam 7 rockets. This type of attack on government forces became an almost daily occurrence, throwing the country into turmoil. The Government retaliated, massing forty thousand soldiers for an attack on the LTTE stronghold in the Jaffna peninsula. To a large degree this succeeded, with government forces taking control of much of the area previously held by the rebels. This led to a reduction in support for the LTTE, not just in funding but also in manpower, the conflict with government troops costing them over two thousand men.

LTTE continued to attack but limited its operations to suicide bombings, one of which killed some ninety people when it went off in the capital, Colombo. Behind the scenes, the LTTE was preparing for a major offensive. With its own navy, the LTTE shipped in arms and ammunition from bases in Thailand and Burma. These ships, mainly old traders, were protected from the Sri Lankan Navy by the LTTE's own Sea Tigers, small launches that carried lots of fire power. The Sea Tigers were also deployed as floating suicide bombs, ramming Sri Lankan shipping before detonating.

July 1996 saw the LTTE mount its largest attack so far when over three thousand of its members assaulted the Sri Lankan Navy base at Mullaitiva on the north-east coast. The government intervened by sending Special Forces (which had been trained by ex-SAS men) and helicopter gunships to support the naval garrison; a seaborne task force was also sent. The latter was once again attacked by Sea Tigers whose craft simply rammed the naval vessels, thus slowing down the government reinforcements. Eventually, the garrison was overrun by the LTTE. The Tigers put most of the government soldiers to the sword. Rough figures quoted for the battle were estimated at over one thousand casualties for the government while LTTE lost just four hundred. Attacks on this scale continued, with both sides taking heavy losses. In September 1998, two thousand members of LTTE assaulted the government barracks in Paranthan with the loss of six hundred government soldiers. The attack was extremely well planned and carried out with the support of mortars and artillery.

Despite the call for peace and several abortive ceasefires, the struggle between Tamil separatists and the Sri Lankan Government still continues. The LTTE has not only established itself as a organised fighting force but it now claims to act as the official voice of the Tamil people worldwide.

America – 11 September 2001

The terrorist attack on the World Trade Centre in New York on 11 September 2001, the simultaneous attack on the Pentagon in Washington and the destruction of another airliner when it plummeted into a field in Pennsylvania – all as part of the same action – created a day that shocked the world. It was the worst ever incident of its kind on US soil, causing massive numbers of casualties and horrendous destruction. By demonstrating how easy it was to turn aircraft into flying bombs, the operatives of Al-Qaida showed how dangerous it was to harbour any complacency towards security issues, especially where bin Laden was concerned.

It is now known that the planning of the atrocities of 11 September began following events that happened years before. In Hamburg, in the late 1990s, three men met at the Al Quds mosque, all from different backgrounds but all with the same zeal for radical Islam. These were the men who were to become the ringleaders of the 11 September attack. One of them was Mohamed Atta, an Egyptian-born architect who had travelled to Hamburg in 1992 to further his studies in urban planning at a college there. The other two were Ziad Jarrah, Lebanese in origin and Marwan al-Shehhi, from the United Arab Emirates. In the summer of 1997, all three travelled to Afghanistan to train in the camps set up by Osama bin Laden.

During late spring 2000, all three men flew to the US, arriving separately on tourist visas. Once there, they made their way to Florida to enrol at aviation schools. During this time it is known that the men were not only doing their flight training, but were also studying flight-deck videos for Boeing 747, 757, 767 and Airbus A320 aircraft. In December, on the premise of wanting to become airline pilots, Atta and al-Shehhi booked six hours on a jet aircraft flight simulator in Opa-Locka, Florida.

In the days leading up to the attack, the gang began to tie up any loose ends. Leaving their rented apartments, the various members, including others who had now flown over from various Arab countries to join their comrades, checked into hotels near the airports they were about to use.

During the early hours of 11 September, the hijackers made their way to the airports and aboard their planes. Atta, seated on American Airlines flight 11 to Los Angeles, made a call to al-Shehhi on his cell phone. Al-Shehhi was aboard another plane, United Flight 175, at the same airport. It was later reported that there were four or five hijackers to each plane, all armed with knives.

At 8.45 a.m. EDT, not long after take off, the American Airline Flight 11 crashed into the north tower of the World Trade Centre, causing a massive explosion and fire. Just over 15 minutes later, the United Airlines Flight ploughed into the south tower, causing similar damage. Within minutes, all airports, bridges and tunnels in the New York area were closed by order of the mayor. This was closely followed by the whole of US airspace being shut down. It was not shut down quickly enough to prevent a third aircraft, American Airlines Flight 77, crashing into the Pentagon, seriously damaging part of the building. The rest of the Pentagon was evacuated immediately, as was the White House.

By 10.05 a.m., the damage sustained by the south tower of the World Trade Centre became too much for the integrity of the structure and it collapsed in a massive cloud of dust and debris. Five minutes later, part of the Pentagon collapsed, too. Then, a fourth aircraft, United Airlines Flight 93, crashed in Somerset County, Pennsylvania, south-east of Pittsburgh. It later transpired that some brave passengers had tackled the terrorists on board and had forced the plane to the ground before it could reach its final target, thought to be the White House.

Back in New York, the north tower of the World Trade Centre collapsed at 10.30 a.m., creating more casualties, including fire department personnel and paramedics who had entered the building to rescue those inside. The world watched on television screens as New York seemed to be locked into a chaos of dust, panic and debris. All large buildings in the city were evacuated for fear of further attacks. The mayor, Rudolph Giuliani, took the helm and rallied the people into pulling together and giving any help they could whether it was providing free meals to rescue workers or simply giving blood.

Later in the afternoon, the adjacent 47-storey Building 7 of the WTC caught fire before finally it, too, collapsed. By the evening, with fires still burning at all the crash sites and thousands of people unaccounted for, President George Bush went on television swearing that the US would not differentiate between terrorists and those who harbour terrorists in its hunt for those responsible. It was already assumed that Osama bin Laden was behind the atrocity.

As photos of those missing started to be placed all around the city, it was believed that the death toll would be more than six thousand. Over the subsequent months, as lists were checked, it became clear that the final death toll was not as great as initially feared. Nevertheless, at the final count, 2,801 people (not including the terrorists) lost their lives in the World Trade Centre attacks, although only a fraction of bodies were recovered. At the Pentagon site 184 died and 40 were killed in the plane crash in Pennsylvania. Following on his promise to hunt down the perpetrators, President Bush sent his troops and planes to Afghanistan, known to harbour bin Laden, attacking various strategic targets and ousting the Taliban regime. Despite intensive searches, US and British Special Forces were unable to locate their chief target. It is suspected that he escaped to a friendly country and, despite rumours of his subsequent death, is still at large and planning further attacks.

Bali – 12 October 2002
On 12 October 2002, at 11.05 p.m., huge explosions tore apart the peace of the idyllic island of Bali. This tropical island, with its beautiful beaches and friendly people, had long been a holiday magnet for young people from around the world. For Australians in particular it was a place for relaxing and having fun. Many were in the Kuta area, enjoying the nightlife and music of the bars and nightclubs. Some were having a drink in Paddy's Bar; the prospect of a terrorist attack could not have been further from their minds.

In just a few seconds that all changed as a bomb, placed on a stool or table near the DJ's booth, exploded in a blast that was strong enough to wrench a row of concrete seats from a wall.

Ten or fifteen seconds later a second massive blast destroyed the nearby Sari Club at Kuta Beach, a popular nightspot packed with clubbers. This bomb had been placed in a white Mitsubishi van parked in front of the building. The blast destroyed the building and caused massive damage to those in the surrounding area. The two blasts killed more than 180 people and injured three hundred more, some seriously.

As the bombs had been aimed at soft targets frequented by Westerners, terrorism was immediately suspected, with the possibility of Al-Qaida being behind it. Subsequent forensic examinations of the scenes revealed that chlorate-based explosives had been used.

Indonesia has long had its own problems with internal violence and racial disputes, but Bali has always managed to remain free of them. Despite the lack of evidence and lack of claims of responsibility, many of those investigating the case suspected it to be the work of a radical Islamic group, Jemaah Islamiyah. This group has been seen for some time as a terrorist threat throughout South-east Asia and is suspected to have strong links with Al-Qaida. Both Malaysia and Singapore have, in the past, arrested operatives of this group and accused them of planning terrorist atrocities but, up until the attacks on Bali, Indonesia has largely turned a blind eye to their existence.

Within days, Indonesian officials had released sketches of three suspects, although it was thought that these people might only have been low-level operatives within the group. A short time later, much to the anger of local protestors, the spiritual head of Jemaah Islamiyah, Abu Bakar Bashir was arrested, despite a complete lack of evidence connecting him to the atrocities. Currently, the investigations are still ongoing and involve detectives not just from Indonesia but also from the US, Australia, Britain, Japan and other countries.

4: ANTI-TERRORIST UNITS

Terrorists can launch an attack in any number of ways, although each incident will have in common its savagery and its aim of achieving a high media profile. To try to prevent such actions taking place, many governments monitor most of their 'in-house' terrorist organisations in order to anticipate any future actions they may be planning.

During World War II, Special Forces were tolerated by the military as those 'amusing' people who would tackle dangerous operations nobody else wanted. Today, they are at the forefront of both military and civilian anti-terrorist operations. These specialised units have acquired all the skills of a modern soldier capable of fighting in a major war zone, yet with equal proficiency they are flexible enough to take on the role of counter-terrorism. Almost any overt operational use of Special Forces creates media interest, be the operation a fantastic success or an unspeakable failure.

Terrorists can launch an attack in any number of ways, although each incident will have in common its savagery and its aim of achieving a high media profile. To try to prevent such actions taking place, many governments monitor most of their 'in-house' terrorist organisations in order to anticipate any future actions they may be planning. In recent years, however, various terrorist organisations have planned their operations to affect not just one government or one country, but to span the continents.

Where terrorists carry out a bombing or shooting attack, the security forces can only react to events. Only when prior information is obtained can countermeasures be initiated to prevent or limit the damage caused by an attack. On the other hand, when a siege situation or hijack takes place, the security services are in a much better position to respond.

To the counter-terrorist units, these actions fall into a number of categories; aircraft hijacking, building assault, vehicle assault, (including trains and coaches) and seaborne (including ships and oil rigs). Outline contingency plans for all these events already exist, and most can be modified and adapted to suit specific circumstances.

In many ways, the terrorist organisations themselves are responsible for the growth and maintenance of the counter-terrorist industry. In direct response to a spate of hijackings and the slaughter of Israeli athletes at the 1972 Olympics, government ministers at the 1973 G7 talks recommended the formation of counter-terrorist units. A few countries such as Israel and Great Britain had already recognised the need and had already implemented plans. Successes at Entebbe and Mogadishu prompted the universal acceptance of such units and most countries raised their own counter-terrorist outfits. Initially, there was mixed reaction to how and where personnel for a counter-terrorist force should be recruited. In most countries, the police are the ones who deal with the terrorist criminals, although military Special Forces are better qualified to deal with certain situations, especially in overseas operations. Many countries have opted for two teams – one police and the other military.

Over the years, increasingly sophisticated or well-orchestrated terrorist incidents have served to highlight the shortfalls in counter-terrorist training, but the security forces have been quick to learn. New equipment and operational techniques are constantly being developed in an effort to keep ahead of the terrorists. One major advancement is the reciprocal training in counter-terrorist techniques provided by various governments. This has helped many counter-terrorist units to appreciate some of the unique problems faced in different environments, while the Third World countries, which produce many of the terrorist factions, learn to fight the terrorists in their own back yards.

Author's note: Many people read and hear about the atrocities caused by various 'Islamic' terrorist groups. There should be no doubt in anyone's mind that almost all Islamic countries support the effort to defeat terrorism, and most have developed counter-terrorist units in order to do so. Many of these are trained by their counterparts in the 'West' and are extremely professional.

Counter-Terrorist Team Formation

While each country has its own problems in relation to terrorism, the formation of counter-terrorist units is quite similar around the world. Clothing and weapons might differ, but tactics and operational procedures are fairly standard. In the main, counter-terrorist units are formed to function on a dry land scenario although some are capable of mounting amphibious operations. This is particularly true of those nations that have a large off-shore oil industry, the STK counter-terrorist unit in Brunei being a perfect example.

Almost all counter-terrorist teams include a command and control element, together with assault teams and sniper units. In addition to these main bodies, various back-up units provide ancillary services such as communications, methods of entry (MOE) and specialist transportation. A dedicated intelligence section may also be attached.

The command and control element of counter-terrorist teams is usually responsible for administration and operational control. The administration will deal with recruitment, liaison, and the day-to-day running of the unit. Operational control will dictate training methods and assault procedures.

Communications are of particular importance to any counter-terrorist unit, especially when they are deployed overseas. The variety of communications equipment required can range from the basic intercom system used to link all team members and issue instructions during any assault, through to a secure communication link directly to the seat of government. Generally, the communications sub-unit will also be responsible for any additional technical assistance such as video links and live surveillance tracking via a laptop.

The main function of the command and control element in any counter-terrorist operation is to establish a briefing area close to the incident site. This requires advance liaison with other emergency services that may also be at the scene. As a terrorist incident becomes apparent, it is normally contained within a confined area. In most situations, the incident will have been reported to the authorities and the local police will respond to confirm the event. Where the call is from a specific person such as an airline pilot whose plane has been hijacked, a full police response team will be put on stand-by and directed accordingly. In all cases, once the incident has been established or it is known at which airport the hijacked aircraft will land, an initial security perimeter will be put in place in order to contain the incident.

A focal point will also be established known as the Forward Control Point (FCP). This can be either a commandeered building or a police mobile support unit. The FCP will try to secure initial links (telephone or radio) directly with the terrorists to establish any demands and to calm the immediate situation. It is normal for the incident commander to order the local police to establish a second outer cordon in order to prevent members of the public, and especially the media, from getting too close. The command and control element will normally find an area between these two cordons where it can bring in and hold the assault teams. This area is generally known as the holding area. The holding area should be large enough to house at least six specialist assault vehicles together with a supporting heavy equipment vehicle; in short a small factory or warehouse building. One part of the holding area will be allocated for operational briefings and communications set-up. Security must be absolute, both from the terrorists, media and non-classified personnel.

The briefing area is set up by men from the intelligence unit. Their task is to see that all information on the terrorist incident is made available and that the team members can absorb it easily. Some of this information may be retrieved from the enormous databases held by counter-terrorist teams. Such information will include individual terrorist profiles or the arrangement of aircraft seating.

The method of briefing will depend on the sophistication and budgets available to individual teams. Some may use a simple magnetic board that details the plan of the aircraft or building. Coloured buttons representing members of the team, hostages and terrorists can be moved as plans and information are acquired. At the top end of the range are computerised systems that have been developed to cope with just about any emergency, terrorist or otherwise. Developed over a number of years, through associations with various police forces and Special Operations Units, the computer software provides both planning and real-time control for any type of major incident, especially terrorist scenarios. A computerised visualisation of what could or will happen can be programmed into the system, providing a massive capability in pre-planning of incidents and events, as well as running 'real-time' monitoring of an operation. Old operations, both successful and unsuccessful can be registered in the database and used as a reference.

For example, if there is a hijacked Boeing 777 sitting on the runway of New York airport, the appropriate counter-terrorist team would have immediate access to the airport plans. Operators can quickly construct a 3D computer model that can be viewed from any angle. Internal layouts of individual buildings and aircraft types can also be retrieved from the system. Pre-planned aircraft parking allocations and sniper locations all help reduce the time it takes to put a team in position, ready to assault.

Incoming data from the perimeter forces that are logging terrorist activity all helps keep the assault team up to date. Most systems also allow for an animated 'walk-through' by the team commander, making sure that everyone is familiar with their positions, where they should go and what they have to do. The integration of such a potentially large amount of intelligence data in a user-friendly format all helps to guarantee a successful operation.

The holding area will also house the support entry team who are responsible for setting up any vehicle, or building, ladder assault systems and abseil equipment. This team will also check and make ready any wall breaching equipment that is required by the assault team.

Transport for the unit comprises a number of Land Rover/Jeep type vehicles. A wide variety of these robust cross-country vehicles have been used by the SAS, for example, since the anti-terrorist team was formed in November 1972. The characteristics of the vehicles should be ideally suited to the role. A drop-down tailgate will allow easy access in an Immediate Action (IA). It should be possible to attach platforms and ladders to the vehicles in order to carry the assault personnel directly to the required height of an aircraft door or building window. Such platforms can be adjusted to suit almost any type of assault entry.

Assault Team

Assault personnel focus primarily on techniques that will ensure they can close with and neutralise the enemy. Most counter-terrorist teams have learned that both speed and aggression play a major role in any successful assault. The basic instinct of survival is strong in all humans, including those who are prepared to die for their cause. Just prior to the 'moment of truth', however, there is a certain amount of hesitation. While the terrorists point guns at their hostages, threatening them with death, they are in control. The moment they are confronted with imminent death, the situation changes. No matter how dedicated, most terrorists will ignore the hostages and concentrate on the immediate threat to their own lives. At this stage there is no contest other than one of speed. Closing with the enemy is vital; the quicker it can be achieved the greater are the chances of success. Moreover, any further risk to the hostages is minimised.

Speed can be achieved through swift delivery of the assault team to an entry point where they can gain immediate access to the incident site. This can be the windows of a building, for example, or the doors of an aircraft. Secondly, there must be minimum delay in breaching the incident site, i.e. doors, walls and windows must be opened instantly. Thirdly, assault members must locate and physically close the distance between themselves and the enemy to the point where any terrorist threat can be neutralised. Selecting multi-entry points will help guarantee a successful assault.

Assault team members wear either camouflage or black, one-piece, fire-retardant suits. On top of this goes their body armour, holsters and weaponry. The modern assault suit is a one-piece outer garment with an outer hood that fits over a fireproof undersuit comprising of vest, trousers and balaclava. These separable layers of clothing give maximum protection from heat and flame by providing air gaps to insulate against and dissipate the heat. In a hot climate, or for operations of longer duration, if fire is not a possible threat, only the outer garment and underwear need to be worn. The outer suit is also fitted with a grab handle for easy dragging should a team member go down. The hood is designed to fit the respirator. All neck, ankle and wrist ends are elasticised to ensure a tight fit.

A respirator, which provides protection against CS gas and other biological and chemical agents, is also carried. The latest type of respirator has a built-in safe speech transmitter that allows for clear and direct communications. In addition, an external voice projection unit can be fitted. The respirator is designed to be carried in its container strapped to the back but, in practice, the pack is discarded and the respirator is shoved up the left arm ready for immediate use. Most actions now involve wearing the respirator, as it not only protects against gas but also projects an anonymous and intimidating image. A radio communications harness is designed to permit anti-terrorist team members to be in full radio communication with the rest of the team. The headset is connected by a lead to the central switching unit on the front of the body armour that contains a press-to-talk switch.

The earliest body armour used by counter-terrorist teams was heavy and cumbersome but the newer generations allow far greater freedom of movement. Most types are now thin, low profile, upper-body sleeveless units with side openings designed to offer the wearer maximum protection against ballistic threats. They are particularly good where space is restricted such as in building or vehicle entry or while abseiling from helicopters and structures. The best units comprise upper-body full wraparound protection with underarm overlap and include protection to the front, back and side body as well as shoulder areas. They have a built-in blunt trauma shield that allows energy absorption to dissipate the effects of the shock energy transmitted by a defeated bullet. As with the assault suit, the body armour material is fire retardant and is easily removable to assist in cleaning. The level of ballistic protection can be adjusted to suit most requirements. Depending on the type of operation the outer webbing of the body armour can be fitted with a series of pockets or elasticated grips that hold varying pieces of equipment saving the need for a separate overvest.

More than half of the world's current counter-terrorist teams use the Heckler & Kock MP5 sub-machine-gun. They do so because it was developed specifically for the job. The gun clips flush across the chest in the snatch mode, making it ready for use in an instant. A separate, low-slung holster system will house any secondary weapon, normally a pistol together with magazine holders for both weapons.

Dressing up in the assault equipment and looking good is the easy part. What most people do not see is the amount of training that goes into creating a highly trained assault team member. In conditions of absolute darkness and uncertain surroundings, and to avoid shooting the wrong person, the average assault team member must identify, confirm and act all in a split second; this can only be achieved by constant and rigorous training in realistic conditions.

Snipers

The role of the sniper unit within a counter-terrorist team is to provide a long-range capability for taking out terrorists. This will be required when an assault team is unable to close quickly with the terrorists, or when an assassination is sanctioned. Opportunities present themselves during the transfer of hostages and terrorists from one venue to another, i.e. in transit from a building siege to an airport. In short, snipers deal with any long-range situation that may present itself. Although assault and sniper teams train and exercise independently, a lot of cross-training takes place, therefore providing the commander with appropriate personnel for just about any situation. A secondary role undertaken by the snipers is one of intelligence gathering. Upon arrival at the incident scene the snipers will deploy to various strategic vantage points, allowing them an uninterrupted view of every aspect of the target area. All movement in and around the area is religiously reported back to the intelligence cell in the holding area. Snipers also cover any approach by the assault team and provide extra security once the assault has been completed.

Unlike the assault teams the choice of weapon used by the snipers varies considerably. In most cases each sniper will carry at least two rifles, one for short distance (300 metres or less, with day and night capability) and one for long range (300–600 metres, day time use only). The combination of sniper rifle and sights will depend on the individual unit. Recently there has been a demand for heavy calibre (.50) sniper rifles which provide the extreme-range accuracy demanded in a war such as Afghanistan.

The typical camouflage 'Gilly' suit remains as the basic sniper clothing, although each member will retain a set of 'blacks' for when he may be required as an assault team member. At present, a new range of 'stealth' clothing is being developed which will allow the snipers to approach the target unseen even by infrared or night-vision equipment. Although there are several prototypes on the market, most have problems with the cooling units and it will be several years before they are ready for operations.

Several systems have been designed allowing the counter-terrorist team commander to exercise split-second control over the members of his sniper team. One system operates via a highly secure digital telemetry radio link. Up to eight sniper radio stations can be included in the standard system. The system is fitted with a Target Indicator Button unit, which is attached to the fore-end of the sniper's rifle. In addition, it also features two further red and green LED displays. Once the sniper has acquired his target and it is in the centre of his crosshairs, reticule of his telescopic sight or image intensifier, he presses his Target Indicator Button, transmitting a constant signal to the unit commander and informing him that he has the target in his sights. Should the sniper lose the target, he releases the button, the signal stops and the commander knows immediately that the target is no longer viable. While the sniper is awaiting the command to fire, the red LED display on his display is illuminated in the 'stand by' mode, indicating to him that the radio link with the commander's set is functioning. When he presses his Target Indicator Button the green LED illuminates, informing him that his set is transmitting properly.

The commander's radio station comprises a radio set which features eight pairs of red and green LED displays, each pair representing a member of the sniper team. Each illuminated red LED display shows the commander that the radio link with each sniper is working properly. As each sniper acquires his pre-allocated target and presses his Target Indicator Button, the respective green LED illuminates and stays lit while the target remains in the sniper's sights. Should a sniper lose his target, when he releases his Target Indicator Button the appropriate green LED on the commander's set ceases to be illuminated. Once all targets are acquired, the commander can give the order to the snipers to fire at the appropriate moment over the separate team voice radio net. A touch-screen visual display is designed to present a graphic display of the situation. The target symbols are ranged along the top of the screen and can be individually drawn by touch into the 'live' area of the screen. Likewise, the symbols representing the members of the sniper team are ranged along the bottom of the screen and can be moved on to the 'live' area and allocated targets. While the snipers are in 'stand by' mode, their individual symbols appear as grey on screen. On switching to 'on target' mode, their symbols change to black. Similarly, the target symbols appear as grey on the screen until acquired by their respective snipers when they turn black. When all targets have been acquired by snipers who are 'on target', a 'totaliser' symbol on the right-hand side of the screen changes colour, notifying the commander that all targets are covered and enabling him to take a rapid decision to give the order to fire if necessary. New sniper control equipment allows the team commander to see what the sniper is seeing, thus allowing him to make a good and accurate assessment of a sniper option. The sniper option might well prove the most effective way of dealing with a hostage situation. For example, if there are four targets and four of the sniper teams can acquire them simultaneously, there is an opportunity to end the problem.

Training

Counter-terrorist teams train in all the basic combat modes required by their profession: these include close quarter armed and unarmed combat. Armed CQB covers a wide range of pistol and sub-machine-gun techniques. This training starts from the very basics of pistol work and encompasses all the problems of movement and weapons stoppages. It then progresses to more advanced techniques using automatic weaponry, rolling movements, and using both primary and secondary weapons. The next level is to progress onto the Heckler & Koch MP5 machine pistol after which both MP5 and pistol are used together. This involves practising stoppage drills on either of the weapons while using the other as immediate back-up. Team members are required to learn stoppage drills, i.e. learning what to do when their weapon jams in the middle of an assault.

From basic weapon handling, students move on to a variety of hostage rescue scenarios including the 'snatch'. This is a drill that is practised as part of the counter-terrorist hostage rescue situation. It involves going into a room shrouded in darkness in which a live hostage is to be found seated amid several paper targets. On average, any member of a good assault team would expend more than 2,000 rounds of ammunition a week practising such drills.

CQB techniques in unarmed combat are typically fast and deadly. They include learning about the defensive and offensive parts of the body, and how best to use them or protect them. In the field team members may be required to carry out a hard arrest (not kill the terrorist), and when the enemy is known to be armed, CQB provides the techniques by which this can be safely done.

Both assault team and sniper personnel work and train in pairs using the 'buddy system'. The buddy system normally runs over from work into the private lives of individuals, making the working bond extremely strong.

Few military or police barracks have full 600-metre firing ranges available, meaning that the team must travel in order to complete its daily training. Although inconvenient, this can isolate the team from any distractions, allowing them to concentrate better. Unsurprisingly, snipers spend a great deal of time shooting, the aim of which is to cover just about any situation that may arise requiring their skills. The individual sniper will generally use one third of his time improving his general shooting skills, using and maintaining all the weapons at his disposal at a high rate of accuracy. Once he is satisfied, he will develop his skills in 'on command' shooting. This means he will acquire a target but only shoot when ordered to. It is vital in the anti-terrorist sniper role that as many targets as possible are acquired simultaneously for sniper 'kill'.

Immediate Action

In any terrorist incident, time is a key factor. The time available to the security services to bring about a resolution of the situation is normally dictated by how long it takes to implement the terrorist demands. At the very least this will run into several hours and, with a viable delaying policy in place, this can be extended to a number of days. This provides the anti-terrorist team enough time to deploy into positions from which, at the very least, it can protect the lives of hostages or property.

The Immediate Action (IA) plan is primarily a simple plan that allows the team to close with the terrorists in order to prevent the loss of further life or destruction of property. Depending on the situation, the IA is put into force the moment the team is assembled in the holding area. It is only activated in an emergency, i.e. prior to a full-scale detailed assault plan being available. To my knowledge, the only time an IA has been used was during the hijacking of an Air France Airbus.

Aircraft Hijack

The hijacking of an aircraft provides two possible threats; the killing of hostages, or the conversion of the aircraft into a flying bomb. Most hijackings take place in the air, which favours the terrorists' chances of success in as much as there will be very little resistance to their initial attack. This is mainly because the passengers are too scared and the crew is too busy flying the aircraft. In addition, any attempt to overpower the hijackers might result in damage to the aircraft, and any damage to the aircraft while in flight can produce fatal results.

The standard terrorist procedure is to smuggle guns, grenades or explosives on board the aircraft and then use these to take command by threatening violence against the crew and passengers or, in the extreme, total aircraft destruction. Demands at this stage are normally simple, 'Recognise that we are in charge and take us to wherever we want to go.'

Due to fuel considerations, aircraft have limited flying time which, under normal circumstances, means they must land to refuel. This is usually, although not always, done at an international airport. Once on the ground, the situation changes; the anti-terrorist team now has an opportunity to assault the aircraft. If time permits, contingency plans are put into operation. Diverting other aircraft in the interest of safety stops the terrorist from changing aircraft. Additionally, snipers can be deployed to prearranged hides prior to the aircraft landing, and assault teams can prepare for an IA should the situation become unstable.

Any assault is divided into three parts: the approach, the entry and the assault. With few exceptions, an assaulting team can approach most aircraft from its 'blind spot' at the rear, an area that cannot be seen from inside the plane. A good team commander will know exactly the amount of room he has to manoeuvre within that 'blind spot'. This silent approach allows the team to reach the outside of the fuselage undetected. Once in position, ladders are placed against the doors and entry points prior to an entry being made.

The size of the aircraft involved and the number of passengers on board will dictate how many entry points the team needs to breach in order to make a successful entry. Almost all aircraft doors, both normal passenger and emergency, can be opened from the outside of the aircraft while it is on the ground. This is a design element that facilitates emergency services access in the event of accident, crash or emergency.

Most aircraft, especially the larger type, require that the assaulting team be elevated several metres in order to gain access. A wide variety of ladder systems are available to the assaulting team, these can be adjusted to reach any type of aircraft door. In some cases, two ladders are used side by side and placed against the aircraft fuselage. The idea being that the first man operates the handle and uses his body weight to swing the door open. This technique normally requires two hands and blocks the view of that particular team member, although the second member is free to fire or enter the moment the door is ajar. Ladders are also used to gain access to the wings whereupon the emergency doors can be opened.

Until recently, stealth has been the most popular method of assaulting hijacked aircraft but many anti-terrorist teams now favour a rapid response vehicle. This vehicle has a pre-assembled platform system attached that can be adjusted to any height. The result is a modern mobile siege tower that transports the assaulting members at the correct elevation directly to the aircraft entry points. While the vehicles can still take advantage of the blind area at the rear of the aircraft, they also offer a rapid delivery. It is incumbent on the team commander to get all his men actually onto the aircraft in order to facilitate a good assault, therefore the vehicle is normally armoured.

The SAS plan for storming a hijacked Lufthansa airliner at Mogadishu is a good example of an aircraft assault (see chapter 5).

Buildings

All building assaults pose the same problems; the number of floors involved; the number and distribution of hostages and the number and distribution of terrorists. Getting close to a building is, in most cases, fairly easy, as is gaining access. The major problem rests in closing with the terrorists quickly enough to prevent them killing any hostages. The best-known building assault was that of the Iranian Embassy in London and this lends itself to being a good example of building assault (see chapter 5).

Ships and Rigs

In the unusual case of a ship that is tied up alongside a dock being hijacked, it will normally be treated similarly to a building assault. This scenario is rare, however, and most terrorist threats against shipping have taken place at sea. As with oil rigs, this poses several problems, especially with approach. A ship or an oil rig is isolated on a flat surface over which would-be terrorists have a clear field of vision for a distance of several miles, much further if radar is used. This limits the element of surprise and thus gives the terrorists time to prepare themselves or execute hostages prior to any assault.

In the past, anti-terrorist team members have been dropped by parachute close to shipping, but this method of deployment is not entirely reliable and is very much dependent on weather. A sub-surface assault offers the best approach. This can be achieved by the use of submarines, sub-skimmers or divers – all offer excellent covert delivery to the target. The problem of getting from the sea surface and onto the ship or rig superstructure has also been overcome. Although oil rigs are high, most offer some form of ladder system which will allow access to the main superstructure. Access to ships that are not too high above water level can be effected using a special grapple and flexible ladder that is hoisted into position. On larger ships, where the superstructure is very high, suction pads can be used to climb the outer surface. This can even be done while the ship is moving. Once the assaulting team has several members on board they will release flexible ladders to enable others to climb aboard. The actual assault is carried out in a similar way to buildings, with each deck being cleared from the top down.

The main threat against both shipping and oil rigs is one of total destruction. A small motor-powered launch fitted with several tons of high explosive is enough to send either to the bottom of the sea. As yet there is no answer to this potential type of terrorist attack

Train and Coach
Trains and coaches are very similar to assault. Both methods of transport are limited in their speed and direction of travel, which means the anti-terrorist team can at least keep up with the hijacked transport, assaulting it when the opportunity arises. Creating that opportunity may involve bringing the train or coach to a halt. With coaches it is possible (if the coach is supplied by the assaulting force) to attach a device capable of stopping the vehicle at any given point. Trains can be stopped in a similar way but not with the same degree of accuracy. To overcome these problems, the SAS worked on a number of assault methods including dropping men from helicopters onto trains and coaches.

Once stopped, both train and coach can be entered in a similar manner. This is simply done by placing ladders against the vehicle and smashing in the windows and doors. As both means of transport are fairly narrow it is not always necessary to enter the coach in order to subdue any terrorists. If there is a need to enter, then stun grenades and CS gas will provide an excellent means of distraction while the tricky business of clambering aboard, when the assault team is at its most vulnerable, is completed.

Counter-Terrorist Teams

As with the terrorist organisations, an in-depth study of every counter-terrorist unit would provide enough information to fill several volumes, so only a select few are described here in any detail.

Much has been learned since the founding of counter-terrorist teams in the early 1970s; some units have achieved success, others have failed – all have striven to do their best. In many cases the techniques and procedures used in counter-terrorist assaults have been freely shared between different countries' units in an effort to stamp out terrorism. This cross-training between countries, and assistance during moments of crisis, has helped produce some breathtaking results, saving the lives of thousands of innocent people. Nevertheless, there have been exceptions, Egypt's Force 777 providing one example.

Egypt – Force 777

As Egypt and Israel negotiated a moderate understanding in the latter part of 1977, so Egypt's relationships with its neighbours declined. Many of the bordering Arab nations did not like Egypt's overtures towards the West and some started to launch terrorist actions against their former ally. In order to protect itself against such attacks from Islamic extremists, Egypt raised a new military unit known simply as Force 777.

The PFLP was one of the first groups to strike when it murdered a well-known Egyptian newspaper editor. The man was a personal friend of President Sadat. Shortly after, the same group hijacked a Cyprus Airways airliner in Larnica. This had been destined for Cairo but after takeoff the aircraft returned to Cyprus. There, the aircraft was moved to a remote stretch of the airfield under the watchful eyes of the Cypriot National Guard. Normally, a Cypriot aircraft on Cypriot soil would come under the jurisdiction of Cyprus, but Egypt had other ideas. With the recent murder of his friend, coupled with the fact that the hijacked plane had several dozen Egyptians on board, President Sadat sent force 777 into action.

The plan was simple. Force 777 flew directly to Nicosia airport in Cyprus, making their plan in midair. Basically they would carry out an Entebbe-style raid. This involved the assaulting troops rushing the hijacked aircraft the moment theirs touched down. While this plan may have worked it would have been prudent to inform the Cypriot authorities that such an assault was about to happen. In fairness, the Egyptians had notified the Cypriots that a negotiation team was on its way. When the aircraft carrying Force 777 landed and rolled to a stop not far from the hijacked plane, however, the Cypriot National Guard were totally unaware of any Egyptian military involvement. As armed men (most with AK47s) started to jump from the newly arrived aircraft, the Cypriots, assuming they were terrorists arriving to help their fellow hijackers, opened fire. Inside the hijacked aircraft, the terrorists watched bewildered as the firefight outside lasted over an hour. The final outcome was that five soldiers from the Cypriot National Guard and fifteen members of Force 777 were killed.

Force 777 returned to Egypt claiming that the fault lay with the Government and the Cypriot authorities, which was partly true. Even so, the unit underwent extensive training, much of which was provided by America. Additionally, it was agreed that all future operations outside Egypt had to be fully sanctioned before Force 777 was deployed.

Force 777 was given a second chance after the hijacking of the Italian cruise ship *Achille Lauro*, which ended with the capture of the four terrorists including their leader Mohammed Abbas. While the Americans saw this as a successful conclusion to the operation, the Palestinian radicals were infuriated, owing to the fact that the Egyptian authorities had covertly assisted in the capture of the hijackers.

The following month a reprisal was swift in coming when members of the Abu Nidal organisation hijacked Egyptair flight 648 at Athens International airport and ordered it to Luga International airport in Malta. The hijackers demanded the release of the *Achille Lauro* terrorists who were languishing in an

Italian jail. As with all Abu Nidal actions, those chosen for the operation were extremely ruthless, killing two Egyptian security sky marshals who had been aboard the flight as well as three women, two of whom were Israelis. The bodies of all those shot were unceremoniously dumped on the tarmac. The Egyptians immediately dispatched Force 777 aboard a military C130 with instructions to carry out an assault in order to release the hostages.

Despite the fact that Force 777 had been retrained by America, their operation remains a classic in how not to assault a hijacked aircraft. Some of the hostages had been released, yet none were interviewed to ascertain information about the hijackers. Such information is vital to any assault. Standard door entry methods into the 737 were also ignored in favour of an explosive entry. At this point in time there had been several successful counter-assaults against the same type of aircraft, and it was considered one of the easiest aircraft to assault. Force 777 also chose to ignore much good advice from outside agencies, such as the CIA, German GSG9 and British SAS.

Instead, Force 777 planned to make their initial entry through a hole in the top of the aircraft, which would be cut by an explosive charge. While this charge used military explosives, it was not of the type developed for such precise work. To add to the problem, this explosion was intended to act as a diversion, therefore more explosive was added. Once the charge had been detonated, those of the assault team who did not go in through the roof would enter the aircraft in a more traditional manner, through the doors. The whole operation would take place under cover of Force 777 snipers who had taken up position around the aircraft.

With everyone in place the 'Go' was given. The explosive entry literally ripped a hole in the aircraft, taking out several rows of seats and killing nineteen passengers. Force 777 members waiting underneath the aircraft managed to open the doors and make entry but the debris and smoke from the blast obliterated their vision inside the aircraft, leading to the deaths of many more passengers who were killed during the crossfire. If this was not bad enough, Force 777 snipers picked off many of the hostages as they struggled to find the exits and fall down the safety slides. In all, the operation cost the lives of 57 of the 90 hostages.

Force 777 retreated back to Egypt never to be used in the anti-hijack role ever again. During 2002, stories surfaced among the anti-terrorist fraternity that Force 777 has once more emerged and has been carrying out operations against its old enemies in Libya and Sudan.

Israel – Sayeret Mat'Kal, Mista'Aravim,Ya'Ma'M

The Israelis were among the first to show their prowess in the field of counter-terrorism. Their raid at Entebbe (see Chapter 5) stands as a template for how to do the impossible. Despite this, the unit did not simply appear, it was forged out of hard work and some early mistakes. Israel's situation in the maelstrom of Middle-Eastern conflicts has meant that it has built up several effective anti-terrorist forces over the years.

Sayeret Mat'Kal, also known as General Staff Recon and 'The Unit' is one of the first and better known of Israel's anti-terrorist forces. It was formed in 1957 by Avraham Arnan for the purpose of carrying out intelligence gathering missions in hostile territory. Basing itself on the SAS, it soon acquired a reputation for being effective and deadly. One of its earlier members was Ehud Barak who later went on to become the IDF Chief of Staff. Their multi-talented teams saw much action along the front line in the Six-Day War of 1967 and they also participated in the well-known hostage rescue at Entebbe Airport in 1976.

The training of a recruit into this unit takes one year and eight months to complete. The best from those that qualify are then inducted into the more specialised Unit 269, which holds responsibility for counter-terrorist operations outside of Israel's borders.

The first operation carried out by the 'Unit' took place on 9 May 1972 when they intervened in a hijacking. A Sabena airliner belonging to Belgium, flight 517, took off from Brussels bound for Tel Aviv with ninety passengers on board. En route, four hijackers, two men and two women belonging to Black September, seized the aircraft. The hijackers instructed the pilot to fly to Lod airport whereupon the plane would be refuelled and the passengers exchanged for Palestinians currently in Israeli jails. Negotiations, which were conducted by the International Red Cross, lasted less than a few hours, enough time for the Unit to get to the airport and prepare an assault.

Their plan was simple and typical of the early days of anti-hijack procedures in as much as they fooled the hijackers by presenting themselves as airline employees in order to get near the aircraft. The port front door was open and steps had been left in place, thus allowing the assault to be swift and clean. Both male hijackers were killed within seconds and the two women surrendered. It was a good start for the Israelis but, four months later, Black September returned. This time the organisation entered the Israeli accommodation at the Olympic village in Munich, killing several athletes and taking the rest hostage. Pleas from Israel to allow the Unit into Germany fell on deaf ears, a decision that cost the lives of the hostages (see Chapter 3).

Mista'Aravim derives from the Hebrew meaning 'to become an Arab'. Mista'Aravim is also a highly secretive group that uses disguise to blend in among the Arab peoples. It was originally composed of two units but one of them, Shimson (Gaza Strip), was disbanded. The other unit, Duvdevan (West Bank), remained and was used to infiltrate agents into occupied territories with the goal of eliminating leading members of the Intifada. Training Duvdevan soldiers requires them not only being able to dress appropriately, but also to think and act like their Arab counterparts. In this way, they are able to move freely in what would otherwise be hostile territory and conduct intelligence gathering, hostage rescues and anti-terrorist missions without drawing as much unwelcome attention as a conventionally dressed IDF soldier.

The training of a Duvdevan soldier has little focus on normal infantry procedures. Instead, they are trained exclusively for the environment they are operating in – the crowded streets of a city. Because of this, more emphasis is placed upon learning different languages, customs and ways of changing appearance. Unarmed combat is also given much attention, as the use of firearms would have disastrous effects in many of the areas in which the agents find themselves. This is not to say the soldiers aren't armed, of course. They tend to carry easily concealed weapons, such as the micro-Uzi or a short-barrelled M16. And, as would be expected, they are highly proficient in their use.

Yechida Meyuchedet Le'Milchama (Ya'Ma'M) was formed after an incident in 1974, when three members of the Democratic Front for the Liberation of Palestine (DFLP) took over 100 students hostage in a school in Ma'a lot.

On Sunday 15 May 1974, a national holiday in Israel, three Palestinian terrorists, armed with AK47s and grenades, took control of a school in the town of Ma'a lot. Crossing the border from Lebanon two days earlier, the terrorists hijacked a workers' van, killing two women in the process. After driving to Ma'a lot they entered a village house, again killing the occupants, one of which was a baby, before going to the school.

Despite the school being closed for the holiday, a festival had taken place and one hundred children, some accompanied by their parents, had used the school for overnight accommodation. Some managed to flee by jumping out of the second floor windows before the three terrorists could round up the children and secure them in one large room. Once this was done, the terrorists immediately demanded the release of Palestinians held in Israeli jails.

Units of Sayeret Mat'Kal were dispatched by helicopter to the scene, but due to the complexity of the situation they could do little more than surround the building and deploy snipers. The remaining eighty children being held hostage posed a major problem for the Israeli government and it was difficult to see how a successful assault could be carried out without a heavy cost in young lives. Defence Minister Moshe Dayan, who was personally at the scene, was not in favour of giving in to the terrorists and advocated an assault – he got his way.

The assault started at dawn with the snipers taking out one of the terrorists, but he was not killed instantly and managed to crawl back inside the building to warn the others. The assault was divided into two, one group covering the bottom floor and one the second. Unfortunately, the second floor group ended up on the third floor and had to make their way back down a level. This gave the terrorists time to react. They threw several grenades in among the children before opening up with their AK's – the result was carnage. Twenty-one children died as a result with fifty more wounded, many seriously. What made matters worse was the fact that one of the terrorists had disguised himself as an Israeli soldier and remained hidden until he had time to kill once more. He was eventually overcome. The incident raised severe criticism, eventually forcing the Prime Minister to resign. In addition, Sayeret Mat'Kal was to take a long look at its assault procedures and Ya'Ma'M was formed.

Interestingly enough, two of the Israeli officers in that assault, Lieutenant Colonel Ehud Barak and Lieutenant Benjamin Netanyahu, both went on to become Prime Ministers of Israel.

Ya'Ma'M hopefuls have to undergo a rigorous selection and have to have served in a combat unit previously. Successful applicants then undergo eight months of rigorous training in the use of all types of weaponry and in surveillance. Ya'Ma'M allegedly produces the best snipers of all the Israeli units. Recent missions have seen members of this unit becoming more versatile, carrying out undercover and long-range reconnaissance missions. Sometimes this unit also operates under the name of Yechida Meyuchedet Le'Milchama Baterror (The Special Unit For War Against Terrorism).

America – Delta Force

Charlie Beckwith was an American Special Forces officer who served with the British SAS for several years. During that time he saw action with the SAS in the Far East. During the Vietnam War he developed a reputation for being both ruthless and courageous. There he commanded a unit called 'Delta'. Upon his return to America he submitted plans for a special unit similar to that of the British SAS.

Beckwith's idea was to raise a unit capable of deep penetration raids, such as prisoner of war rescues, hostage rescue and intelligence gathering for larger operations – in brief, a unit that could operate like the British SAS. The selection course was comparable to that of the British, with Beckwith choosing just seven out of the original thirty candidates. Consecutive selections took place and each time a few more men were chosen, most of whom came from the established Special Forces units or Ranger Battalions.

By early 1978 the unit numbered seventy men, enough, Beckwith thought, to start counter-terrorist training. Again, this mimicked the British SAS format: CQB shooting, assault techniques and medical training, and those that were not parachute qualified were sent to jump school. A special 'House of Horrors' equivalent to the British 'killing house' was constructed in order to aid in rescue hostage scenarios. A defunct 727 aircraft was made available allowing Delta to work on anti-hijack procedures.

Offshore operations are normally handled by SEAL Team 6. SEAL Team 6 works in a similar way to the British SBS (Special Boat Section). They have been fully integrated with Delta since 1980, but still retain the capability to operate as an individual unit.

Weaponry for both Delta and SEAL Team 6 was fairly conventional in the beginning but the unit soon switched to the 'classic' MP5 machine gun, although their range of handguns remained varied. The normal allotment of CS gas, and stun grenades, were also used as were night-vision aids and purpose-built surveillance equipment. By early 1979 Delta was demonstrating its capabilities and they looked good, so much so that the original date for the unit becoming operational was brought forward. On 5 November the American Embassy in Iran was seized and Delta was tasked to respond.

Intelligence for the operation was plentiful, with the CIA and the media producing satellite images and film footage of the embassy in an effort to highlight the problems involved in any rescue attempt. Delta took full advantage of all this and prepared itself accordingly, eventually coming up with a workable plan (see Chapter 5).

The rescue attempt failed. The fault, however, lay with the American military administration and not with Delta. To make things worse, the administration and chain of command was never reviewed and thus further disasters were inevitable. Their second disappointment came when Delta was sent as part of the task force assembled for Grenada. Due to miscalculations, helicopters and mission arrival times were missed. The problem seemed to be one of organisation, especially where transport was concerned. While it is recognised that Delta cannot work in isolation, and needs to be supported by special flights and other units, it must also be recognised that these external elements must be dedicated and trained to work with Delta. Direction and authority for Delta has also been tightened. As one American general put it, 'It's no good having the best sword in the world if the user cannot wield it correctly.' Things have improved and Delta has gone on to show its capabilities in many roles, such as the Gulf and Afghan wars.

In conjunction with Delta force, as previously mentioned, the Americans also use a unit known as SEAL Team 6. This unit almost always accompanies Delta on special operations. Formed in October 1980, the unit totals some 150 to 170 men and is now based in Norfolk, Virginia. Both Delta and SEAL Team 6 are supported by the 160th Aviation Group. This is a large and varied collection of helicopters and fixed-wing aircraft. The reputation of the pilots in the 'Night Stalkers', as they are known, is as renowned as the units they ferry around on operations.

Britain – Special Air Service (SAS)

The British Special Air Service (SAS) stands alone, the envy of the world's security services. In the words of the late Charlie Beckwith of Delta Force, 'There is the SAS, and then there's everyone else.' This reputation is not based on bravado but has been earned the hard way. The reason for their exulted position is their overall success rate in countering terrorism.

Within every member of the SAS burns a special motivation, a desire to achieve the impossible, or die trying. This quality was evident in the original members of the SAS during World War II and has remained the ethos supporting the backbone of the regiment.

While the SAS is commanded by a Lieutenant Colonel and has the normal quantity of officers, training and operational procedures are firmly under the control of the senior NCOs. Over the past twenty years most senior NCOs have been promoted to officer status, therefore ensuring the regiment's potency and expertise remain intact and free from external military and political change.

Unlike the military units of many nations the SAS was not thrust into the counter-terrorist role following the 1973 G7 conference decision to establish specialist anti-terrorist teams. The SAS had already anticipated the threat and had plans prepared immediately to begin equipping the new unit that became known by a variety of names, including the anti-terrorist team, SP Team (Special Patrol) and the Pagoda Team. New equipment was purchased and the SAS responded to the training with unmatched keenness. Within days of the Commanding Officer receiving his orders from the Ministry of Defence, six SAS troopers were sent to the Range Rover factory and, through the direct intervention of the British Government, took the next six white Range Rovers that came off the assembly line.

At first the SAS counter-terrorist team was a fairly uncomplicated unit, but as the enormity of the terrorist problem developed and hijackings increased, so did the professionalism and the training. The team developed tactics to counter any type of terrorist threat and in the process the SAS produced the first outline strategy for counter-terrorist operations, including the make-up of the counter-terrorist team. The team is divided into two main groups, the assault teams and the sniper teams. These, together with a small command and communication group, make up the unit. The number of men involved was variable and would be dictated by individual terrorist situations. The overall strength was approximately fifty men per unit.

The assault teams were to concentrate mainly on assault entry, covering all the methods of getting in, be the target an aircraft, train or building. Snipers, on the other hand, were to deal with any long-range situation that might present itself. All team members had to be flexible in their roles, therefore providing the required numbers to suit the specific terrorist situation.

General rules for personal and group training were also ratified and written into the training manuals. These included CQB, high-speed driving, MOE, and communications. New training facilities were built both at the SAS's Hereford base and at their secret camp in Pontrilas, a few miles south of Hereford. All members of the SAS counter-terrorist team spent hundreds of hours in the famous 'Killing House', the name given to a flat-roofed block building in the grounds of the SAS base. This structure was designed and built with the express purpose of perfecting individual shooting skills of the SAS, and allows for many different scenarios to be set up. At the Pontrilas facility a variety of aircraft were installed, and a complete mock-up embassy building constructed. Equipment was also high on the list; stun grenades and other devices designed to create distractions during an assault were developed, as were assault ladders and specialist vehicles. These were just some of the major advances the SAS had achieved by the mid-1970s.

Since that time, the SAS has stayed at the very forefront of counter-terrorist operations. Its soldiers, the best Britain can find, are trained to the very pinnacle of excellence but, above all, SAS soldiers are constantly 'combat active'. The SAS works on a rota system that is broken down into roughly five-month blocks. For example, an SAS soldier may serve five months in Bosnia, Colombia, Northern Ireland, Afghanistan or any other small war. They will then rotate and do a similar length of time on the counter-terrorist team, where they will spend most of their time training on new techniques and equipment. Whatever they are doing, the SAS soldier is always combat active.

During any major terrorist incident in the UK where the SAS is involved, Hereford is normally given the tip-off to stand by, via the excellent network that exists between the chief constables of Britain's various police regions and the SAS. Control of all terrorist incidents in Britain rests firmly in the hands of the civilian authority. Even when the SAS are at the incident site they only make ready for any assault. Only when the situation demands the use of military action to stop the further loss of life will the SAS be given the official 'green light'. Counter-terrorist operations overseas depend totally on the country and the situation.

Today the SAS anti-terrorist team is housed in a purpose-built building just outside Hereford which is manned by two teams, Red and Blue, 24 hours a day. Each team member is issued with an alert device and his movements are restricted to allow for a quick response. On call-out the vehicles are loaded with a vast array of weapons and equipment, before a briefing is given on the operational requirement. The anti-terrorist team will only move into position when requested by the Home Office. There are, at present, two teams, each capable of working independently or together, as the task dictates. The SAS anti-terrorist team is regarded, by most of its peers, to be the best in the world.

France – Groupement d'Intervention de la Gendarmerie Nationale (GIGN)

Groupement d'Intervention de la Gendarmerie Nationale, France's elite counter-terrorism unit was formed in November 1973 shortly after the takeover of the Saudi Arabian Embassy in Paris, in September of the same year. The GIGN was initially split into four separate units with GIGN 1 (Paris) under the command of Lt Prouteau. Prouteau was a very capable officer who believed in doing better than the rest of his men. Both units merged in 1976, under the command of Prouteau, who was promoted to Captain.

The GIGN will never be larger than one hundred members and usually only has about ninety operatives at any one time. It is organised into four fifteen-man teams, five officers including the CO, a deputy CO, captains and lieutenants. It also has a command and support group and a negotiation unit. It accepts only eight new recruits each year, recruited from the Gendarmerie. Prospects have to have served for at least five years and have a clean record. Those who are then accepted have to undergo a further eight months of training in which they learn to operate in all types of environment and with all types of weaponry. They learn to do parachute insertion as well as underwater (SCUBA) work and close combat training. Apart from the physical training, the GIGN members are also trained to think fast and to avoid casualties wherever possible.

Counter-terrorist training for the GIGN is not dissimilar to that of the SAS, although the French place great emphasis on unit fitness, especially swimming. While under control of the French Ministry of Defence, they are basically policemen and certain military skills have to be taught, including parachute training at the school in Pau.

As with other counter-terrorist units, GIGN often undertakes exchange training with similar units, including the SAS, in order to practise hostage rescue and counter-terrorist tactics. They also send out training teams to such countries as Saudi Arabia, where they trained the National Guard. These forces were also trained by the SAS and were later used against radicals who had occupied the Mosque at Mecca. The GIGN displayed its full potential when it successfully assaulted Air France flight 8969 which had been hijacked from Algiers and flown to Marseilles (see Chapter 5).

Germany – GSG9 & KSK

GSG9 is an acronym for Grenzschutzgruppe 9, an elite German counter-terrorist unit formed from the Federal Border Police. Although the German Army had available several prime military units, each capable of doing the job, it was deemed more appropriate to put a police unit in the role of counter-terrorism. Like many of the counter-terrorist units, it was formed as a response to the massacre at the Olympic games in Munich in 1972. It consists of approximately 220 men who are stationed at St Augustin, a typical German military barracks on the outskirts of Bonn. It has close links with the SAS, not only through training but also through operations. GSG9's first leader, Ulrich Wegener, led the German unit's assault on the hijacked aircraft at Mogadishu airport in 1977. Two members of the SAS were also present during the rescue attempt.

From the start, GSG9 was well equipped and extremely well trained. Ulrich Wegener's style was always positive and very direct, an element which helped the Germans develop at a very quick rate. The unit has a range of Mercedes cars and 4x4's that convey them to an incident. If required, they also have access to dedicated police helicopters and fixed-wing aircraft. It goes without saying that their standard weaponry is H&K, with side arms from the same stable, although some SIG sniper rifles were used in the early days. CQB had a very high priority and Wegener sent a team to study the British ranges in Lyde and Hythe. Although these ranges are not used very often by the SAS they are excellent for counter-terrorist training.

After Entebbe and Mogadishu, but before the British Iranian Embassy siege, GSG9 held the first ever conference of counter-terrorist teams at their base in St Augustin. The idea was to swap tactics and techniques and hold inter-unit competitions. The idea was sound and well attended by units from America, Canada, France, Great Britain, Israel and several other countries.

Due to the success of the Germans at Mogadishu, they soon found that they were in heavy demand, with many of the world's teams demanding to be trained by GSG9. The Germans sent numerous training teams to various countries but, just as the SAS had found, this overseas training only served to water down the operational ability of the unit back in Germany. Despite this, GSG9 remained in the top echelon of counter-terrorist teams. Then in 1993 the bubble burst.

On 27 June 1993 two of Germany's most wanted were trapped in a train station in the village of Bad Kleinen. They were Wolfgang Grams and Birgit Hogefeld, both members of the Red Army Faction. The German security service BKA (Bundeskriminalt) had for many years been rounding up members of the shrinking renegade group, and had tracked the pair down. They called in GSG9. As the unit closed in Grams opened fire, killing one of the team members and seriously wounding another before he himself was shot and killed. This was not how the media saw the event. Some eye witnesses stated quite clearly that they had seen a GSG9 member stand over Grams and kill him in cold blood. Whatever the truth, GSG9 was slaughtered by the media. Two months later, on 17 August, a lone Egyptian hijacked a KLM flight from Tunis to Amsterdam. As fate would have it, the hijacker ordered the aircraft to land in Düsseldorf, whereupon GSG9 was ordered to assault it. This they did in excellent style, capturing the hijacker without firing a single shot. GSG9 had proved it had no 'shoot to kill' policy.

KSK is the German Kommando Spezialkraefte anti-terrorist group formed in 1996 in response to the new and different threats posed by the unification of East and West Germany. More specifically, it was created to protect German lives and interests not just within its borders, but all over the world. In all probability, the incident that prompted its formation was during the 1994 Rwandan civil war when eleven German nationals needed to be rescued. Because there was no suitable German force available, specialist troops from France and Belgium were sent in instead.

KSK operates alongside Germany's other counter-terrorist force, GSG9, but its operations are more military than civil in scope and it has wider-ranging jurisdiction. Like GSG9, however, KSK also maintains a hostage rescue team capable of going into any situation. Similar in many ways to the SAS and US Special Forces, KSK is able to undertake missions that include defence of German or NATO territories, long-range reconnaissance and raids into hostile territory, peacekeeping and crisis-management as well as counter-terrorist operations.

Most of today's KSK force came from the combined numbers of Three Airborne Brigade's commando companies and two of the army's Long Range Scout companies. With a fierce training regime of three years for the original members, the unit finally became operational in a limited capacity in April 1997. With recruitment and training ongoing KSK will eventually consist of one thousand troops split into various companies and platoons, all specialising in a different area of operation. For example, each platoon, which will consist of four teams of four men, will be trained either in land infiltration techniques, air infiltration (HALO), amphibious operations or mountain/arctic operations. In addition there will also be an HQ platoon and various platoons specialising in signals. The individuals in each platoon also have to become highly skilled in one of the following: explosives, medical, intelligence or communications. Other training covers operating in all terrain and conditions, survival and high-speed driving.

New recruits into KSK undergo a selection process and training similar to the SAS. To be accepted for selection, each prospective recruit needs to have served in the army and be airborne qualified. They must also be prepared to sign up for at least six years with KSK. The selection procedure then involves several days of psychological and physical tests, including swimming five hundred metres in under fifteen minutes and a seven-kilometre field run with a twenty-kilo backpack in 52 minutes. Once successful, the applicant then passes on to approximately three months of training including orienteering, abseiling, survival, high-speed driving, weapons handling and close quarter combat.

Weapons at KSK's disposal include the HK G36 5.56mm assault rifle, the P8 9mm pistol; the HK MP5 SD3 9mm SMG; the HK G8 assault rifle; the G22 Sniper Weapon System; HK PII underwater pistols; HK 21 5.56mm LMG and the Milan anti-tank weapon.

KSK members have already been operational. In 1999, a small number were sent to Kosovo to provide protection for German VIPs. It is also known to have sent over 100 troops to Afghanistan to aid in the operation against Al-Qaida and bin Laden.

Russia – Alpha Units

Alpha is an elite KGB unit whose main functions are counter-terrorism, VIP protection and Special Forces operations, roles bearing more than a little similarity to those of the British SAS, with a structure that is almost identical. Little was known about Alpha prior to the coup against President Gorbachev in 1991, during which they reversed the direction of the coup by standing alongside Yeltsin rather than attacking him in the White House of the Russian Parliament, as they had been requested to do by the coup directors. As a consequence of their actions, they gained a great deal of kudos and the unit itself is no longer under the direction of the KGB. Units known as 'Bravo' also work under similar direction but their exact role has not been identified.

There are many unconfirmed stories about the Russian unit, almost all conclude with a violent ending. One early story relates how they tricked hijackers into believing they had left the Soviet sphere of influence allowing them to land in a neutral country. They had not and, as the aircraft came to a halt, it was rushed by members of Alpha. So fearsome was their reputation that most of the hijackers preferred to commit suicide rather that surrender.

The hard-line approach taken by Alpha also proved to be effective in other areas, one example was Beirut. While the American and British were spending their time concocting elaborate deals, such as the arms for hostages debacle, Alpha used a much more direct line of reasoning. When, in October 1985, three Russian diplomats were taken hostage by Sunni Muslims, Alpha was dispatched to deal with the situation. Before they reached Beirut, one of the diplomats, Arkady Katkov, had been shot dead with his body dumped on waste ground. It did not take the local KGB agents long to identify the perpetrators, and once they had done so they then spent time tracking down relatives of the perpetrators. Alpha proceeded to arrest some of these as counter hostages, and just to show they could be equally as savage, they cut off several body parts and sent them to the kidnappers with the stern warning that other bits would follow if the kidnapped Russians were not released immediately. The tactic worked and since that time no other Russian has been taken hostage by any of the warring factions in the Middle East.

Alpha continues to be a highly secret organisation with very little information available about its operations. In 1991, however, a private organisation known as Alpha A was established and officially registered with the approval of the Russian Government. Its directors are drawn from former professional security and anti-terrorist officers of Government Special Security and the anti-terrorist forces unit Alpha. Alpha A is a unique company in the Russian marketplace, where they face little or no competition in expertise, capabilities and personnel. Alpha A actively employs a varied group of professional experts in security consultancy and support, giving the company the ability to respond effectively to any demand for security, nationally or internationally. They currently have their offices in Cyprus and provide security for many of the 'Blue Chip' Western companies that operate in the former Soviet Union.

Alpha's most recent operation involved trying to save the lives of more than six hundred hostages when, on the evening of 23 October 2002, fifty Chechen guerrillas stormed a Moscow Theatre (see Chapter 5).

Saudi Arabia

Saudi Arabia has one of the best anti-terrorist teams in the Middle East, having received training from both the British SAS and the German GSG9. The SAS training team was first involved in 1978 when a six-man team arrived in Jeddah. A preliminary recce had been carried out by an Arabic-speaking major one month prior to the main team arriving. Both the SAS and the students, all selected from the palace guard, were housed in a barracks on the western edge of the city, close to the old disused Royal Palace grounds. These grounds became the primary training area.

The SAS team used a training programme similar to its own, starting with the basics of weapon training and working up to full practice attacks on both buildings and aircraft. The daily programme was adjusted to accommodate both the midday heat and religious prayer. Morning classes would normally start with physical exercises at 5.00 a.m. followed by classroom lessons. Breakfast was taken around 9.00 a.m., with lunch at 1.00 p.m. There would then follow a sleep break until lessons resumed between 5.00 p.m. and 7.00 p.m.

Classroom lessons covered dry weapons training, including the Browning Hi-Power and the H&K MP5. On week two, range work began. Special ranges had been constructed in the desert, both to cover normal CQB shooting and 'Killing House' techniques. In the case of the latter, the walls of the building were constructed out of hessian cloth, secured behind a sandbank. Safety was paramount, thus command and control on the ranges required several team members at one time. The students would progress from basic pistol work, firing double taps, to short controlled bursts with the H&K. As the students moved on to the makeshift killing house, they were formed into teams, learning the more difficult house clearing techniques.

As previously mentioned, the training area allocated to the SAS was the old Palace grounds, which contained about three hundred houses of different styles and layout, stretching through a variety of streets. The entire complex was surrounded by a ten-foot high wall, which afforded excellent security. This proved to be a major asset in training the Saudi anti-terrorist team, especially in-house clearing and vehicle ambush drills. Given that the SAS was allowed to blow off doors and generally wreck a building before moving on to another, it added a great deal of authenticity to the assaults. Towards the end of the training, with several Royal members present, a full-scale exercise was carried out, both on the buildings and in the streets.

Aircraft assaults were practised at the airport. At first a military C130 was used, due to the fact that at the time the Saudi household used a converted C130 to travel around. An accident happened during one practice assault on the rear door of the C130; when the door was opened, an SAS instructor had his thumb completely severed. The thumb was saved by a doctor who sewed it back on. Later, the students practised on a Boeing 727 and, again, a final exercise included an aircraft assault. Less than a year later the Saudi unit went into operation when a group of fanatics took over the main Mosque in Mecca. They did a great job.

5: SUCCESSFUL COUNTER-TERRORISM

Anti-terrorist teams must act within the law. This means they must try to stop the terrorist from killing the hostages. In most cases, stopping the terrorist means killing the terrorist. At the initial moment of assault the health of the hostages is of little relevance and pacifying the terrorist takes priority. As the assault personnel gain control of the incident, so the safety of the hostages becomes more of a priority.

As we have seen, success in fighting terrorism is based on overturning the events of a terrorist threat and not by the numbers of terrorists killed. Whereas the reason for any terrorist act is to perpetrate fear, those opposing the act must react within certain restraints. In short, anti-terrorist teams must act within the law. This means they must try to stop the terrorist from killing the hostages. In most cases, stopping the terrorist means killing the terrorist. At the initial moment of assault the health of the hostages is of little relevance and pacifying the terrorist takes priority. As the assault personnel gain control of the incident, so the safety of the hostages becomes more of a priority.

The performance of anti-terrorist teams since their conception has varied from spectacular to downright disastrous. There are many reasons why an operation becomes a success or turns into a failure but none more than the skill and professionalism of the individual unit. Most counter-terrorist personnel will tell you that good planning and lots of luck have a lot to do with success.

The first counter-terrorist teams became operational around the mid-1970s and, while the manoeuvre by the Israelis at Entebbe was stunning, it was not the first counter-terrorist operation.

Djibouti – 3 February 1976

The French GIGN (Groupement d'Intervention de la Gendarmerie Nationale) carried out one of the first counter-terrorist operations. Although this event is overshadowed by the Israeli assault at Entebbe later in the same year, it was extremely well planned.

The French Government had sent the GIGN to the small French colony of Djibouti in north-east Africa after a school bus containing thirty children was hijacked by four members of the FLCS (Front de la Cote des Somalis). The bus was on its regular round trip from the airbase to the primary school in the town's port district. The rebels forced the driver to take them towards the Somali border, a distance of 180 kilometres. The bus finally stopped in open ground between the French and Somali frontier posts. In front of the bus two military trucks had been positioned by the French Legionnaires who initially controlled the situation. At this stage, a fifth hijacker joined the bus from the Somali side under protection from soldiers guarding the frontier post. The Legionnaires reacted by moving into a position to ensure that the terrorists could not move the children over the Somali border.

As the situation stabilised, the FLCS issued its demands. The demands, most of which were totally unattainable, dragged on for hours, with the terrorists threatening to cut the throats of the children. Added to this torment was the unbearable heat that caused terrible conditions inside the bus.

The GIGN arrived in Djibouti on 4 February and immediately put a rescue plan into operation. A hijacked bus is normally open to a sniper assault and for this the GIGN dispatched snipers to cover every angle of the bus. However, the terrorists showed no sign of exposing themselves and conditions inside the bus grew worse. Lunchtime food, which had been demanded by the terrorists, was drugged with a tranquilliser and sent to the bus. By 3.30 in the afternoon the effects of the drug and the afternoon heat ensured that almost all the children were asleep. This gave the snipers a clear line of fire to take out the terrorists. At 3.47 p.m. there was a single volley of rifle fire and four of the five terrorists fell dead. The GIGN assault squad stormed aboard the bus but not before the fifth terrorist, who had managed to survive, shot and killed one of the children. Five other children, the conductor and a woman teacher were wounded during the assault; the remaining children were successfully rescued. Somali soldiers at the frontier post opened fire to provide cover for the terrorist but this was quickly silenced by the French Legionnaires.

Entebbe – 27 June 1976

Wilfred Boese, a 28-year-old West German, was a tall, good-looking man with fair hair and penetrating blue eyes. Boese was a lawyer by profession but when he wasn't practising law, he was a full-time member of the Baader-Meinhof gang. He was described as an intelligent man, with a smooth persuasive manner, a manner he used to coerce four other terrorists into hijacking a French aircraft.

At this time, most of the Baader-Meinhof gang were under strict supervision in German jails. In May 1976, Ulrike Meinhof, one of the founding members, was found dead, hanging in her cell at Stammheim Jail, Stuttgart. Boese had always respected Meinhof so, in retaliation, he began his planning with the Palestinians for the hijacking of the airliner. The chosen team consisted of two Palestinians from the PFLP and another German woman, also a member of the Baader-Meinhof, Gabrielle Tiedemann. Like Boese, she knew Ulrike Meinhof well and the action they were to carry out was to be in Meinhof's name.

Somewhere between May and June 1976, the group gathered together in the city of Kuwait in order to plan and train for the operation. It was to be the most spectacular hijacking ever, their target, an Air France Airbus bound for Paris from Tel Aviv, via Athens. The whole operation was to be overseen by the master of hijackings, Dr Wadi Haddad, who would direct events from his operational base in Mogadishu, Somalia. Also playing a vital key role in the whole operation was the President of Uganda, Idi Amin. Amin had already declared himself a sympathiser of the Palestinian movement and had welcomed the PFLP training camps into Uganda. In exchange for this protection and the facilities of his country, the Ugandan President would be given the role of mediator. Such a role was irresistible to Idi Amin, hoping that this would establish him as a prominent statesman to the rest of the world. By this time, Idi Amin was well known for the atrocities instigated by himself and his henchmen throughout Uganda, the country was in rapid decline and the only law was that of the gun.

Author's note: It is widely thought that the Israeli Security Services played a major part in the conspiracy which overthrew Milton Obote and brought Idi Amin to power.

The hijack team of two Germans and two Palestinians would fly from Kuwait and board the Air France aircraft during its stopover in Athens. Once airborne from there, they would hijack the aircraft and force it to fly south to Bengasi in Libya. After refuelling, and under the defensive shield of Libya, they would continue south to Entebbe. Once at Entebbe, they would come under the protection of Idi Amin, with his 20,000-strong army. At this stage, there would be little chance of them not having their aims fulfilled.

In the early hours of 27 June, the team left their apartment in Kuwait and, travelling in pairs, drove to the international airport. Here they boarded the scheduled flight for Paris via Athens. The flight to Athens was uneventful and upon arrival both groups went straight to the transfer lounge. As they boarded flight 139 for Paris, the aircraft that had arrived from Tel Aviv was already carrying more than a hundred Israelis. The two Germans had booked first-class tickets, while the two Palestinians were seated in economy. Many of the first-class passengers recall the ugly German female getting on board. It would seem that someone had taken her seat and she created hell. During the flight, Boese went to the rear toilets were he met up with one of the Palestinians. Here Boese collected his weapons. Boese then returned to his seat at the side of Tiedemann and gave her a weapon. It would seem at the outset that the Germans had entered the aircraft clean, and the risk of carrying the weapons on board had been undertaken by the Palestinians.

Once the captain, Michael Bacos, had established his aircraft on the correct flight path, he handed over control to his co-pilot. Back in the cabin, the crew of nine stewardesses started the mammoth task of serving courtesy drinks to the 258 passengers on board. As one of the stewardesses was passing out the drinks, a young girl stood up in the aisle and raised her arms above her head. At first the stewardess thought she might be stretching then to her horror, she realised that the girl was holding two grenades.

Suddenly everyone started screaming – 'Sit down, sit down, everyone must sit down.' At the same time a tall, well-dressed German with fair hair walked up the aisle waving a pistol at everyone and repeated the order for everyone to sit down. Walking past the girl, he made his way to the flight deck. Then the two Palestinians stood up with weapons and again started to repeat the girl's call for everyone to sit down and keep quiet. 'We are Palestinians,' they said. 'If you remain seated and do as you are told, no one will be harmed.' The message was repeated over and over, and slowly the turmoil subsided. Quickly, the two Palestinians strapped boxes, which they told the passengers contained explosives, to the two emergency doors halfway down the aircraft. They now warned all the passengers that if anyone tried to do anything silly, they would blow up the plane.

Suddenly, the intercom was switched on and the frightened passengers listened in horror as a man with a heavy German accent told them that they were being hijacked by members of the Che Guevara Commando Unit of the Popular Front for the Liberation of Palestine. The German spoke for roughly ten minutes, telling them why the aircraft had been hijacked and that it was to convince Israel of the rights of the Palestinian people. He went on to inform the terrified passengers that they would be held hostage for the release of many freedom fighters presently in prison in Israel and Germany.

Back on the flight deck, Boese made his instructions clear to Captain Bacos. The Captain in return reassured him that he would have no problem, they would fly wherever they were required to go and made it quite clear that his main concern was for the safety of the passengers. He also asked to speak to the chief stewardess, to instruct that his crew should co-operate fully with the hijackers and offer no resistance. Boese's instructions to the Captain were to take the Air France Airbus into Bengasi. The stop at Bengasi was required in order to refuel so that the aircraft could reach Entebbe. While it was only intended to remain for a short while at Bengasi, they met with a problem. The problem was that a British woman by the name of Patricia Hayman, who was heavily pregnant at the time, had suffered severe pains in her abdomen and these were now getting worse. Fearing that the pregnant woman may cause some unplanned problem on the southward journey to Entebbe, it was agreed with Boese that she should be left in Libya. Finally, after three hours, the lady concerned was taken by ambulance to a Bengasi hospital.

Later that evening the aircraft took off, with the passengers heading for their unknown destination. In the early hours of the following morning, the Air France Airbus brushed over Lake Victoria and touched down at Entebbe airport. The moment it landed the whole aircraft was ringed with Ugandan troops. To the passengers, this would seem a normal precaution in the event of a hijacking. A little later, a service vehicle pulled up next to the aircraft. Within minutes the stewardesses were dispensing cartons of drinks, this familiar procedure was putting everyone in a relaxed mood. As the day progressed, however, so did the heat inside the aircraft. No one had moved for several hours and now many people became restless. Slowly, the mistrust started to creep back again. At last the 257 passengers were allowed to leave the aircraft and, under a tight cordon of Ugandan soldiers, were forced into the old terminal building of the airport. Many of the passengers thought that the Ugandan soldiers were there to assist them but it soon became obvious to everybody that they were co-operating with the hijackers.

In Israel, parliament had called an emergency session of the Knesset where Prime Minister Yitzhak Rabin informed the members of his Government about the hijack. There was no doubt in the minds of the Israelis that the hijack situation had been painstakingly planned, and now the hostages were being held in a hostile country. It also became obvious that the hijackers were being assisted by Idi Amin and his soldiers. It was clear to everyone that any rescue attempt would have to be on a large-scale military footing.

First on the agenda was the Israeli secret service, Mossad. They required information from their eyes and ears around the world. The second task was to assemble a strike force and get them to Entebbe undetected, rescue 270 people, and get them home safely. Defence Minister, General Gur, issued orders for the recall of Israel's finest soldiers. Together they formed what was to be known as 'The Unit'.

Back in Entebbe, the hostages were crowded into the old terminal building, which was a long, two-storey structure and was now derelict, falling into decay. Outside, the whole building was surrounded by Ugandan troops, together with the four hijackers, who sometimes were present and sometimes disappeared for talks with Idi Amin. Throughout the night food and drink were supplied and the toilets were initially usable.

On Tuesday 29 June, the German Boese came into the room and announced that because of the crowded conditions in the old terminal building they intended to move some of the hostages to a different room. This all seemed like a very good idea to everyone until the list of names was called out. It was then realised that all the names they were calling were either Israeli or had a Jewish sound. The following day, 47 passengers from the larger room holding the non-Israelis, were all taken out and flown to Paris. Again, Idi Amin arrived to let the hostages know that he had already sent some of them home, although he neglected to say that none of them were Israelis.

Meanwhile, plans for rescuing the hostages were well advanced, but it would seem the more they planned the more problems arose. Even though the number of hostages had been reduced, it still left some 200 people in Entebbe to rescue and this would involve several aircraft. A courtesy American AWAC flight had also discovered that there were two squadrons of Mig 17s and 21s sitting on the tarmac at Entebbe. Added to this, the bulk of Idi Amin's army was only about an hour's drive away at Kampala. Irrespective of all this, the Israelis still thought it was possible to mount a successful operation and rescue the hostages.

An entry could be made into Entebbe by using three C130 transport aircraft flying in very tight formation at a height of no more than two hundred feet, in order to avoid the radar. These would be shielded by a Boeing 707 scheduled flight from Tel Aviv on its normal route to Kenya, which would be at twenty thousand feet. Any of the neighbouring Arab nations watching the radar would merely assume that the 707 scheduled flight was giving off some sort of echo. The main problem lay with the Israeli's communications for the operation. This was solved by having an Air Force Boeing 707 fly in a holding pattern above Entebbe to act as a communications relay. In the final analysis, the Israelis estimated that, once on the ground, they would have no more than fifty minutes in order to complete the whole operation. For this, the overall command was given to one of Israel's top soldiers, Brigadier Dan Shonron.

Shonron broke his force into three defined groups, the first (the largest one) was to attack the primary targets at the old terminal building and provide protection for the hostages. Additionally they were to knock out the radar and communication system. This larger group would also deal with any Ugandan soldiers on duty guarding the hostages. A second, smaller squad would take out the Mig 21s and Mig 17s that were parked at the airport to avoid any follow-up once the C130s had completed their mission and taken off. The third group would set up an ambush at the entrance of the airfield in case any soldiers came from the Army camp a short distance away once the shooting had started.

One of the biggest problems that faced the whole mission was the distance involved in flying from Israel to Entebbe. It was almost impossible to refuel en route due to the amount of air activity this would require. Secondly, should the C130s be spotted on Egyptian or Libyan radar, fighters would be scrambled immediately. To offer some protection against being spotted, it was decided that the Israelis would put up Mirage and Phantom fighters. These fighters would escort the C130s to the limit of their range.

The only way for the three C130s to avoid enemy radar, was to fly on the deck in close formation for over two thousand miles. Such a task requires not just skill but great daring. With the 707 El Al aircraft on a scheduled flight flying down to Nairobi, the Israeli Air Force command 707 would fly just above it, shielded by its radar image. The flight path for all the aircraft would take them down the Red Sea and then, turning right, they would cut across Ethiopia directly into Uganda. It is worth pointing out at this stage that this is right through the middle of enemy territory. On the left they had Egypt, and on the right they had Saudi Arabia, both of whom had sophisticated radar and missile systems.

The Air Force 707, once over Uganda, would climb to 60,000 feet and circle in the 'blind zone'. Using highly sophisticated radar jamming equipment to block out any possibility of the operation being seen, it would also serve as excellent communication relay for everyone concerned. The assault force on the ground could relay messages directly from the soldiers into Israel.

The man chosen by Brigadier Shonron to lead the main assault, was Lieutenant Colonel Jonathan Netanyahu. He was chosen for one thing above all else – his qualities of leadership. He had a rare ability to get a job done by firing his soldiers with enthusiasm.

On Friday 2 July, he practised all day with his men at the military air base where they used positions marked out in the sand to represent the buildings at Entebbe. Time after time they practised unloading the armoured jeeps from the C130s, racing across the five hundred metres of tarmac and assaulting the buildings. An old black Mercedes car was found and given a thorough once-over by Israeli mechanics and the finished item was made to look like a car that was currently used by Idi Amin.

Eventually, the Israelis were ready, the assault team and all their equipment boarded the C130s, the rescue bid had started. Soon after takeoff the aircraft reached their maximum speed of just over 350 miles an hour and together the three C130s flew almost at zero feet above the waves. As they flew further south, to add to their already difficult flying conditions, the weather increasingly deteriorated and the C130s found it difficult to maintain altitude or hold such a tight formation. Directly above them, at 30,000 feet flew the normal El Al scheduled flight for Nairobi, and again above that was the airforce 707. Anyone watching their radar screens would merely assume that they had a shadow blip.

Back in Uganda, conditions had deteriorated, with the toilets now being blocked, the food almost inedible, and there was a serious fear of sickness and diarrhoea. Again, Idi Amin made several visits to the Israeli hostages, assuring them that he was doing everything he could and that, hopefully, the situation would be resolved.

Mossad had also been busy, awakening its agents in Kenya and Uganda. All were given tasks of minor sabotage, cutting telephone wires, or relaying vital information back directly to the command aircraft. As the rescue aircraft flew southwards, a special task force of Mossad agents left Kenya by boat, skimming across the smooth waters of Lake Victoria. Less than five hundred feet above them the three C130s flew in and landed at Entebbe totally unnoticed by the radar operators there. As they touched down, one of the C130s broke the radio silence and said 'This is El Al flight 166 with the prisoners from Tel Aviv' and without waiting for the reply. 'Can I have permission to land?' The Entebbe control tower was taken completely by surprise. They obviously knew that some arrangements had been made but had not been kept in the picture, therefore they had little option but to let the flight in, thinking that only one C130 had landed. At the same time, Mossad agents cut all telephone lines between the airport and Kampala. Thus, the confused control tower watched as a C130 landed and came taxiing towards the old terminal building. As the Hercules taxied to the edge of the tarmac facing the old building, a large black Mercedes, complete with an escort of two British Land Rovers, rolled off the tail gate out of the back of the C130. This small convoy drove across the tarmac, quickly followed by the main assault group, all making directly for the main doors of the old terminal building.

Caught unawares, both Tiedemann and Boese, together with some Ugandan officers, watched in amazement as the C130s arrived. The presence of the convoy, including the black Mercedes, swept towards them, stopping just feet away. Too late the Ugandan officers realised that something was desperately wrong. By this time the Israelis had opened fire. Boese ran inside the building to find his machine gun as behind him gunfire broke out. Men were jumping out from the convoy of vehicles firing as they ran. The weight of fire put down by the Israelis was quite terrifying, but served initially to drive a lot of the Ugandan soldiers back. Gabrielle Tiedemann, who had also been outside the building, raised her pistol and fired one shot, before she was cut down. Seconds later Boese reappeared, this time with his machine gun. As he emerged, Wilfred Boese realised he was outgunned and decided to surrender – a burst of automatic fire killed him instantly.

The Israeli soldiers reached the building holding the hostages, trapping and killing the two PFLP Arabs in the process. Another group took control of the terminal and killed several Ugandan soldiers, while others placed charges on the Mig fighters. Suddenly huge fireballs erupted into the sky as the Migs were destroyed on the ground. A fourth group had gone to the main entrance gate and met up with the Mossad agents who had already positioned an ambush for any support coming from the Ugandan barracks which lay just a few hundred yards away.

Slowly, but surely, the whole situation became under control, and the hostages were taken across the tarmac and placed aboard the C130s. Desperately, the engineers aboard had removed the pumping equipment and were working furiously to fill the empty tanks of the C130s. As the soldiers loaded the hostages on board the planes, the medics and doctors rushed to treat the wounded. Meticulously, all the hostages and soldiers were counted, making sure that no one was left behind. Even the Land Rovers and the Mercedes were put on board and returned to Israel. As the three aircraft took off, they left behind them a ruined airport terminal and two squadrons of Mig 21s and 17s destroyed. Over one hundred Ugandan soldiers lay dead or dying in the darkness. The whole operation had taken no more than 95 minutes. Once more, the C130s flew up the Red Sea towards Israel, as squadrons of Phantoms and Mirages were scrambled to give them maximum air cover. The Israelis had carried out one of the most daring counter-terrorist operations of all time.

The Netherlands – 23 May 1977

The Depont Train hijacking was one of the earliest instances of such a terrorist act. A train travelling between Assen and Groningen in the Netherlands was hijacked by nine Moluccan terrorists on 23 May 1977, with 51 hostages being taken. At the same time 110 hostages, in the main children, were seized at an elementary school at Bovensmilde, although 106 were released a few days later with a stomach virus. The stand-off lasted for three weeks until the psychiatrist who was conducting negotiations on behalf of the Dutch government disclosed his concern that the terrorists were about to start killing the hostages.

The Royal Dutch Marines Close Combat Unit prepared to storm the train at 4.53 a.m., working in five-man teams. SAS advisors were in close contact throughout the hijack and recommended the use of stun grenades, but the Dutch decided against this form of action, preferring instead to instigate the assault under the distraction of six F104 Starfighters flying low over the train. Six of the terrorists were killed and three surrendered. Two hostages, who panicked when the firing began, were killed. One other hostage was also shot, albeit not fatally.

In a simultaneous assault at the school, the results were much better. Three of the four terrorists were caught unawares, asleep in their underwear, when the Marines broke through the school wall with an armoured vehicle. All four terrorists were captured and the hostages safely released.

Mogadishu – 13 October 1977

The hijack to Mogadishu came sixteen months after Entebbe and, although the hijack team were all Palestinian, the operation was jointly co-ordinated with the Baader-Meinhof which, by this time, had become known as the RAF (Red Army Faction). For their part, the RAF had kidnapped a top German industrialist, Hans-Martin Schleyer, a month earlier. As it later transpired, both the kidnapping and the hijack were allied to the same demands.

Lufthansa flight LH181 took off from Palma, Majorca, for Frankfurt on the afternoon of Thursday 13 October 1977. Only the eleven German beauty queens attracted any particular attention among the 87 passengers. No one suspected that there were also four terrorists on board. Taking off at 12.57 p.m., the journey should have been completed within two hours; instead it lasted five days.

The in-flight meal had just been served when the hijackers struck. All four terrorists seized control of LH181, brandishing pistols and hand grenades, starting a drama that was to ricochet around the Middle East. Refuelling at Rome and Larnica in Cyprus, the plane flew on to Bahrain. Here it refuelled yet again before making its way to Dubai, Union of Arab Emirates. The terrorists were demanding the release of the Baader-Meinhof gang, currently held in a top security German prison, as well as two other terrorists held in Turkish prisons. They also demanded fifteen million dollars. Their demands were identical to those issued for the release of the kidnapped German industrialist Hans-Martin Schleyer a month previously. During the first 48 hours of negotiation, the Bonn Government took a firm line, refusing any concessions to the terrorists. At the same time they looked to Europe for support in their stand against terrorism, receiving assurances from both France and Britain that they had their full support.

Author's Note: The British Prime Minister sent myself and Major Alastair Morrison to assist the GSG9 German anti-terrorist team throughout the hijack. The following is my version of events.

During the week preceding the hijack, I was on duty at Heathrow with eight other members of the SAS anti-terrorist team. We were training on various types of aircraft, familiarising ourselves with their basic internal layouts and the variations employed by different airlines. On the afternoon of Friday 14 October, I returned with my crew to Hereford through the beginnings of fog that was thickening dramatically across the country. Ensuring that all the crew were on call, I released them for the weekend, before setting off for my own home. I had only just arrived when the phone rang, ordering me back to camp. Back at the anti-terrorist team office, I found the team commander, who informed me that the British and German Governments had agreed on the need for a joint anti-terrorist effort, and that the two of us were to leave immediately for London. As the fog was so thick, we took the command chopper that flew us directly to Battersea heliport.

Unfortunately, due to the fog, the heliport had been closed, so that when we landed, we had no option but to climb over the heliport gates to get into the street. Luckily, one of the first vehicles we saw was a police patrol car, which we flagged down. We asked the driver to take us to Whitehall. He was, not surprisingly, dubious about such a request from two scruffy individuals but our manner, backed up by ID cards, persuaded him to check with his control. Arriving outside 10 Downing Street, we were met by senior military personnel, who briefed us on the current situation.

Major Morrison of SAS HQ, London, joined us at this time. We were further briefed regarding the areas of national secrecy concerning the operation and the equipment employed. We were also told that a couple of politicians from Bonn had arrived, together with two members of a unit barely known to us at the time – GSG9. (Grenzschutzgruppe 9, a division of the border police trained in anti-terrorism). We attended a meeting inside No.10 at which the hijack situation was more fully discussed. Present were various Heads of Security Departments, Ministers, Major Morrison, my anti-terrorist team commander and myself. It was quickly established that the plane's position was still as reported by the media that afternoon – in Dubai. We reported that there was an ex-SAS man currently in position in Dubai working under contract for the Palace Guard.

We were then introduced to the GSG9 members and within minutes realised how much in common the SAS anti-terrorist team had with them, for we had each developed tactics and equipment that would later be of great benefit to both teams. I mentioned that we had developed a new type of stun grenade which would detonate almost instantaneously when thrown, effectively stunning anyone in close proximity. The grenade emits a very loud bang and a very bright flash of light in a set sequence, not dissimilar to the effect of strobes in a disco as they flash on and off. The combination of the effectiveness of these grenades in momentarily incapacitating the target by disorientation, together with our expertise and knowledge gathered from the Middle East, plus our recent training on aircraft interiors was of such great value to the Germans that we were immediately asked to return with them to Germany. They also suggested that once we had talked to the people in Germany, we would, if requested, fly on to Dubai to give further assistance. Major Morrison and I were selected to accompany the GSG9 and arranged for eight stun grenades to be sent from Hereford to meet us at Brize Norton. We left shortly afterwards, the intention being to travel by helicopter, but due to the very thick fog we had to endure a very tedious drive – sometimes at not more than 10–15 mph – arriving at Brize Norton at about 4.00 a.m. Here we met the crew of the C130 that was placed at our disposal and ready for an immediate take off. The weather was so bad we crossed the channel using low level radar during the flight.

Already aboard – and under guard – were the two boxes containing the stun grenades. I checked them at once to make certain that we had fully operational grenades, and not the dummy training variety. The C130 then took off, landing in Bonn, Germany at 6.30 a.m. on Saturday 15 October.

There to meet us were the two GSG9 officers we had previously met in London. They immediately took us directly to GSG9 HQ. Here we had a very short discussion with the GSG9 second-in-command (the commander, Ulrich Wegener, was already in Dubai) and it was decided to demonstrate the British stun grenades to the Germans. The most convenient space, which was similar in size and shape to the interior of a plane, was a long corridor in the cellars of the HQ building. About a dozen GSG9 soldiers took up positions in various recessed doorways. With the lights out, I tossed in a stun grenade. The language was pretty blue as some very shocked GSG9 soldiers emerged from the cellar corridor. Nevertheless, it proved how effective they were. The second-in-command then made an instant decision to send Alastair and me on to Dubai by the fastest means. Unfortunately, this meant getting the 12.12 p.m. plane out of Frankfurt for Dubai, but changing aircraft in Kuwait. All went smoothly until we arrived in Kuwait. As you can imagine, the entire Middle East was alarmed by the hijack in Dubai. For this reason, Kuwait airport was on full military alert and even passengers in transit had their luggage re-checked before being allowed back aboard the plane for Dubai.

Although Alastair and I hung further and further back in the queue, it was inevitable that we had to put our bag containing the boxes of stun grenades through the X-ray machine. I can still envisage the screen clearly showing those grenades and I still recall, very vividly, the commotion it caused. We were at once slapped under heavy guard and manhandled quite ruthlessly by Kuwaiti soldiers into the main Security Officer's room, followed by our hand luggage.

The bag was opened for examination, a procedure that I had to terminate when one of the Arabs tried to remove the pin from a grenade. At this stage, realisation dawned on everybody in the room that we were taking the grenades from Germany to Dubai. Luckily for us, at this moment the General Manager for Lufthansa in Kuwait came into the security room. In a few moments, he left the Security Officer in no doubt that, unless we were released immediately, together with our grenades, to rejoin our original flight to Dubai, no other Lufthansa aircraft would ever again fly into Kuwait Airport. It worked and we were hassled across the tarmac to the waiting plane before physically being pushed into our seats. Then the bag with the stun grenades was dropped into my lap for me to nurse.

We arrived in Dubai at around 3.00 a.m. on Sunday, only to be arrested at the airport for lack of documentation. Our passports were taken from us. This allowed one of the Western news reporters, covering the hijack, to pick up our names. Later, he realised our true identities, and that we were SAS. Alastair made numerous attempts during the early hours of the morning to contact the British Embassy, but got no further than the gate man who was manning the night phone. Then, luck came our way in the form of an ex-SAS officer called David Bullig. He had left the SAS and had been seconded to work training the Dubai Palace Guard. We both shouted and the moment he recognised us, events took a completely different turn. Within minutes we were able to roam freely about the airport to assess the situation. David was extremely helpful in many other ways, not least that he had already primed some of the best soldiers from the Palace Guard to be ready to attempt an immediate action assault on the aircraft should the terrorists actually start killing the hostages.

We toured the airport and then spoke to the German Minister, Wischnewski, who was acting representative for the West German Government. We also met and talked with the Defence Minister of Dubai, who had taken charge of the situation directly (this was the second hijack he had dealt with). Having fully assessed the situation, we went with David Bullig to talk to Colonel Ulrich Wegener, head of GSG9 anti-terrorist unit, who was resting with several other Germans in the airport hotel. We all agreed that there was very little we could do until the morning. We would be better off refreshing ourselves with a little sleep and meeting later in the morning.

David Bullig took Alastair and I to his home, where his charming wife plied us with sandwiches and coffee while we laid out our plan of action. David scribbled notes, listing our demands for kit and equipment. Our most expensive request was for the use of a 737 for training and practice purposes. About 5.00 a.m. both Alastair and I fell asleep. After a couple of hours dozing, we were awakened by Mrs Bullig with the news that David had managed to fulfil most of our demands. All three of us left for the airport to meet with the GSG9 and three other officers David had found from various units in Dubai. In addition, he had selected eight of the best men from the Dubai Palace Guard.

We set about a very quick immediate action drill to meet the needs of the worst possible scenario. That's when we would have no choice but to assault the plane with the limited force available. Of course, the more time we had available, the more our plan would improve. By now, most of the kit and equipment we needed had arrived – shotguns, masking tape, walkie-talkies, various ladders, padding and a myriad of other items. We had two quartermasters standing by with four jeeps and an apparently endless supply of cash to obtain anything else required. Most importantly, a Gulf Air 737 had been given on loan and was parked at the far end of the airfield, out of sight of the hijacked plane. I was about to start a crash course in anti-terrorist techniques.

On the personnel side, my resources were limited to a hard core of five men who had received at least some professional CBQ (Close Quarter Battle) training or anti-terrorist training. These included Alastair, David, myself and the two GSG9 officers. Additionally, I had three other officers and the eight soldiers from the Palace Guard. I concentrated our first efforts on the immediate action drill needed to counter any terrorist deadline.

The Boeing 737 is a simple little animal where anti-terrorist drills are concerned. There are only three options for entry – tail, wing and front catering area. We thought that if the terrorists began to carry out any threatened shootings, they would naturally take the precaution of covering the main doors. It seemed less likely that they would cover the two emergency exit doors leading on to the wings, so the plan that basically fell into shape was to attack through these. The fact that the wing emergency exits were designed to be opened easily from the outside was another strong factor in favour of adopting this mode of attack – and there were others. We had also discovered a blind spot were the wing joins the aircraft body. Two men could sit beneath the emergency doors and not be visible from any of the windows.

By comparison, the entry and exit points at front and rear require considerable manhandling and some time to get them open. For instance, the front door is operable through a small hatch on the outside of the plane that allows the door to be opened and brought down with the stairs extending automatically.

The basic moves involved in our plan were to make a single file approach to the aircraft from its blind spot at the rear, assemble our ladders quietly and erect them at the wings and the rear door. The two leading assault teams would covertly climb onto the wings, one outside the port emergency exit, the other outside the starboard, with the second assault pairs waiting on the top rungs of the ladders. Each of these assault teams consisted of an SAS man or a GSG9 man backed up by one of the best of the soldiers from the Palace Guard. Back-up squads would be positioned beneath the rear area of the plane ready to scale their ladder, open the rear door and effect their entry as quickly as possible. At the same time, a second back-up squad would move quietly forward until they were beneath the front door area, ready to erect their ladders and follow suit. The back-ups would co-ordinate their moves with those of the assault teams.

Once everyone was in position, and the 'Go' was given, the leading assault teams were to stand, punch the emergency exit panels and drop the doors into the laps of the passengers in the mid-section of the cabin. The teams would then enter, the port side pair clearing to the front of the cabin, the starboard team clearing to the rear. The leading teams were to receive immediate back-up from the second assault pairs entering behind them from their stations at the tops of the ladders to maintain control of the centre of the aircraft. Simultaneous with the assault, the outside squads were to open both front and rear doors and enter the plane. The intention here was to provide further back-up in case of any problems and also provide routes for the hostages to leave the plane, which by this time would be full of smoke from the stun grenades. Once entry had been effected to the centre of the aircraft, the starboard assault team would have a clear line of sight to the toilet doors at the rear of the cabin. The port team, moving forward through the economy area, would arrive in the first-class section which leads into the front catering area. Directly beyond this is the flight deck, the door to which is usually closed.

The only obstacles the team would encounter were the flight deck door and the curtains that separate economy and first class. Although this basic plan is quite uncomplicated, we calculated that it would require a great deal of practice to get the timing right, particularly the time it would take the assault teams to effect their entry and make their way to the front and rear of the passenger cabin. We reckoned that as soon as we dominated these points, the only people in serious danger would be the crew in the cockpit.

By 8.00 a.m. on 16 October, 67 hours after LH181 had left Palma, the training and practice began. We took a break around 2.00 p.m., using the time to iron out every detail, searching for anything that might increase the odds in our favour. We now felt fairly confident that if the terrorists forced us into immediate action, we had better than a 50-50 chance of success. We were now sure that we could approach the aircraft and establish all our people in their starting positions unobserved. Next we would put eight men – the four assault pairs – inside the plane, and we had worked out a way to momentarily distract the terrorists. We considered how best we could locate their positions inside the aircraft – extremely valuable information if we could get it. We also gave considerable thought to the possibility of an attack at night during which, if it came off, we would have an extra man underneath the plane to shut down the APU, or Auxiliary Power Unit. This is located inside the rear of the wheel housing, and one yank on the red and yellow handle would kill all the lights and power in the plane at the moment which suited us.

At about 3.30 p.m. the Dubai Defence Minister left his careful watch in the control tower and came to check on our progress. We went through our operation on the Gulf Air 737, and I have to admit that it looked pretty impressive. Then just as we finished our demonstration, the unexpected happened. LH181 came to life and took off, taking with her any hope that the hijack would end in Dubai. Fortunately the Germans had a Boeing 707, being used by the negotiators. Everybody from Germany concerned with the hijack, as well as Alastair and I, went aboard and we took off to follow the hijacked plane. First indications were that it was going to land at Salala, Southern Oman. This sounded like good news, for the SAS had men stationed in the area with anti-hijack skills. Our expectations were dashed, however, when we learned that LH181 had, in fact, landed at Khormaksa Airport in Aden. Captain Schumann, piloting LH181, had been too low on fuel to fly anywhere else, and he skilfully put the aircraft down on the hard sand alongside the runway. Our 707 had to fly on to the International airport in Saudi Arabia. Here, confined in the aircraft, we sat on the ground awaiting further developments. During this waiting period, the negotiating psychologists attempted to persuade the hijackers to release the hostages in exchange for the fifteen million dollars that we held in a large suitcase in our plane. Then came the shocking news that brought an immediate end to negotiation.

Captain Schumann had been shot dead aboard LH181. Now the decision more or less made itself. Wherever LH181 was, wherever she was forced to fly, we would make our rescue attempt. For the first time I saw the true determination of our German partners. The killing of Captain Schumann decided the matter. Any further ideas about peaceful negotiation were dismissed.

Our next news was that LH181 had again taken off from Aden with the dead pilot aboard, and had flown to Mogadishu, capital of the Somali Republic. We got airborne in the 707 and sought permission to land there also. On our approach to Mogadishu we were given permission to land, but the situation was complicated by the presence of LH181 sitting in the middle of the main runway. Our pilot was equal to the challenge, however. Using only a short length of runway, he brought off a superb landing, using every yard of concrete available and rolling to within feet of buildings and houses on the airfield perimeter. Even the intensity of the overall situation didn't dim this brilliant feat of professional skill, and everyone aboard broke into spontaneous applause.

On the ground, two top Somali officials collected all passports and were surprised to discover two of the British variety among them. They were most courteous and friendly. The German Minister went off to meet the Somali Prime Minister to discuss the developing political aspects of the hijack. The rest of us were taken to one of Mogadishu's top hotels and given accommodation and a meal. We were kept in constant contact regarding the hijack situation through the Mogadishu security services who were very friendly and helpful.

The terrorists now announced that their deadline was 3.00 p.m. on that same day, Monday 17 October. Negotiators from Mogadishu tower asked for an extension, explaining that the Baader-Meinhof terrorists jailed in Germany, together with the two Palestinians held in Turkey, would be released. They could not, however, be flown to Mogadishu in less than ten hours. After prolonged discussion, the terrorist leader, Captain Mahmud Martyr agreed on a final deadline of 3.00 a.m. the next morning.

In the meantime, Minister Wischnewski obtained permission to bring in the German anti-terrorist team, flying to Mogadishu to provide the option of an assault on LH181. While awaiting their arrival, we all worked together to modify the assault plan to match it with the current situation. Joining us in our planning was a Colonel from the Somalia Special Forces.

We stuck to the basic plan to approach the plane in a single column from the rear, breaking into four sub-sections, each moving to its assigned position to make simultaneous entry through both wing emergency exits and the port front and starboard rear doors. We modified the choice of ladders for the assault on the doors, using double (i.e. side-by-side) ladders instead of single. The advantage of these was that two men could go up together. At the top, the left-hand man could turn the door handle and swing his full weight away from the fuselage, so pulling the door open quickly. This made it possible for the second, right-hand man to penetrate the plane immediately.

We asked for outside help in two regards. First, before the assault began, we wanted the negotiators to start talking positively to the terrorists to ascertain as closely as possible their whereabouts inside LH181. We also thought we might distract them, encourage them to come to the cockpit by lighting a very large fire at the far end of the runway. This job was entrusted to the Somali soldiers, who were also responsible for ground defence around the aircraft.

The GSG9 arrived in a second Boeing 707 at five minutes past eight on the evening of 17 October. Immediately, their commander briefed them, and they set about preparing their equipment for the assault. We ran through a quick rehearsal, using the GSG9 707 that was parked out of sight of LH181. By 11.30 p.m. the whole group was in position about seventy metres to the rear of the plane. In file, we approached the plane, and in complete silence the ladders were put in position at each wing root and against the chosen doors. Major Morrison and I were on either side of the fuselage, at the rear of the wing roots. Our initial task was to throw stun grenades over the fuselage just as the doors were opened, to achieve the penetrating effect of noise and light in the cabin. I was also to throw a stun grenade over the front of the cockpit to assist further in the disorientation of the terrorist leader, Captain Mahmud Martyr.

The approach to the aircraft was very slick and smooth. The only problem we had was that the airfield lighting around the control tower created long shadows. Had the window blinds been up, any one of the terrorists looking out could have seen them. But this was not the case. The GSG9 commander was in direct contact with the tower. Just before the operation began he transmitted to all his assault teams that the two male terrorists had been heard in the cockpit. At this moment, the fire was ignited at the end of the runway. In spite of the tension, this caused some amusement, for it was plain that the Somali soldiers had let their enthusiasm run away with them. It looked as if they had set fire to a complete tanker-load of petrol.

The GSG9 commander counted down and gave the 'Go' signal. Everything happened at once. The quiet African night erupted. The front and rear doors opened as the left-hand ladder-men swung on them; their right-hand partners heaved themselves out of sight into the plane. The wing assault teams stood up, punched the emergency exit panels and vaulted in as the doors fell into the cabin – all these actions orchestrated by the bangs and flashes from the stun grenades. Immediately the rear starboard door swung open the first terrorist was sighted, absolutely amazed by this turn of events. She was shot instantly by a GSG9 soldier, who then threw himself flat into the rear catering area alongside the toilets, firing up the aisle where the other female terrorist had been spotted. The front assault team were involved in a brief firefight with the two male terrorists. Lasting for about a minute, it ended when they had both been fatally shot. During the firefight we heard two dull explosions inside LH181. These were hand grenades exploding as the terrorists' strength drained away and their grip on the grenades relaxed involuntarily. So, as the first few minutes of Tuesday 18 October ticked away, thus ended the hijacking of Flight LH181.

As soon as the firing died away, the passengers began to disembark. And now occurred one of those unforeseen circumstances which could have led to quite serious injury among the passengers, who seemed convinced that every plane is equipped with those inflatable rubber chutes into which they could jump and slide happily down to the ground. In this case they didn't exist, but several of the passengers, young and old alike, tried to slide down the assault ladders. To say that this caused us some concern would be an understatement. The thought of the passengers injuring themselves this late in the game was too much to take. The GSG9 men on the ground took swift and firm command of the exits, guiding people down the assault ladders or assisting them through the mid-section emergency exits down to the ground via the wings.

The passengers were in a state of sheer bewilderment. They had, after all, spent five long days cooped up in a very confined space, in hot, filthy conditions and with failing sanitary facilities. On top of all this physical discomfort, every hour would have been heavily weighted by the fear feeding on the uncertainty of their future. The climactic few minutes of the assault, involving loud explosions, flashes, smoke, rapid movement, gunfire and raw danger must have disoriented many of them. As they disembarked they were ushered to the rear, where a fleet of ambulances and other vehicles ferried them to the passenger lounge in the terminal building.

The casualty list showed three of the terrorists dead – two men and one woman – and the second woman terrorist severely wounded. Incidentally, as she was taken away for medical treatment she gave the V-sign and screamed an assortment of slogans. One member of GSG9, one member of the aircrew and five of the passengers were slightly wounded. After any necessary medical attention, the passengers were soon taken aboard the negotiators' 707, while the negotiators, the GSG9 men and we two SAS boarded the GSG9 707, all to be flown back to Germany.

Although apparently over, the hijack of LH181 still had a twist in its tail, still posed questions, this time questions to which no answers have been found. During the flight we heard on the radio that the leading members of the Baader-Meinhof terrorist gang, confined in separate cells in Stammheim Jail in Stuttgart, had committed suicide. Andreas Baader and Jan-Carl Raspe had shot themselves; Gudrun Ensslin hanged herself, while Irmgard Möller had made an unsuccessful attempt to kill herself using a stolen bread knife. How did the terrorists, locked in separate cells in a maximum security prison, simultaneously learn of the German Government's success in Mogadishu, 3,500 miles away – and this within a very few hours of its occurrence? How did the two male terrorists obtain pistols and ammunition in that same jail? These mysteries remain unexplained to this day.

Upon arrival at Frankfurt we SAS men were separated from the GSG9 people and taken to the VIP lounge. Here we were instructed to retain our scruffy appearance until and during our flight to the UK. Arriving in London at around 9.00 p.m. we were moved off to a secret rendezvous for full debriefing regarding the operation. So came the final end to the hijacking of LH181, together with the SAS/GSG9 operation to rescue hostages and crew. The success of our joint operation was only marred, for me, by the death of Captain Jurgen Schumann, shot in Aden. He was a very brave man and, like so many other aircraft captains, upheld his professional responsibilities to the end in seeking to protect all those in his care, passengers and crew alike. The success was soon worldwide news, and governments all over the free world applauded Germany's determination in the face of an international terrorist threat. As a postscript to this account, it may be worth mentioning the kidnapping of a Dr Hans-Martin Schleyer, which took place just before the hijack. There were suspicions that the two events were linked in some way. Within a few days of the rescue, the body of Dr Schleyer, who had been kidnapped a month prior to the hijack, was found in the boot of a car – he had three bullets in his head.

Beirut – 22 January 1979

Not all counter-terrorist operations work out, and in the process innocent people die. This next story is just one example of how poor intelligence and hearsay can lead to the death of someone who just happens to be in the wrong place at the wrong time.

When the Israeli Prime Minister, Golda Meir, decided to seek revenge for the Olympic games massacre in Munich, her advisors, both military and civil, advocated clinical vengeance, although personally she had misgivings. Nevertheless, the deaths in Germany had pushed her to the edge and the voices of her nation rang out for revenge. Mossad hit teams were sanctioned.

First the Israelis compiled a list of Arabs who had been involved in the Munich operation. The assassination teams then began to trail the men on their 'wanted' list, most of whom had remained in Europe engaged in various terrorist activities. The Mossad wanted them silenced forever. Yet what they were doing was not inside Israel, so caution was needed, months of intensive training and painstaking attention to detail. Assassination is not a weapon governments like to use. There can be embarrassing mistakes. If anyone was caught, he was on his own.

On 16 October they took out their first victim in Rome. Abel Wael Zwieter was a noted academic of some stature, seemingly opposed to terrorism; but in reality he was one of Black September's very able architects. Using two innocent English girls, he had planted a bomb on an El Al flight. It was designed to explode after the aircraft had taken off. It misfired, but Israeli retaliation did not. Following him home one night, the hit team struck just as he was about to use the lift; ten bullets from a .22 Beretta colandered his body.

December saw the hit team in France. Here was another academic living in Paris, Dr Mahmud Hamshari. Known as an historian, he lectured and wrote. Mossad believed him to be Black September's number two in France, and planned his death. Careful observation established Hamshari's wife and child left around eight each day. Using this information, the Mossad agents lured Hamshari to a nearby café, pretending to be Italian reporters interested in an interview. At the same time, a bomb was placed in his flat; next morning when his wife and child left the house the bomb was detonated.

Number three also died by a bomb. Abd el Hir, was Black September's man in Cyprus, using his close connections with the USSR to support the Palestinian cause by organising weapons and training. The bomb that killed him was detonated one night as he went to bed before switching off the light.

By this time, Ali Hassan and some of the others were beginning to get the picture, giving their response by killing a Mossad agent in Madrid. The man known as The Red Prince was far from finished. At a reception in Khartoum, Black September struck, seizing the building and holding many foreign dignitaries hostage. When the West failed to negotiate, three diplomats – two Americans and one Belgian – were murdered on the express instruction of Ali Hassan. But the incident did not end well, as all seven of the Black September surrendered to the police. Losing all semblance of sanity at this weakness, The Red Prince went on a killing spree – actions that lost him all sympathy from the outside world, encouraging the Israeli hit teams to continue their work.

In the middle of March 1973, a full-scale raid against Black September and other Palestinians living in Beirut was sanctioned. Dressed as tourists, a small, six-man advance team entered the city and hired cars to carry out precise reconnaissance on their targets. Around midnight on 9 April, the hire cars were parked on the beach ready to receive a trained commando team together with several explosive experts. By 1.30 a.m. they were at their target areas. One group took a seven-storey block of flats in Verdun Street; while a larger force went off to the PDF HQ in Khartoum Street. The block of flats was quiet, with most of its inhabitants already in bed asleep. Kamal Nasser, was the first to die. Unable to sleep, he was writing a letter when he was cut down. On the second floor, Kamal Adwan died in front of his wife and children, while on the sixth floor Abu Yussef was shot locked in the arms of his wife. One little old lady woken by the noise stepped from her flat – an Israeli killed her on the spot. Before leaving, they searched the victims' quarters and valuable files giving names and locations were discovered, an added bonus for the hit team.

Meanwhile, at Khartoum Street on the other side of Beirut, two Israelis approached the guards in a friendly manner – then they shot them. A third guard saw the shooting and returned fire, killing the two Israelis, and a pitched battle broke out. The Israelis held their ground as the demolition charges were put in place. A mushroom cloud followed the ear-shattering blast, lighting the night sky over Beirut. Slowly the whole building crumbled. Without stopping to admire their handiwork, the hit teams raced for the beach; dumped the hire cars and made off by boat and helicopters that had come in to collect the wounded. Despite the success of their mission, one man, Ali Hassan, was once more in a different place at the right time.

For some reason, the West seemed to glorify these murders, arguing, like the Israelis, that they had a right to retaliate. But how did they know they were hitting the right targets? This point was to become painfully obvious when Israel shot down an unarmed aircraft. The Libyan airliner had been blown off course by a sandstorm en route to Cairo. The deviation in flight path took it over Israeli airspace. The Israelis knew full well that it was a commercial passenger aircraft, but were paranoid that it was a flying bomb destined for Israel; two fighter aircraft were dispatched to blow it from the skies – 104 innocent Libyans were scattered across the desert.

Next on the hit list was a man called Abu Zaiad, a member of Black September who had been sent to Athens and told to await instructions from Beirut. For several days he remained in his hotel room at the 'Aristedes' worried that he had had no communication. The answer came as he listened to a radio news bulletin of the Beirut raid; for the first time he left his hotel in search of a newspaper. During his short absence the hit team placed a bomb in his room, yes, under the bed. He died when it exploded in the night.

The hit team then went back to Paris, this time in search of an Algerian called Boudia. The Israelis believed that he had masterminded the oil refinery bombings at Trieste and Rotterdam, attacks claimed by the PFLP. But he proved difficult to find. Their only lead was information that he was one for the women. So, with the help of a young Algerian female professor, who sang of Boudia's sexual prowess, they found him. While he was busy with a new conquest, the hit team kindly filled up his petrol tank. The car was destroyed with him in it.

Success after success followed the hit team but still the man they really wanted, Ali Hassan, was nowhere to be found. Every time they got wind of his whereabouts he would simply disappear. Then, in July 1973, a report was received that Ali Hassan was in Germany. All efforts were made to locate him. It paid off. A Palestinian by the name of Kamal Benamane, a minor member of Black September, was spotted and followed to Norway. While the tracking team located Benamane in an Oslo hotel, a hit team was assembled in Israel. When Benamane checked out of his hotel, he headed north to Lillehammer; the whole Israeli team, fifteen in all, in hot pursuit. When they arrived in Lillehammer, a small town of little more than 20,000 inhabitants, the Israelis split themselves between three hotels before covering the town in the hope of locating Benamane. They found him, and he was talking to another Arab. A rapid discussion over the identity of the new Arab then took place and, despite the fact that the guy had no moustache and the photograph was somewhat old, they where convinced that they had located Ali Hassan. In fact, they had the wrong man, resulting in the state-authorised murder of a Moroccan waiter (see Chapter 1).

Meanwhile, the real Ali Hassan was under heavy security in Beirut. He had just married a beautiful woman, 'Miss World'. On the afternoon of 22 January 1979, Ali Hassan left his wife, now six months pregnant and set off in his distinctive 'Chevvy'. Sitting in the back, he was squashed between two bodyguards. Several more heavies accompanied him in a white Land Rover. The Chevvy moved slowly down Verdun Street and into Madame Curie Street. Someone had badly parked a white Volkswagen, making the street much narrower. As the Chevvy negotiated its way past, the Volkswagen, which had been packed with explosives, detonated. Finally, the Mossad had got their man. Ali Hassan's body was blown to bits together with those of his bodyguards. Unfortunately, several other innocent tourists died in the explosion, including an English nurse. Yasser Arafat helped carry Hassan's coffin.

Iran – 4 November 1979

Raised in 1977, Delta Force was late entering the world of counter-terrorism, but America had lots of friends willing to give advice or lend expertise in training and the unit got off to a really promising start. Good men, coupled with excellent training and equipment, brought Delta Force up to the standard of the top echelon of the world's counter-terrorist units. Two years later, they were called upon to carry out their first real rescue attempt. Their target, the American Embassy in Tehran, was not only 'out-country' it was also hostile territory.

The problem started when a revolutionary coup in Iran toppled the Shah from power. The country declined and the once-proud army was replaced with a rabble known as the Iranian Revolutionary Guards. On 4 November 1979, the militants took over the American Embassy in Tehran and held over a hundred Americans hostage. From the earliest days of the crisis, one of the options under constant review and development was a military rescue. One of the main problems was the remoteness of Tehran from any available US bases. The plan finally narrowed down to an Entebbe-style raid by Delta.

The name of the operation was 'Eagle Claw'. The basic outline plan was to insert Delta into Iran covertly, using an old airbase at Masirah Island in Oman, and from the aircraft carrier Nimitz, which was sailing somewhere in the Gulf of Oman. The first part of the plan was to establish a firm base about two hundred miles south of Tehran, called Desert One. Delta would fly from Masirah to Desert One by C130 transport aircraft. Three would carry fuel and three would carry Delta plus a section of Rangers who would supply protection. Shortly after they had landed at Desert One, eight RH 53D helicopters would take off from the aircraft carrier to join them.

Once the helicopters had arrived at Desert One, they would refuel and carry Delta force to a hide area just outside Tehran, while the C130s would return to Masirah. Delta Force was then to hide for the day just outside the city, ready to attack at night. Special agents of DOD (Department of Defence) had been inserted to assist with vehicles and transport to move Delta to the city. The helicopters, once they had dropped off Delta, would fly south and hide in the mountains until required for pick-up. That night, with the assistance of the DOD agents, Delta Force would covertly assault the embassy and rescue the hostages. They would then use the helicopters to extract them.

Any resistance by the Iranian Revolutionary Guard was to be suppressed and, to stop any supporting Iranian troops coming to the embassy, helicopter gunships were on stand-by. As the operation was going on around the embassy, a force of US Rangers would fly in and secure an airfield called Manzariyeh thirty miles south of Tehran, from where everyone would be lifted out by a giant C141 Starlifter aircraft. This plan involved and relied on many aircraft and, as a precaution, special SAR (Search and Rescue) teams were put on stand-by should one of them go down.

The daring plan had presidential approval, and started late on the evening of 24 April.

Author's Note: I would add that, before the mission got under way, Ulrich Wegener, commander of GSG9, sent a message to Charlie Beckwith stating that the Germans wanted to insert a television camera crew into Iran to cover the American hostage situation. Was there any way Charlie could help? I think Charlie would have jumped at it but his superiors would never have allowed it. This was to be purely an American operation.

Problems started a few minutes after the C130s carrying Delta touched down at Desert One. A Mercedes bus came along and was stopped by the rescue force. It was found to have about thirty passengers on board. As they were being held hostage a petrol tanker also came along from the other direction. For some reason, one of the Rangers providing security fired a LAW anti-tank rocket at the tanker. The tanker burst into flames.

At the same time, the driver of a smaller truck coming up behind the tanker saw the fire and the soldiers. Before the Americans could do anything, the driver of the tanker leaped from the burning vehicle and jumped into the smaller truck, which made off at speed. Despite the potential hazard of having been compromised, Charlie Beckwith continued with the plan, and a little later, all six C130s arrived. After dropping off their troops, three of them returned to Sharjah. All they had to do now was detain any Iranian civilians until the helicopters arrived in about thirty minutes time. During this wait, kit and equipment were camouflaged and a SATCOM radio link was set up.

Then the real problems started. The choppers were late, and daylight was coming fast. Finally, only six of the choppers arrived. They were an hour and a half late. It would seem that they had hit a bad sandstorm. Then, as the troops started to load, one of the choppers developed problems and became unserviceable. Charlie needed all six and almost begged the pilot to fly but it was no good, the mission was called off.

As Delta was about to get back into the remaining three C130s one of the choppers that had just taken off crashed into one of the C130s. Instantly, the whole area was lit by a fireball, ammunition and rockets carried by the aircraft ignited like some giant fireworks display. Five USAF aircrew in the C130 and three Marines in the RH-53 died.

That was it. Charlie put all his men and the chopper pilots on the remaining C130s and flew back to Masirah. A jet strike was called in to destroy the choppers that were left behind. After all the years of training, for such a disaster to happen was beyond belief. It should be pointed out that this was not the fault of Delta, but many looked in that direction. A few days after Delta had returned to the US, President Carter paid them a visit. He had nothing but praise for the unit.

London – 30 April 1980

At 11.25 a.m. on the morning of Wednesday 30 April 1980, six armed gunmen took over No. 16 Princess Gate, the Iranian Embassy in London's Kensington district. It was understood that the terrorists were opposed to the regime of Ayatollah Khomeini and were seeking the liberation of Khuzestan from Iran. As they took control of the embassy, they captured 26 hostages including the British policeman who had been on duty at the entrance. The terrorists' entire takeover of the embassy was something that might have gone almost completely unnoticed but for the fact that a few minutes later a burst of machine-gun fire was heard. The police were on the scene immediately. Their swiftness was in part due to the captured policeman, Trevor Lock, who had managed to alert his headquarters before being taken by the terrorists. Armed police marksmen soon surrounded the building and siege negotiation plans were put into operation.

By 11.47 a.m., Dusty Grey, an ex-D Squadron SAS man who now worked with the Metropolitan Police, was talking to the Commanding Officer of the SAS in Hereford. His information gave the briefest details, but it was enough to alert the regiment. Several minutes later, the duty signaller activated the 'call-in' bleepers carried by every member of the anti-terrorist team. Although the SAS had prior warning, it could make no move before its deployment was officially sanctioned by the Home Secretary who, at the request of the police, would contact the MoD. Despite this red tape, it makes sense for the SAS to think ahead and positioning the anti-terrorist team closer to the scene can save time. Around midnight on the first day, most of the team had made their way to Regents Park Barracks, which had been selected as a holding area. From here various pieces of information could be assembled and assessed. A scale model of No. 16 Princess Gate was ordered to be constructed. This task fell to two pioneers, drafted in from the nearby Guards unit. Additionally, an intelligence cell was set up to gather and collate every snippet of information that would aid an assault.

By this time, the terrorist leader, Oan, had secured his 26 hostages and issued his demands. These included the autonomy and recognition of the Arabistan people, and the release of 91 Arabistani prisoners. The line taken by the terrorists was tough but, despite several threats to blow up the embassy and kill the hostages, by Thursday 1 May, they released a sick woman. Later that same day, Oan managed to get a telephone call through to Sadegh Ghotzbadeh, Iran's Foreign Minister. The conversation did not go well. Oan was accused of being an American agent and was informed that the Iranian hostages held in the embassy would consider it an honour to die for their country and the Iranian revolutionary movement.

Around this time, Chris Cramer, a BBC sound man, had became sick with acute stomach pains. His partner, BBC sound recordist Sim Harris, pleaded with Oan to call for a doctor immediately. This was done but the police refused to comply and, in the end, Cramer was released, whereupon he stumbled out of the embassy door and into a waiting ambulance.

Later that night, again under the cover of darkness, three Avis rental vans pulled up in a small side street by Princess Gate. Men carrying holdalls quickly made their way into No. 14, just two doors down from the embassy. Within minutes they had laid out their equipment and made ready for an immediate action. If the terrorists started shooting, they would run to the front door of No. 16 and beat their way in. It wasn't a very sophisticated plan, but it would have to do until a more clearly defined scheme could be organised.

By 6.00 a.m. on the morning of Saturday 2 May, the situation inside No. 16 was getting very agitated. Oan rang the phone that had been set up between the embassy and No. 25 Princess Gate – The Royal School of Needlework – which now housed Alpha Control (the main forward control point) and the police negotiator. Oan's main criticism was that there had been no media broadcasts about the siege, so how could his cause be heard? By late afternoon on the same day, Oan was allowed to make a statement that was to be broadcast on the next news slot. In return for this, two more hostages were released, one of whom was a pregnant woman. The trouble was, Oan would not release the hostages before the statement was read out. Likewise, the police wanted the hostages first. In the end a compromise was reached and the broadcast went out on the evening *Nine O'clock News*.

Two hours later, eight members of the SAS team climbed onto the rear roof of No. 14 and made their way amid a jungle of television antennae, to No. 16. Two of the men went directly to a glass skylight and, after some effort, managed to get it open. They found that it opened directly into a small bathroom on the top floor of the Iranian Embassy, and would provide an excellent entry point. Meanwhile, other members secured ropes to several chimneys and made ready for a quick descent to the lower floors where they could smash in through the windows.

By 9.00 a.m. on Sunday morning, things seemed to be heading for a peaceful settlement. Oan had agreed to reduce his demands and, at the same time, Arab ambassadors had attended a Cobra Committee (Cabinet Office Briefing Room) meeting in Whitehall. This committee was chaired by the Home Secretary, William Whitelaw, who was, to all intents and purposes, in charge of the whole operation. He was aware that the SAS anti-terrorist team now had access to the embassy and that efforts were being made to penetrate the wall. To avoid the sound of the drilling being heard, various sound distractions were supplied by the Gas Board working in the vicinity. COBRA was also aware that a basic plan had been formulated. This plan involved attacking all floors simultaneously, with clearly defined areas of demarcation to avoid overshoot. Mock-ups of the floor layouts were constructed from timber and hessian sheeting and assembled at Regents Park Barracks so that the SAS could practice the raid.

The police, who had adopted a softly-softly negotiating approach, managed to keep control of the siege for several days, time that was desperately needed for the SAS to carry out covert recces, study plans, build models and, more importantly, locate the hostages and terrorists within the embassy building. A major break was talking to the hostage Chris Cramer, the BBC sound engineer. Letting him go was a big mistake by the terrorists; in his debrief to the SAS he was able to give them precise and detailed information about the situation inside the embassy.

By the sixth day of the siege, 5 May, the terrorists were becoming frustrated and the situation inside the embassy began to deteriorate. All morning, threats were made about executing hostages and at 1.31 p.m. three shots were heard. At 6.50 p.m. more shots were heard and the body of the embassy press officer was thrown out. Immediately, the police appeared to capitulate, stalling for time, while SAS plans to storm the embassy were advanced. At this stage, the police negotiator worked hard to convince the terrorist leader not to shoot any further hostages and that a bus would be with them shortly to take them to the airport. From there they could fly to the Middle East. During this telephone conversation, the SAS took up their start positions.

A handwritten note transferring control of the situation from the police to the SAS was handed over. Shortly after, while a negotiator from Alpha control talked to Oan, the SAS moved in.

Author's Note: Oan heard the first crashes and complained that the embassy was being attacked. This conversation was recorded, and on tape one can clearly hear the stun grenades going off. Oan's conversation is cut short by a long burst of machine-gun fire.

For the assault team, the waiting was over and the words guaranteed to send their adrenaline pumping, where given. 'Go. Go. Go.' At 7.23 p.m., eight men abseiled down to the first floor balcony, on ropes secured from the embassy roof. The assault came from three directions, with the main assault from the rear. Frame charges were quickly fitted to the windows and blown. Stun grenades were thrown in advance of the assaulting men and the SAS went into action. Systematically, the building was cleared from the top down, room by room. The telex room on the second floor, which housed the male hostages and three of the terrorists, was of utmost priority. Realising that an assault was in progress, the terrorists shot and killed one hostage and wounded two others before the lead SAS team broke into the room. Immediately they shot two gunmen that were visible, the third hid among the hostages and was not discovered until later. As rooms were cleared, hostages were literally thrown from one SAS soldier to another, down the stairs and out into the back garden. At this stage they were all laid face down on the ground while a search was conducted for the missing terrorist.

Breaking the siege took just seventeen minutes. The SAS took no casualties, other than one man who got caught up in his rope harness and was badly burned. Once the embassy had been cleared, and all the terrorists and hostages had been identified the problem was handed back to the police. Meanwhile, the SAS vacated No. 14 and went back to Regents Park Barracks in time to watch themselves on television. Still dressed in assault gear, and clutching cans of Fosters lager, (someone was on the ball) they crowded around, eager to see themselves in action. Halfway through, Prime Minister Margaret Thatcher, who had left a dinner date, arrived to personally thank the SAS. She circulated, as one man put it, 'Like a triumphant Caesar returning to the Senate', her face glowing with pride and admiration at her Imperial Guard. Then, as the news started to show the full event, she sat down on the floor amid her warriors and watched with them.

In total there were 26 hostages taken in the embassy when the siege started. Of these, five were released before the SAS assault. Two died, but the remaining nineteen survived. Of the six terrorists, only one survived.

Loughall – 8 May 1987

Another classic SAS operation took place in Loughall, Northern Ireland on Friday 8 May 1987. Intelligence had been received indicating that the police station at Loughall was to be attacked by the method used a year before in County Armagh. There, a mechanical digger packed with explosives had been driven into the RUC station at the Birches. It had caused widespread damage.

A report that another JCB had been stolen in East Tyrone gave rise to the suspicion that an identical IRA operation was being planned. All efforts were made to locate the digger and identify the target. After intensive covert searches, the weapons and explosives were located. Subsequently, the digger was also located in a derelict building some fifteen kilometres away. Surveillance provided more information and eventually the target was assessed as being the RUC station at Loughall. This station was only manned part time and consisted of one main building running parallel to the main road and surrounded by a high wire fence. The time and date of the attack was eventually confirmed through a telephone tap.

Two of the IRA activists were named as Patrick Kelly and Jim Lynagh, who commanded the East Tyrone active service unit. When masked men stole a Toyota van from Dungannon, Jim Lynagh was spotted in the town, leading to the possibility that the van was to be used in the Loughall attack. Not long after, the OP reported that the JCB was being moved from the derelict farm. At this stage the SAS, who had been reinforced from Hereford, took up their ambush positions. It was reported that some were in the police station itself, but this was not true. Instead, most of the main ambush party was hiding in a row of small fir trees that lines the fence on the opposite side of the road to the station. Several heavily armed stops were also in position covering all avenues of escape.

At a little past 7.00 p.m., the blue Toyota van drove down the road in front of the police station. Several people were seen to be inside. It shortly returned from the Portadown side, this time followed by the JCB, together with three hooded IRA terrorists. Declan Arthurs was driving, with Michael Gormley and Gerald O'Callaghan riding shotgun. The bucket was filled with explosives contained in an oil drum. This had been partly concealed with rubble. While the blue van charged past the station, the JCB slammed through the gate. One of the two riding shotgun, it was not very clear which, ignited the bomb and all three made a run for it. Back at the van, several hooded men jumped clear and started to open fire in the direction of the RUC station. At this stage the SAS ambush was activated.

The sudden hail of SAS fire was terrifying. The eight members of the IRA fell under its ferocity. At the height of the firefight, the bomb exploded, taking with it half the RUC station and scattering debris over all concerned. As the dust settled, the SAS closed on the bodies. At that moment a white car entered the ambush area. Both the occupants, dressed in blue boiler suits similar to those worn by the IRA, were unfortunately mistaken for terrorists. It did not help their cause when, on seeing the ambush in progress, they stopped and started to reverse. One of the SAS stops opened fire, killing one of the occupants and wounding the other. It later transpired that the dead motorist, Anthony Hughes, had nothing to do with the IRA. Several other vehicles and pedestrians soon appeared on the scene, but by this time the situation was stabilised. For this quiet village, it was an awesome sight – the RUC station half demolished, the mangled yellow metal, that was once a JCB, and the numerous bodies littering the street.

Without doubt, Loughall was one of the most successful operations ever mounted against the IRA, marred only by the tragic death of Anthony Hughes.

The IRA were totally stunned by the loss of two complete active service cells and, thinking that there was a spy in their organisation, went into a period of self assessment. They did not lick their wounds for long. Shortly after, on Remembrance Day at a ceremony in Enniskillen, the IRA detonated a massive bomb. Eleven were killed, with more than sixty injured.

Gibraltar – 4 March 1988

In the war against the IRA, the SAS has been relentless in their hard-hitting attacks. Most of these end the same way: a quick shoot-out followed by several dead terrorists. At times, the SAS has been called upon to work in mainland Britain against the IRA and, just occasionally, abroad.

So it was in March 1988 when information filtered through the security channels that a bomb was to be exploded in Gibraltar. The IRA team consisted of three people, Sean Savage, Daniel McCann and a woman, Maraid Farrell. Each had a history of terrorist activity. The three, later acknowledged by the IRA as an active cell, had been spotted by British security services. They had been trailed for months and many conversations between the three had been recorded. This led to the identification of the target – the British garrison in Gibraltar. The method of attack was to be a car bomb. As events came into focus, the target was narrowed to a military ceremony where several military bands would be parading. It was also known that the IRA had developed a new type of remote control device that could detonate a car bomb from a distance.

In late 1987, a well-known IRA bomb-maker, Sean Savage, had been spotted in Spain. With him was Daniel McCann, another IRA suspect. MI5 spent the next six months watching the two, gathering vital information that they were certain was leading to a bombing. When, on 4 March 1988, Maraid Farrell arrived in Malaga airport and was met by the two men, it seemed likely that the bombing was on. At this stage, the SAS were invited to send in a team. The SAS and the security services have had a good working relationship since the mid-70s and the Gibraltar police were informed of the operation. They were told that the IRA active service unit was to be apprehended. For a while, contact with the IRA cell was lost, but by this time the target had been defined. It was suspected that one car would be delivered on to the Rock, and parked in a position along the route taken by the military parade. This car would be clean, a dummy to guarantee a parking space for the real car bomb. The best spot to cause the most damage was suggested as the plaza, where the troops and public would assemble. This proved to be correct.

At 2.00 p.m. on the afternoon of 5 March a report was received that Savage had been spotted in a parked white Renault 5. There was a suspicion that he was setting up the bomb's triggering device. Not long after, another report was received that Farrell and McCann had crossed the border and were making their way into town.

The SAS men were immediately deployed and, once Savage was out of the way, an explosives expert did a walk-past of the Renault. No visual tell-tale signs were observed, such as the rear suspension being depressed, indicating the presence of a bomb. If they were using Semtex, however, thirty pounds or more could easily be concealed. After consultation, it was considered probable that the car did contain a bomb. At this stage, the local police chief, Joseph Canepa, signed an order passing control to the SAS. Operation Favius, as it was known, was about to be concluded. The orders given to the SAS men were to capture the three bombers if possible but, as in all such situations, if there is a direct threat to life, be it the SAS or anyone else, they hold the right to shoot. It was stressed that the bomb would more than likely be detonated using a push-button trigger.

The SAS men, dressed in casual clothes, were kept in contact through small radios hidden about their person. Each soldier was also armed with a 9mm Browning Hi-Power pistol. Savage met up with McCann and Farrell and after a short discussion all three made their way back towards the Spanish border. Four of the SAS team shadowed the trio. Suddenly, for some unexplained reason, Savage turned around and started to make his way back into the town. The SAS team split; two with Savage, two staying on McCann and Farrell.

A few moments later, fate took a hand. A local policeman, driving in heavy traffic, was recalled to the station. To expedite his orders, he activated his siren. This happened close to McCann and Farrell, making the pair turn nervously. McCann made eye contact with one of the SAS soldiers, who was no more than ten metres away. The soldier, who was about to issue a challenge, later said in evidence that McCann's arm moved distinctly across his body. Fearing that he may detonate the bomb, the soldier fired. McCann was hit in the back and went down. Farrell, it is said, made a movement for her bag, she was shot with a single round. By this point, the second soldier had drawn his pistol and opened fire, hitting both terrorists. On hearing the shots, Savage turned to be confronted by the other two SAS men. A warning was shouted this time, but Savage continued to reach into his pocket. Both SAS men fired and Savage was killed.

As the first news of the event hit the media, it looked like a professional job, but the euphoria was short-lived. No bomb was found in the car and all three terrorists were found to be unarmed. Although a bomb was later discovered in Malaga, the press and the IRA had a field day. Allegations were made and witnesses were found who claimed to have seen the whole thing. The trio had surrendered; their arms had been in the air; they had been shot at point-blank range while they lay on the ground, and so on. Once again, the SAS was accused of being a bunch of state-authorised killers. No matter that they had probably saved the lives of many people, and dispatched three well-known IRA terrorists, they would stand trial.

In September 1988, after a two-week inquest and by a majority of nine to two, a verdict was passed of lawful killing. Although this satisfied most people, the story did not end there. The SAS soldiers that took part in the shooting in Gibraltar, were taken to court by relatives of the three IRA members killed. The European Commission of Human Rights in Strasbourg decided eleven to six, that the SAS did not use unnecessary force. They said that the soldiers were justified in opening fire as the IRA members were about to detonate a bomb. However, they did refer the case to the European Court of Human Rights. As a result of this court case, the British Government was forced to pay compensation.

Mogadishu – 1993

In 1993, US Army Rangers were deployed in Somalia, East Africa, as a part of a United Nations peacekeeping force. Somalia had been embroiled in a vicious civil war for many years with fourteen armed factions and their warlords causing anarchy and misery throughout the country. The factions' 'soldiers' were usually teenagers high on a local narcotic called Quat, a substance that gave them a false sense of bravery. With the most successful warlord, Mohammed Farah Aideed causing problems for the international peacekeeping force, a decision was made to try to bring him to justice. To that end, in August 1993, 440 elite troops, consisting of Delta Force and Rangers were flown into the country and based in a hangar at Mogadishu's main airport.

During the afternoon of Sunday 3 October, the task force commanders received intelligence that Aideed was about to hold a meeting with some of his top aides in a housing compound next to the city's Olympic hotel. Immediately, a raiding force was prepped and just after 3.00 p.m., seventeen helicopters and a ground convoy started to make its way towards the target. The Delta operators were dropped at the house, making an immediate entry and taking those inside by surprise. Meanwhile, other helicopters dropped the Rangers off around the perimeter of the area so that they could keep it secure. At first, everything seemed to be going almost to plan. Delta had taken about 20 prisoners, although Aideed was not among them. They were loaded onto the convoy, along with a couple of wounded Rangers and it prepared to head back to the airport.

Suddenly, an RPG rocket hit the Blackhawk helicopter 'Super 61' in the tail, sending it crashing into an alley five blocks away. Some of the Rangers rushed to the crash site to form a protective barrier around it while others tried to help those inside. A Little Bird helicopter containing an SAR team managed to land in the alleyway and get some of the wounded on board before taking off again, but by now the area was under heavy fire by Aideed's troops. The ground convoy also tried to reach the crash site but such a journey was not going to be easy as more and more of Aideed's men had been alerted to the Rangers' presence and were setting up roadblocks of burning tyres along the route.

Meanwhile, the ninety Rangers became pinned down either at the crash site or nearby, with hostile Somalis closing in on every side. By now it was late afternoon and they should have been safely back at base. Then, at 4.40 p.m., the news was broadcast that nobody wanted to hear: a second Blackhawk had been shot down half a mile from the first. This helicopter, Super 64, was piloted by Mike Durant and had also been hit by an RPG. Although it landed upright, all inside had either been seriously injured or killed and, as with the other site, Somalis were closing in fast. The ground convoy was ordered to try to get to the second site but got lost on the way. After spending more than two hours under fire, it was eventually ordered back to base.

At the site of the second crash, the situation seemed hopeless. Two Delta operators Gary Gordon and Randy Shughart, circling above in one of the other helicopters decided they would be more use on the ground. Fast roping down, they took up positions and prepared to hold off the onslaught they knew was about to come. Sure enough, they were soon engaged in a fierce firefight in which both were shot and killed. At the end of it only Mike Durant was left alive. He was taken prisoner.

Back at the airport, a second rescue convoy was being sent out to rescue the trapped Rangers. The plan was to take the Rangers to a nearby sports stadium, held by the Pakistanis in a safe area of the city, where they could then be airlifted out by helicopters. On the way in, the convoy suffered badly under heavy fire and was forced quickly to return to the airfield. It was decided that reinforcement with armour from Pakistani and Malaysian units was needed. By the time the larger convoy was organised it was 11.23 p.m. Despite getting lost again and again, the first vehicles of the convoy finally made it to the first crash site where a casualty collection point had been set up for the wounded in a nearby house. With limited space in the vehicles, anyone not wounded was forced to run alongside the convoy towards the pick-up point, all the time taking heavy gunfire from all around. Once there, all the Rangers were packed into Humvees and taken to the sports stadium. Then, as planned, they were airlifted back to base.

The next morning the aftermath of the event became clear. Nineteen US soldiers had lost their lives with eighty injured. One man had been captured (but was later released alive) and the body of another soldier had been dragged through the streets of Mogadishu to the horror of all who saw it on television later. Somali casualties numbered 1,000 with many of those being innocent civilians who got caught in the indiscriminate gunfire of that day. President Carter decided enough was enough and abandoned the hunt for Aideed, ordering all US troops to be withdrawn.

Algeria – 24 December 1994

The first reports came as French television gave news of a hijack that had taken place at Algiers airport. It reported that an Air France Airbus had been boarded by four Islamic fundamentalists, who had taken the 220 passengers and twelve crew hostage. They had managed to gain access to the airfield where, dressed as officials, they entered the aircraft just prior to takeoff. This ploy allowed them to bring weapons aboard the aircraft without anyone getting too suspicious. Once on board, they closed the doors and forced the pilot to taxi away from the main airport building. On demand, the passengers handed over their passports, still believing that these men were airport officials instead of a unit of the Armed

Islamic Group (GIA). The GIA, which is an Algerian-based terrorist group, view France in very much the same way as Iran views America. Their demands were for the release of GIA prisoners held in Algeria and France.

The French Government was informed of the situation and immediately put their anti-terrorist team, GIGN (Groupement d'Intervention de la Gendarmerie Nationale), on full alert. Despite being Christmas the unit was ready to deploy in just a few hours, whereupon they flew to Palma airport in Majorca. A planned assault on the aircraft was ruled out when the Algerian Government refused to allow the GIGN into the country.

Shortly after, the terrorists drew more media attention and a certain amount of public sympathy by releasing nineteen people, mainly women and children. This act of mercy was soon overshadowed when the terrorists shot and killed two hostages, an Algerian policeman and a Vietnamese diplomat. Hours later, early on Christmas morning, they released more women and children, bringing the total freed to 63. A few hours later, a third hostage was shot, a 27-year-old Frenchman, a cook with the French Embassy in Algiers. Soon after, the Algerian Government gave in and allowed the aircraft to take off. Instead of taking its planned route to Paris, the aircraft was diverted to Marseilles where it landed early next morning. The GIGN had already taken off from Palma and arrived in Marseilles in plenty of time to prepare a warm reception.

By 4.00 p.m. the GIGN took up their positions ready to assault. Then the aircraft started moving. This presented the GIGN with one of the worst hijack scenarios possible, and required an IA (Immediate Action). This is only carried out as a last resort, when people are being killed. There is nothing sophisticated about an IA assault. The GIGN had to get on board the airbus as quickly as possible to neutralise the terrorists and free the hostages. The risks to both the assaulting force and the hostages would be very high, due to the lack of surprise or diversion.

The aircraft continued to move towards the control tower and demands from the authorities for the aircraft to stop and move no further prompted the hijackers to fire several shots at the control tower. By this time, the GIGN commander must have realised the

SUCCESSFUL COUNTER-TERRORISM

terrorists intentions and ordered the IA. By 5.17 p.m., assault units of the GIGN could be seen racing towards the rear of the aircraft, and sniper fire could be heard. The team commander, Denis Favier, together with his second-in-command, Oliver Kim, stormed the front right door. They used normal airport landing steps to gain entry and, despite trouble with the door, and considering the conditions, the entry was very slick. At the same time, Captain Tardy led another unit in via the right rear door, using the same entry method. Once on board, both groups made their way towards the cockpit where most of the terrorists had gathered. A third group of the GIGN moved into position under the belly of the aircraft, ready to receive the hostages. Inside the Airbus, the two teams moved quickly, separating the terrorists from the hostages, disembarking the latter as quickly as possible.

By 5.39 p.m. the four terrorists lay dead and, although the hostages got away with a few minor cuts and bruises, the cost to the GIGN and the crew was heavy. Nine GIGN were wounded, two quite severely, one lost two fingers of his hand and one was shot in the foot. The three members of the crew that were hurt had, unfortunately, been trapped with the terrorists in the cockpit area. During the assault by the GIGN, the co-pilot managed to climb out of a small window and throw himself to the ground. Despite a broken leg, he managed to effect his escape.

Later reports indicated that the terrorist plan was to fill the aircraft full of fuel and blow it up over Paris. This theory was supported by the discovery of twenty sticks of dynamite under the front and mid-section seats. Parisians can count themselves very lucky, as this is believed to be the first attempt to use a large commercial aircraft as a flying bomb.

Peru – 17 December 1996

On Tuesday 17 December 1996, fourteen Peruvian rebels belonging to the Tupac Amaru, known by the Spanish initials MRTA, (see Chapter 2) stormed the Japanese Embassy in Lima. The stunning attack occurred during a party celebrating the Japanese emperor's birthday, which was attended by diplomats, Peruvian government officials and business leaders. In all some six hundred people, most of whom were VIPs, were attending the party when the assault began. According to accounts provided by hostages who were later released, the guerrillas entered between 8.15 p.m. and 8.25 p.m., as many of the guests were working their way down the buffet table set up in a tent in the grounds. An explosion, followed by a volley of gunfire, announced the takeover.

It has never been established exactly how the rebels gained access to the embassy but reports state that most of the attacking guerrillas apparently rushed over the high concrete walls that surround the embassy compound. Other unconfirmed reports say that they entered disguised as waiters, while one newspaper described how the rebels had spent three months tunnelling their way into the grounds of the residence. While this later method may sound a bit implausible it did have some merit.

Whatever their method of entry, the MRTA rebels had certainly researched their target. The hostage list read like a who's who and included Peru's Foreign Minister, Francisco Tudela; Agriculture Minister, Rodolfo Munante Sanguineti and the speaker of the parliament. Peru's Supreme Court President Moises Pantoja was also present as were at least three Peruvian legislators. Japan's Ambassador Morihisa Aoki and seventeen Japanese Embassy staff members were attending the party along with other foreign diplomats including the ambassadors of Austria, Brazil, Bulgaria, Cuba, Guatemala, Panama, Poland, Romania, South Korea, Spain and Venezuela. There were also seven Americans. Without doubt, the hostage list was the best ever taken by any terrorist group.

The hostages were immediately divided into groups and ushered into rooms on the second floor of the residence. The ambassadors were separated and held in one room that was heavily guarded by the rebels. During the raid, some were lucky enough to escape being held captive; Fernando Andrade, the mayor of the Miraflores section of Lima, managed to escape by sneaking into a bathroom and then climbing out of a window. US Ambassador Dennis Jett was at the party but left around 7.45 p.m., about half an hour before the attack. Despite a pitched gun battle during the takeover and the guerrillas' threats, by nightfall the siege had resulted in no deaths and only minor injuries. Once the siege had settled down, the rebels issued their demands via a telephone call to a local radio station; these were:

1. The release of three hundred imprisoned rebels, including Tupac Amaru's leader Victor Polay who had been in solitary confinement for the past four years.
2. Transfer of the freed prisoners and the hostage takers to a jungle hideout with their hostages; the hostages would be released once they had reached their destination.
3. Payment of an unspecified amount as a 'war tax'.
4. An economic programme to help Peru's poor.

Although the demands centred on the release of imprisoned rebels there was also strong reference to what the rebels called Japan's 'constant interference with Peru's internal politics'. The Peruvian Government and the President, Alberto Fujimori, who is of Japanese descent, had sworn never to negotiate with terrorists. Fujimori, who was elected president in 1990 had managed to severely weaken the guerrilla movements, capturing most of the leaders and jailing thousands of militants and sympathisers. The takeover of the Japanese Embassy now put Peru's image at stake. It was because of President Fujimori's hard-line action in the past that Japan invested so heavily in Peru, leading to the Tupac Amaru's resentment of Japanese influence on their country. With so much in the balance, Fujimori spent most of his time presiding over a closed-door meeting of his Council of Ministers, including the chief of police, Kentin Vidal, a legendary figure who had led the operation that captured the rebel leader Abimael Guzman.

When medicine was delivered to the embassy 24 hours into the siege, the rebels released four more diplomats – the ambassadors of Canada, Germany and Greece, and the French cultural attaché. The men read out a statement in which they said they had been sent to 'search for a negotiated solution' that would avoid deaths. During the next few days, the rebels released more hostages, including President Fujimori's mother and sister. In return, Christmas turkeys were delivered to the besieged embassy. Fujimori, however, rejected an opportunity to make a separate deal for other relatives trapped in the embassy and flatly refused to release Peru's guerrilla prisoners. Instead, he offered the terrorists safe passage to some location outside Peru as an incentive to them to lay down their arms and free all their hostages.

The rebels refused this offer and set several deadlines, each accompanied with the threat to kill hostages. All these deadlines passed without the loss of life. By 6 January 1997, the rebels were becoming agitated and refused to release any further hostages until the Government started negotiations.

Within minutes of the original attack, Peru's security forces had begun showing their strength. They started to implement anti-terrorist procedures straight away. All services where disconnected and the Government refused to allow fuel into the residence for the generator which had provided power to the rebels and hostages since the electricity was cut off. It ignored repeated demands to restore running water and telephone connections.

As the weeks went by, the Peruvian intelligence services started to monitor activities and set up a series of listening devices. The CIA sent an Air Force RG-8A aircraft with a forward-looking infrared camera to monitor the remaining 72 hostages and their fourteen rebel guards. The unmanned, 29-foot, single-engined aircraft makes very little noise and, in addition to its infrared camera, carries several high-resolution television cameras. This information was vital before any planned assault could take place. It is also believed that one of the hostages, a former military officer, was using a concealed two-way radio to supply information on the rebels.

While both the United States and Britain deny any direct role in the rescue operation, both have supplied Peru with experts in anti-terrorism training and this was no ordinary terrorist incident. The taking of so many foreign nationals forced many nations to become involved. Some openly offered help. The British Ambassador to Peru, John Illman, voiced Britain's concern, 'We are ready to respond and are, in fact, making preparations in advance to respond to any such request. And we've made it clear that the experience that we have is totally at the disposal of the Peruvian authorities should they require it.'

This response came in the guise of four members of the British

SAS, the world's foremost experts in counter-terrorism. Their brief was to evaluate the situation and offer solutions – all of these solutions included an assault of some form. In this case there were two options: assault the embassy or assault the rebels while in transit to freedom.

The first option would entail identifying the behaviour patterns and routines used by the rebels in order to establish their whereabouts at any given time. They would also need to know where the hostages where located. Once these two variables were known they would have to decide how they were going to enter the embassy and close with the rebels. While this may sound an impossible task, a modern computer software system especially designed for such incidents is available to the SAS. Within hours of reaching an incident scene, this software can produce amazing results, such as 3D images of the embassy, locations of the rebels and hostages and much, much more.

The second option is to get the rebels to move from the embassy compound to an airport or some other location that involves the use of transport. Due to the large amount of hostages, this transport would come in the form of buses. In such an eventuality there are two assault options open; one during the move from the embassy to the bus, and one while the vehicles are en route. Both expose the rebels to sniper fire and a planned assault.

While the military planned and gathered information, the politicians tried to work out some form of compromise, one of which was to release the rebels and give them asylum in Cuba. To this end, President Alberto Fujimori had talks with the Cuban President Fidel Castro. Eleven weeks into the siege, a basic agreement was in place whereby a military aircraft would take the rebels to Cuba. Whether or not this was a deception or a plan to assault the rebels en route, we shall never know. For while these discussions were taking place, another plan was being conceived by the shadowy figure of the unofficial head of Peruvian intelligence, Ivan Vladimiro Montesinos.

Montesinos is a cashiered army captain, former lawyer of drug barons, and a figure who inspires fear and fascination in Peru. While he has not appeared before news cameras for several years, the fact that he strode victoriously, wearing dark glasses, with the army chief of staff into the liberated Japanese compound after the assault was a sure sign of his involvement. It was Montesinos who had raised the 150-man commando unit that carried out the raid. Using his strong personality he was able to combine the best of the elite special forces units from the police and army and get President Fujimori's permission to use them in a daring plan.

Montesinos's plan was to tunnel under the embassy from several different directions then, at the right moment, the assaulting force would blast its way through the floor and walls. To facilitate the plan, 24 miners were shipped in from the government-owned Centromin mining company. Over a period of several weeks, they excavated a number of tunnels from nearby buildings, all of which ran to precise positions under the Japanese Embassy. This was not an easy task as the work needed to be done in secret, so both noise and vibration diversions were put into operation. The end result was a series of tunnels equipped with electric light and ventilation. While the tunnels were being dug the assembled group of elite commandos was painstakingly training at a crude wooden replica of the ambassador's home in the hills outside Lima.

But there was one small problem with the method of entry; the final flooring, which was concrete, had to be breached. If explosives were used the blast in the confined tunnel would mean that the assaulting force would be in no fit state to jump out and close with the rebels, if they survived at all. Added to this, there was a great danger of a cave in. The SAS have for many years contemplated such a problem and have developed a wall-breaching cannon. This ingenious device not only creates a hole, it can do so with the assaulting force standing within a few feet. There would be no violent shock wave, thus reducing the risk of a cave in. The plan was to make sudden breaches into the embassy from five different directions. Twenty of the commandos would enter rapidly through the floor while the remainder would enter at ground level through he compound walls. With all the assaulting forces in position the plan was initiated.

On 22 April 1997, at 3.00 p.m., after four months of captivity, the hostages heard several explosions rapidly followed by blistering

Counter-terrorist teams train for every emergency; here they can be seen entering a bus.

Room combat is the very basis of counter-terrorist work. The soldiers must be able to enter a room in total darkness and kill all the terrorists without harming the hostages.

Above Counter-terrorist teams have devised a whole range of specialist equipment to help them succeed in their task. These range from stun grenades to devices that can blow precise holes in walls without harming anyone on the other side.

Above The modern day counter-terrorist soldier is protected by state-of-the-art clothing. The helmet and face visor are capable of stopping small arms ammunition even when it is fired at close range.

Above America's elite counter-terrorist unit is known as Delta Force. Like Britain's SAS it
s not reserved purely for hijacks; here it can be seen operating in Afghanistan.

Above The British counter-terrorist team pose for a unit photograph. The SAS is
renowned worldwide for its efficiency in combating terrorism. Small units of the SAS
operate all over the world.

Methods of entry (MOE) sometimes provide a challenge for counter-terrorist units. Here a unit is testing a new device that allows divers to get from the surface of the sea up on to a ship.

Left In the mid-1970s, the German GSG9 proved to be one of the most effective counter-terrorist teams in the world. Most of its members were drawn from the various police forces in Germany. Much of the work carried out by the GSG9 has now been allocated to a new force, the KSK.

Right The leader of the Palestinian group that hijacked flight LH181 lies dead after the aircraft was successfully assaulted by the GSG9 in 1977. The operation was carried out with textbook style, resulting in the deaths of three of the four terrorists, while all the hostages were safely evacuated.

Above Storming the Iranian Embassy in London proved to be a difficult task for the British SAS. The multi-storey building had to be penetrated at every level to ensure the safety of the hostages. The operation was successfully completed in less than eight minutes on 5 May 1980.

Left The siege at the Japanese Embassy in Lima began on 17 December 1996 and lasted for several months. In the end the Peruvian Special Forces entered the embassy by tunnelling under the building. All the terrorists died in the assault.

above The conversion of a commercial aircraft into a flying bomb has given terrorist organisations yet another method of inflicting carnage. One of the ways to prevent this from happening is to restrict access to the flight deck by make the door bullet-proof and unbreakable.

Left Biological weapons pose one of the most terrifying threats if used terrorists. Several attempt to use them have been made already in Japan ar the USA.

Below Retaliation against terrorist leaders has demanded the use of assassination. America ha reintroduced the age-old tradition albeit with the use of modern day technology. New sniper systems can now guarant a kill at up to half a mile just about any weather conditions.

gunfire. The rebels had become lethargic and at the moment of assault half of them had been playing football in the main hall while some were sleeping upstairs. Those rebels outside the building were killed instantly while those inside met their fate as the commando team carried out a room-by-room clearance. In all, the assault took only fifteen minutes. During the assault only one hostage, Supreme Court Judge Carlo Giusti Acuna, died after being shot and this was as the result of a heart attack. Two police officers in the assault also died, one being a member of the security detail assigned to protect the President's son. In all, 25 hostages received minor wounds with two others needing surgery. All fourteen of the rebels were killed, although at least two dropped their weapons and were seen by several hostages surrendering to the commandos. The Government reported that all the rebels had been killed during the assault but TV footage later showed that some of their bodies had been mutilated and even dismembered by the soldiers. The bodies of the rebels were buried in unmarked graves to prevent closer examination.

There is no doubt that Peru's security forces pulled off a raid that rivalled some of the most stunning anti-terrorist assaults of the decade. The deaths of the fourteen rebels has, however, highlighted what many see as a just and worthy cause. There remains a quiet distrust in Peru and the heavy Japanese presence within the country is not helping matters.

Sierra Leone – 25 August 2000

Soldiers from the Royal Irish Regiment were sent to Sierra Leone as part of the 200-strong British training team assisting the country. On 25 August 2000, for reasons unknown, eleven of the solders in two vehicles left a safe road and entered rebel territory controlled by a 'renegade militia' known as the West Side Boys. As they drove along an isolated jungle track, the soldiers were stopped and taken hostage. Once it became obvious that the men were overdue, other British forces in the country launched a search operation using helicopters; they failed to locate the missing soldiers.

Two days later, an exchange offer was received from the West Side Boys asking for the release of their leader, General Papa, from prison, along with food and medicine. One of the soldiers was allowed to meet and negotiate on behalf of the rebels. He assured the British commander that they were being well treated and that no one was injured. On Wednesday 30 August, the situation looked somewhat better when five of the British soldiers were released in exchange for a satellite phone and medical supplies. The remaining six soldiers would not be released until all the demands were met.

As negotiations continued, the British Government, keen to show no weakness, ordered 120 soldiers from the 1st Battalion Parachute Regiment to Sierra Leone. It was also rumoured that a small force of British SAS had been sent to the region some days before; both units were there as a possible military solution to the problem. The SAS unit supplied deep penetration patrols that located the West Side Boys' camp in the area known as Rokel creek. The six remaining hostages were being held there. One of these witnessed several mock executions of the hostages when they were lined up in front of firing squads. This prompted the British Government to sanction a rescue attempt.

At dawn on 11 September, the plan was put into operation. Three Chinook helicopters and two Westland Lynx gunships headed directly towards Rokel creek. By 6.30 a.m., they were overhead and the two Lynx helicopters began strafing the banks of the river. Moments later, one of the Chinooks landed, dropping the paratroopers directly near the rebel huts. An immediate firefight broke out with the rebel guards, who had been alerted by the approaching helicopters. As these were taken care of, a special hostage rescue unit of SAS men ran to the hut that contained the hostages. At that moment, a heavy machine gun opened up on the assaulting forces, killing one of the paratroopers. This served only to rally the British, who moved forward, overrunning the position and forcing the West Side Boys to retreat. By this time, the SAS had located the hostages who were hustled into one of the helicopters. This immediately took off and flew directly to the warship HMS *Sir Percival* which was anchored off the coast of Freetown. As the hostage rescue was taking place, the remaining two Chinooks landed at a secondary camp south of the first position. Under support of the Lynx gunships, the paratroopers engaged in a vicious firefight with the rebels. The fighting continued for several hours but by mid-afternoon mopping up operations were complete and the rescue party was airlifted out.

The British had lost one man with another seriously wounded, together with eleven slightly injured. In addition to the six rescued hostages, the British had captured one of the rebel leaders, Foday Kallay, killed 25 West Side Boys and captured a further eighteen.

Afghanistan – 2002

The British SAS was part of the Coalition force sent to fight in Afghanistan against the Taliban and Al-Qaida network. As in the Gulf War, they operated closely with Delta Force. The SAS had been in Afghanistan for several weeks when they were ordered by the American Central Command in Florida to raid an opium storage plant to the south-east area of Kandahar. The target location was said to hold around £50 million worth of pure opium and was heavily guarded. In addition to the opium it was believed that, due to the large number of guards (estimated at eighty plus) on site, Al-Qaida may have some interesting intelligence documents at the location.

Unfortunately, maps of the area were virtually non-existent and the SAS was forced to rely on aerial photographs that had been taken by an unmanned US spy drone. The American command requested that the site be attacked almost immediately, leaving no time for a CTR. This would have enabled the SAS assaulting forces better to determine the strengths and weaknesses of the Al-Qaida positions and refine their strategy accordingly. Timing also meant that the attack would have to go in during daylight hours, abandoning the element of surprise and the use of their technically advanced night-vision equipment.

The SAS mustered two full squadrons, almost 120 men, the largest force it had fielded in a single operation for many years. With this in mind, the final assault was to rest on fire power. The SAS had thirty 'Pink Panthers' (110 Land Rovers specially made for desert warfare) all armed to the teeth with ferocious weaponry. The Pinkies carried both front- and rear-mounted GPMGs (General Purpose Machine Guns), while the roll bar was mounted either with a Milan anti-tank rocket system or a Mk19 automatic grenade launcher. The Pinkies were supported with big 2.5 tonne ACMAC lorries acting as 'mother' vehicles. Just prior to the assault, the US Air Force would carry out two precise air strikes. These would be close enough to destroy the drug warehouses but leave the headquarters building intact.

The journey to the target started long before dawn. It was a long journey over dreadful, rocky terrain. As the area was hostile, the column was forced to stop at regular intervals and send out scouts. For this they used off-road bikes just as they had done in the Gulf War.

Dressed in light order, which means no rucksack, each SAS man carried his personal weapon, either an M16 rifle with an under-slung M203 grenade launcher or a Minimi light machine gun. During such an assault the SAS prefer to forgo any body armour depending instead on speed of movement, but in this case both body armour and Kevlar helmets were used. Belt equipment consisted mainly of grenades, ammunition, food, water and emergency equipment such as a SARBE beacon with which to call for help. By 10.00 a.m. the force was within two kilometres of the Al-Qaida camp but the going was slow due to soft sand. This meant an on-the-spot change of plan.

Midday saw the start of the action as half the SAS lined up their Pinkies and started to lay down covering fire ready for the other half to assault. The ground was not suited for a direct assault and the Al-Qaida rebels had chosen their defensive positions accordingly. By 1.00 p.m. a serious firefight had developed but the assaulting squadron continued to push forward. The assault was helped at this stage by the arrival of US Air Force F-16s. The first pass caused massive explosions in and around the compound but, as requested, didn't touch the building serving as the headquarters. The second air strike came close to wiping out the assaulting force but by this time the drug-laden dust from the destroyed warehouses had thickened the air and nobody really cared very much.

Despite the horrendous fire put down by the SAS, the Al-Qaida fighters refused to give ground, preferring to die. By 2.30 p.m.

most resistance had been overwhelmed and the headquarters raided for laptop computers, papers and maps. The ground was littered with dead and wounded Al-Qaida fighters while several SAS men had been hit. Thanks to the body armour and Kevlar helmets, most of the wounds were to the limbs but several were extremely serious and it required all of the skills of the SAS medics to keep the most badly wounded soldiers alive.

Finally the word was sent to 'bug-out'. Everyone jumped back in their vehicles and headed south. The first port of call was a rendezvous at a makeshift airfield where a C130 complete with doctors and medics evacuated the wounded, flying them directly back to the UK. Although several of the wounded were serious, the mission had been accomplished without the loss of a single SAS soldier.

Moscow – 23 October 2002

During the evening of Wednesday 23 October 2002, fifty Chechen guerrillas – 32 men and eighteen women – stormed a Moscow theatre, taking everyone inside as hostages. The audience, numbering around seven hundred, had been watching a performance of the popular classic Russian musical 'Nord Ost' when the heavily armed rebels took the stage during the second act and ordered the actors off at gunpoint.

In what was obviously a well-planned operation, more gun-wielding terrorists raced into the complex and rounded everyone up into the auditorium. As well as the explosives carried by the women, other, larger explosive charges were placed around the building and threats were made that these would be detonated if any rescue by the Russian military was attempted. The leader of the group, 23-year-old Movsar Barayev, then issued a statement that they would start to execute the hostages unless the Russian authorities ordered an end to the Russian occupation and war in Chechnya. No deadline was given but Barayev mentioned that the group was prepared to hold out for a week.

Barayev was no unknown idealist but the nephew of the notorious Chechen warlord, Arbi Barayev, a man responsible for the kidnapping and beheading of three Britons and a New

Zealander in 1998. Movsar had already led many rebels against Russian forces inside Chechnya and was known to be ruthless and determined. His threats were taken seriously by the Russian authorities who continued to negotiate with the terrorist leader. They offered the terrorists safe passage out of the country if they released all hostages unharmed. Barayev refused, saying they were prepared to die for their cause. As a gesture of goodwill 41 hostages, including children, Muslims, citizens of Georgia and a pregnant woman, were released within the first few hours.

Late on Thursday morning, Barayev allowed cameramen from the Russian television channel NTV to film him and some of his fellow rebels. Barayev, defiant and the only one to show his face, explained that the women with him, dressed in black chadors and with bundles of explosives tied around their waists, were prepared to die because they had lost their husbands and brothers in the war in Chechnya. During that morning a Russian parliamentary official and representatives of the International Red Cross were also allowed in. As a result, five more people were released. By now, many relatives and friends of the remaining hostages had gathered outside the theatre and were protesting against the war in Chechnya, hoping to sway President Putin's mind into ending the war and saving those they loved. Putin refused to move from his hard-line position of not giving in to threats from terrorists.

By Friday morning, conditions began to worsen inside the theatre. A burst water pipe had begun to flood the ground floor. Although water had been delivered, none of the hostages had eaten a proper meal since the siege had begun. The only toilet available to all was the orchestra pit. The rebels too, seemed to be getting more anxious as there were no signs of their demands being met. Once more they threatened to start executing the hostages 'ten an hour' if no progress was seen. Once again the Red Cross intervened and secured the release of a few more people. Then, for no apparent reason, even these negotiations began to break down. The tension was increasing and it was obvious that cracks were beginning to appear.

According to some reports, the breaking point occurred on Friday evening when a small boy threw a tantrum and ran screaming down the aisle. The terrorists fired on him but missed, hitting some of the seated hostages instead, killing two and wounding two others. Hearing the gunshots, the authorities outside thought that the executions had begun and prepared to storm the building.

At 5.30 a.m. on Saturday morning a potent gas was released into the building through the air conditioning system of the theatre. This gas, now identified as an opiate-based anaesthetic, quickly put those inside to sleep before any explosives could be detonated. An Alpha team of the Russian Special Forces then stormed the building, shooting dead all the Chechens and bringing out the hostages. Gunfire and explosions were heard for approximately fifteen minutes before the all clear was sounded.

Tragically, the gas proved lethal for some hostages with heart or respiratory conditions and 115 died as a result of the rescue. A further 42 were seriously ill and hospitalised. The use of the gas, at first unidentified, brought massive criticism of the Russian authorities but when it was revealed that the hostage-takers had planted the equivalent of 110 kilos (242lbs) of TNT in the building, it became evident that this measure, although drastic, had averted an even greater tragedy.

In the days that followed, amid the mourning for those who had died, the Russian authorities put pressure on Denmark to extradite Ahkmed Zakayev, a former senior member of the previous Chechen Government who was suspected of being involved with the attack. The Russians also threatened that the terrorists would be buried in pigskin – considered unclean in Islam and therefore a barrier for the soul to reach heaven. In doing this they hoped to deter other Chechen Martyrs hoping to die for their country and claim their reward in eternity.

Author's Note: The problems associated with a mass hostage scenario and proposed rescue have long been debated by many anti-terrorist teams. Attacking any installation where numerous hostages are held will almost certainly create a reaction from either the terrorists or the hostages themselves. In either case, the terrorists have time to kill. Where explosives are known to be present, the death toll will be even higher, causing total mayhem just as the assaulting forces make their entry. One answer is to incapacitate everyone with gas. This allows both hostages and terrorists to be separated. It has long been established that the types of gas available for such use are extremely limited and require immediate medical backup on a large scale.

6: THE FUTURE OF TERRORISM

We also have to recognise that a new breed of terrorist has emerged, one that has developed outside the normal profile. For example, Al-Qaida is a network that has the means to spread its terror across continents. In addition, it has the ability to organise many of the radical Islamic groups in order to co-ordinate their attacks. They are also prepared to accept the retaliation levied on them by the West, as much of this rarely harms their organisation but kills instead many innocent people. The present terrorist mode of operation seems to be, strike, wait and suffer any retaliation, then rebuild and attack once more.

The future of terrorism is not that hard to define; neither is the response to terrorism, as both phenomena are being acted out at the moment. While it is possible for the terrorist organisations to repeat events similar to those of 11 September or, as many claim, evolve tactics of a more deadly kind, there is no indication that they plan to do so. Likewise, the response of many countries has been to increase their defences against world terrorism to the point where aggressive operations, such as those seen in Afghanistan and those (as I write) about to be undertaken against Iraq, take the fight to the enemy and states that support terrorism.

The response to terrorism in the 1970s eventually led to the creation of national counter-terrorist units. Some battles were won and some were lost. Most countries have learned from past events and adjusted their planning and countermeasures to combat the tactics of the various terrorist organisations. In the same way, the events of 11 September have forged a new united front against international terrorism that in itself will help solve the problem.

Despite this united front, terrorism was given a major boost, when, in 1990, the former Soviet Union disintegrated. The military hold it had had for years over various regions around the world suddenly evaporated. The growth of terrorism can be seen to have changed from this point. Nevertheless, to understand the future of terrorism we must take stock of the terrorist incidents that have taken place over the past fifty years. Even a simple analysis shows that terrorism is not only on the increase, but the incidents have also increased in brutality, producing ever more casualties. For example, the hijacking of the late 1960s produced few casualties compared with those incidents that have taken place at the start of the twenty-first century. The attacks on America, the Bali bombing and the Chechen siege in Moscow are all evidence of this. Such incidents provide governments with an insight into the future of terrorism by demonstrating what terror-ist acts are feasible.

We also have to recognise that a new breed of terrorist has emerged, one that has developed outside the normal profile. For example, Al-Qaida is a network that has the means to spread its terror across continents. In addition, it has the ability to organise many of the radical Islamic groups in order to co-ordinate their attacks. They are also prepared to accept the retaliation levied on them by the West, as much of this rarely harms their organisation but kills instead many innocent people. The present terrorist mode of operation seems to be, strike, wait and suffer any retaliation, then rebuild and attack once more.

Another aspect of terrorism is the success of some of its attacks. Apart from the damage in human lives and property, successful incidents by one group are more likely to be imitated by another. It seems almost a supporting necessity for the perpetrators of each new atrocity to raise the death toll and therefore secure more media attention. In order to continue with this escalating trend, terrorist organisations must look to use more powerful weapons. If this is the case, then the future will involve preventing weapons of mass destruction from falling into terrorist hands.

It is at this point that the problem of media exposure raises its head. While we all wish to receive open and accurate information, the effects of overreaction can trigger the very thing terrorists hope to create — fear. While no one denies that envelopes containing anthrax being distributed to certain individuals in America was something about which everyone needed to be aware, the emotionally charged media reporting only exacerbated the situation. Pictures of men walking around in bright orange protective suits, decontamination units being set up, and a report providing a detailed history of the effects of biological agents, served only to turn most of us to jelly. This type of hysterical reporting is done not to protect the people, but simply to create headlines and boost programme ratings. Without thinking, the media is doing much of the terrorists' work by creating fear.

*　　*　　*

Government initiatives in fighting terrorism vary from continent to continent, but most have taken an unequivocal stand against terrorism. Both America and Europe have at last instigated policies to protect their homelands but, unlike in Israel for example, precious little information or instruction has filtered down to the man on the street. While the general public is aware of the threat through the media, most have received no specific information about how they should combat a terrorist hazard. True, many individual establishments such as airports, government offices and military bases (all of which are classified as high risk) have taken preventative steps. Awareness at the individual level for the 'man on the street', still leaves much to be desired, yet it is here where the most good could be achieved.

It remains a mystery why Western governments have not jumped at the opportunity to utilise the general public in a vast 'eyes and ears' campaign. The cost of a national awareness promotion would be minimal by comparison to the damage caused by a major terrorist incident. The eyes and ears of a nation, especially when it is in their express interest, could provide a major defensive shield against acts of terrorism. Vigilance should not be limited to the domain of the security guard. An effective collective awareness would provide a much tougher barrier against the terrorist. Airport security, with its constant reminders about unattended baggage, is a perfect example of this. An unremitting government campaign along comparable lines, aimed directly at the public through the media, would serve to highlight the methods used by terrorists and possibly forestall an attack.

This collective awareness has been forced upon the state of Israel to the point where would-be suicide bombers have been apprehended just seconds before they have detonated their bombs. There have been around 85 suicide attacks against Israel during the past two years, for which HAMAS is mainly responsible. The population of Israel knows that HAMAS is likely to continue with this policy for the foreseeable future. The Israeli people know the pattern these suicide bombings take and are, therefore, watchful for any warning signs.

*　　*　　*

In the fight against terrorism, it is sensible to consider a serious effort by governments to target individual members of the more radical terrorist organisations. This entails covert operations against the leadership, their paymasters and their weapons suppliers. Such tactics have been tried before and it is difficult to quantify the effects of an arrest or assassination policy against individual terrorist leaders. Such policies do, of course, already exist. The number of covert operations have increased dramatically over the past two years and America has publicly declared that assassination is back in its arsenal.

On a much broader front, America is also trying hard to curtail the activities of terrorist organisations by consolidating international co-operation. At the moment, this is based on four main principles:

1. Make no concessions. While this remains the backbone of most countries' policies in the fight against terrorism, it is not always an easy position to maintain. Terrorist groups have long since learned that pressure in one form or another can, and has, caused governments to capitulate and give in to their demands. While America and Israel stand firmly behind the principle of no concessions, what would be their response if threatened by a nuclear bomb? What price could you put on the lives of all those living in Tel Aviv or Washington, if terrorists had the means to detonate a nuclear device in the heart of a city? If we are to believe the analysts, that day is not far off and this type of scenario will be put to the test.

2. Pursue and prosecute. The second basic principle is to seek out and bring terrorists to justice. This is the aim of many governments but unfortunately, as we saw in the Afghan War, it is proving harder than first thought. True, many members of Al-Qaida were captured and shipped off to the American facility known as Camp X-ray, where they await trial. Other countries, such as Germany, have also captured Al-Qaida members and these, too, are now being tried for their alleged crimes.

3. Pressurise terrorist sympathisers. The third principle is to bring pressure on all those who would harbour terrorists and provide

terrorist funding. When it comes to freezing assets or confiscating money, most governments are quick off the mark but it remains an enigma that terrorist funding is not always seen as such. The IRA received much of its funding from donations provided by those of Irish descent living in America. Despite the events of 11 September and the decline in the amount, funding from America for the IRA still continues. As for harbouring terrorists or allowing them to recruit and train on your territory, again we must take our example from America. Many Jewish Americans are raised and educated in the United States. They become doctors, military experts, even nuclear physicists. Many seek to return to the land of their forefathers, Israel, where their skills are used to serve fundamental Jewish groups. While many may not see this as a fair example, those in countries being charged by America with harbouring terrorists tend to see things differently.

4. Counter-terrorist units. Finally, governments must improve their counter-terrorist capabilities through both their intelligence agencies and their counter-terrorist teams. Since the early 1970s the growth in counter-terrorist teams and equipment has been little short of a revolution. Most countries now possess some specialist team (see Chapter 4) capable of defeating terrorist organisations when the opportunity arises. Conversely, intelligence on terrorist organisations and their mode of operations is much in need of a rethink.

Options and Reality

To ascertain what and where the terrorist organisations will strike next we must not only study their past operations but also look at what is achievable. Nuclear bombs, nerve gas, suicide bombers, assassinations and even conventional warfare are all options open to terrorist groups. In reality the options open to most terrorist groups are fairly restricted.

While it is possible, in theory, for a terrorist group to construct a nuclear bomb, it is almost impossible in practice. Therefore, it will be a long time before we see a terrorist threaten nuclear attack. Unfortunately, the same cannot be said for biological or chemical weapons, some of which, although highly dangerous, are simple to produce. The sarin attacks on the Tokyo subway (see Chapter 3) provide a prime example.

For the moment, the growth areas of terrorism are in the use of the suicide bomber and assassin. In both cases we have much to fear. We have seen that an individual can strap a bomb around his or her waist and walk onto a bus before detonating the device and causing many casualties. More worrying is the collective use of intelligent suicide bombers. These can plan a combined attack that could take a horrendous toll of the civilian population. An example of this is the attacks on America.

The Suicide Bomber
Although we have seen chemical attacks in Japan and anthrax being delivered in America, we must judge the 'suicide bomber' to be our current main threat. This particular technique has undergone many improvements over the years. Suicide bombers are now on par with smart bombs, laser guided missiles and multi-million-dollar fighter aircraft. While we in the West require a defence budget running into billions, terrorist organisations simply breed young men and women to fulfil the same role. They offer a perfect guidance system with full stealth facilities. When in range, they can identify their target with one hundred per cent accuracy. If threatened, they can abort and go immediately to a secondary target without being re-programmed. Their lethality is unlimited and thousands more become available every day. The suicide bombers are human beings who are prepared to sacrifice their lives at a cost, the greater the cost to the enemy the greater their death.

Suicide bombers have been with us for many years. In their basic form they simply strapped huge amounts of explosive around their bodies and walked into a place where the enemy was to be found in numbers. At the opportune moment, they detonated the explosives killing themselves and all those in the immediate vicinity. A more advanced suicide bomber uses a larger amount of explosive, contained in either a car or a truck. This is then driven to a location where again the enemy is in substantial numbers. This type of suicide bomber is normally deployed against military or government installations where a degree of resistance is offered. The car or truck is generally rammed into the weakest point in order to breach the enemy compound before the bomb is detonated.

The latest and most specialised suicide bombers are highly intelligent. They spend months, even years, working on an operation. They will research and utilise impressive intelligence on their enemy before choosing a target. Next, they will train to acquire any required skill, such as learning to fly a commercial aircraft. At the given moment, they will seize several aircraft and fly them into buildings with devastating effect. The frightening thing is they can, when required, work together with other suicide bombers, increasing their effectiveness beyond the wildest dreams of any weapons manufacturer. So how and where will the specialised suicide bomber strike next?

From a terrorist point of view, improving on the results of 11 September may prove difficult. The effect caused by crashing a commercial aircraft into a nuclear reactor, may or may not cause it to become unstable. There would be a massive explosion, but there is unlikely to be a nuclear blast of the type seen when a military nuclear device is detonated. There would be a severe radiation leak and residual fallout over the local area. At worst such an impact might cause a Chernobyl-type melt down. If such a scenario were to be acted out, nuclear reactors would soon be protected by a 'no fly zone' and surface to air missiles.

The suicide bomber requires one important element, explosives or a combustible material. Unfortunately, military explosives can be purchased from many countries, and their commercial equivalent is to be found in just about every quarry worldwide. In most countries, laws exist to control explosives but these are mainly enforced more through safety than for counter-terrorist reasons. Additionally, high explosive is extremely simple to make with most supermarkets stocking the basic ingredients. The know-how is easily obtained over the internet. Even when no explosive is available, combustible material such as gasoline is always accessible, and one gallon of gasoline has the blast power of seven pounds of high explosive when detonated. It is interesting to note that the IRA mainly used home-made explosives in the majority of their larger culvert and car bombs. The utilisation of commercial fertiliser and diesel oil would make up the bulk of the bomb, which would then be initiated by commercial explosive in order to achieve the required detonation speed. Given this availability of raw bomb-making materials and information, we must recognise that the suicide bomber has the means available to carry out his mission.

Preventing the suicide bombers from achieving their goal may not always prove feasible but we could make commercial passenger flying more secure. Back in 1960, Sky Marshals were introduced after a series of hijackings in the Middle East. They are still used today, especially with such airlines as Israel's El Al. Since 11 September the use of Sky Marshals has seen a massive increase. Even the British have acknowledged their presence on certain international flights. They can, of course, be a double-edged sword. If they are professional, acting as one of the passengers while sitting in a dominating seat with a concealed weapon ready at hand, they can be of great benefit. Unfortunately, cost is a factor and many airlines employ armed men who really have no idea about how to exercise their duties with any sense of responsibility.

Author's Note: I once travelled on a Middle Eastern airline that employed a Sky Marshal. He spent most of his time walking up and down the aisle frowning at the passengers, showing his hardware and fraternising with the stewardess. I could have taken this guy out with a catapult and then used his gun to hijack the aircraft. Therefore, there are points for and against Sky Marshals.

Repetition of 11 September is highly unlikely for another reason – the passengers. As we saw with one of the hijacked aircraft, the passengers refused to tolerate their lives being taken for nothing, leaving them with no option than to assault the hijackers. Furthermore, in any future event where an aircraft is suspected of being a flying bomb, it will almost certainly be shot down. The risk of killing several hundred is preferable to several thousand deaths and, under such circumstances, responsible governments would have no other choice. Moreover, if the events of 11 September were to happen on a frequent basis, air travel as we know it would cease to exist.

A better compromise would be to introduce stricter passenger control and identification. To some degree this has already been done, but how far do the authorities go before the paying passenger says 'enough is enough' and refuses to fly? The effect of this can already be seen in America, where entry has become so strict that it threatens to undermine the tourist industry.

Another answer is to make it harder to gain access to the flight deck. That means no one enters during the flight. A camera outside the door could also be mounted to watch over the aisle. The crew could also be given small arms training and be equipped with a gun. This would at least negate the chance of the aircraft being taken over by someone with a knife. Even where the intended hijackers had a gun, the restricted flight deck would provide time to alert the authorities of the situation.

But aircraft are not the sole domain of the suicide bomber. Cities and places of intense population, i.e. sports stadiums or airports, offer the opportunity for mass murder. Almost every major city in the Western world has a main airport within a few miles of its centre; in some cases the airports are actually within the city limits. Any attack does not necessarily have to come from a hijacked aircraft. The most popular option to date is the car bomb, individual bomber or gunman. Three members of the JRA, after all, walked calmly into Tel Aviv's Lod airport, collected their suitcases from the carrousel and proceeded to open fire on the packed hallway (see Chapter 2).

What can we do to protect the cities? By the time a hijacked airliner has been converted into a flying bomb, there is very little we can do. Once it is over the city, shooting it down only serves to guarantee the attack. Attacks from terrestrial bombers, on the other hand, can be prevented. The Israelis, who have suffered horrendously at the hands of suicide bombers, have managed to detect the presence of individual bombers prior to them detonating their bomb. Admittedly, most of this is down to public vigilance and the restricted access to security areas. They have also re-instigated the policy of destroying the bomber's home. To some degree, this may seem a pointless exercise but the safety of his family left behind is something the suicide bomber must consider.

Finally, we ask the question, are suicide bombers insane? This depends on your point of view, but for the most part, they are at best misguided. How many terrorist commanders would risk strapping a bomb to a crazy individual? It would be far better if they used someone who is deeply committed to their cause, someone who will go to the required target. Among the various terrorist groups that use suicide bombers, there is a certain amount of individual glory for those who willingly give their lives. This act in itself perpetuates the cult of the suicide bomber and inspires others to follow suit.

Given that many terrorist organisations do not have a lot of sophisticated weaponry, the suicide bomber is a highly prized asset. The suicide bomber is a valuable and flexible weapon that can be used for either mass destruction or to attack a precise target as was clearly illustrated by the attacks on America and the murder of Indian Prime Minister Gandhi in 1991 by the Tamil Tigers.

Bio-terrorism

The next major threat must come from bio-terrorism. Long ignored and denied, this threat has heightened over the past few years. Both extremist nations and terrorist organisations have access to the skills required to selectively cultivate some of the most dangerous pathogens and to deploy them as agents in acts of terror.

In 1995, Iraq was discovered to have a large biological weapons programme. They produced, filled, and deployed bombs, rockets, and aircraft spray tanks containing bacillus anthracis and botulinum toxin. In the same year, the Japanese cult, Aum Shinrikyo, released the nerve gas Sarin in the Tokyo subway. The Sarin had been manufactured by the cult's own chemists. Members of this group are also known to have travelled to Zaire in 1992 to obtain samples of Ebola virus.

Yet, in the main, two candidate agents are of special concern. These are anthrax and smallpox. Anthrax is an organism that is easy to produce in large quantity and extremely stable in its dried form. The effect of aerosolised anthrax on humans is highly lethal. In 1979 an anthrax epidemic broke out in Sverdlovsk in the Soviet Union. Sverdlovsk was also the home of a military bioweapons facility. Around 66 people died, all living within four kilometres of the facility. Sheep and cattle also died along the same wind axis, some as far away as fifty kilometres.

Anthrax also raised its head shortly after America suffered the attacks of 11 September. A strange white powder was sent through the ordinary mail system. The powder was later confirmed as weapons grade anthrax. Several people became contaminated and some even died. The government took all reasonable precautions to protect both postal workers and the general public and the problem seems to have diminished but even this recent anthrax scare slips into insignificance when compared to other diseases such as smallpox.

Smallpox is caused by a virus spread from person to person; infected persons have a characteristic fever and rash. After an incubation period of ten to twelve days, the patient has high fever and pain. Then a rash begins with small papules developing into pustules on days seven to eight and finally changing to scabs around day twelve. Between 25% and 30% of all unvaccinated patients die of the disease. There was, until 1980, a vaccination programme against smallpox. Other than that there is no specific treatment.

The terrorist potential of aerosolised smallpox was demonstrated by an outbreak in Germany in 1970. A German who had been working in Pakistan became ill with high fever and diarrhoea. He was admitted to a local hospital on 11 January where he was isolated due to the fact that they thought he might have typhoid fever. Three days later, a rash appeared and by 16 January he was diagnosed as having smallpox. He was immediately transported to one of Germany's special isolation hospitals and more than 100,000 people were swiftly vaccinated. But the smallpox patient had had a cough, a cough that had acted as a large-volume, small-particle aerosol. Consequently, nineteen cases of smallpox occurred in the hospital and one person died.

Two years later, in February 1972, a similar outbreak went undetected in Yugoslavia. It was four weeks before a correct diagnosis was made, by which time the original carrier was dead and buried. Twenty million people were vaccinated. Almost ten thousand people spent several weeks in isolation, while neighbouring countries closed their borders. By the time the situation was under control, 175 patients had contracted smallpox, and 35 had died.

At the moment we are ill-prepared to deal with a terrorist attack that deploys biological weapons. We need to focus on detection and be able to diagnose and respond quickly. This means stockpiling vaccines and drugs in addition to training and practising the mobilisation of health workers at all levels. When an attack comes it will require all our efforts to contain it. Some countries, such as America, have already gone down this route, producing millions of vaccines as well as educating the American people on how to react under such an attack.

Nuclear Terrorism

As previously stated, the principles behind the construction of a nuclear bomb are fairly straightforward, but the practicality of making such a bomb is somewhat different. It would be safe to say that none of the present fifty or so terrorist organisations scattered around the world have the capability to manufacture such a device.

That said, there are hostile nations that have proved themselves capable of manufacturing nuclear weapons, North Korea being a prime example. This same country also has a reputation for selling its finished produce to anyone with the money to pay for it. Proof of this was seen recently when the Spanish Navy intercepted a shipment of missiles from North Korea. The missiles, which were en route to South Yemen, were hidden beneath tons of cement bags.

If a terrorist organisation could procure a nuclear weapon, and many can afford to do so, it would create a dilemma. If the device was secreted in a major city and detonated, the result would be catastrophic, especially if that country had a nuclear arsenal of its own. If, for example, Tel Aviv were to be the target, the retaliation by the Israelis might well be to launch a full-scale attack on all the major Arab nations. At worst, the Palestinian people would be badly affected and it is foreseeable that Israel would demand their total removal from the region. The impact of killing hundreds of thousands with a nuclear device would serve to make the world a very unstable place, one where terrorist freedom would not be tolerated even in the smallest degree.

The other option open to terrorist organisations is the use of a conventional bomb which has been 'seeded' with nuclear waste – the so-called 'dirty bomb'. The explosion from such a bomb would cause minimal damage compared to that of a pure nuclear device but the fallout and resulting contamination would be widespread. Cities could become deserted after such an explosion as, depending on the type of radioactive material used, the resulting half-life radiation could last for hundreds of years. The dirty bomb is presently considered a serious threat by many Western nations.

Cyber Terrorism

Dirty bombs and biochemical sprays are not the only weapons in the modern terrorist's arsenal. Many Western nations are heavily reliant on their economic infrastructure, much of which relies totally on computer-based systems. It is hard to imagine everyday life without computers. In fact, it would be almost impossible for the West to go back to the old days of paper business. The demands on a modern society are so great that it requires machines to control its functions. Being so reliant on computers also makes us vulnerable.

Computers support the delivery of goods and services, aid manufacturing, governance, banking and finance. What would happen if, say, the stock exchange computers were put off line for several days or the banks could not issue money to their customers because all the accounts had been wiped out? While both would have a continuous back-up system, it is feasible that someone in the know could, after years of research, also find ways of destroying these.

All political, military and economic interests depend on information technology, including critical infrastructures such as electric power, telecommunications and transportation. The information technology infrastructure is at risk not only from disruptions and intrusions, but also from serious attacks. Hardly a day goes by without the world waking up to yet another 'I Love You' virus. But this is just the beginning. What happens when the information technology system is deliberately violated in order to achieve a specific aim? Cyber warfare also offers a cloak of obscurity to potential attackers. All they need is access to a computer and a telephone line.

The military rely heavily on computerised weaponry. Smart bombs and cruise missiles are guided to target via the GPS (Global Positioning System) as are many of the ground troops. Find a way of shutting down the 27 or so satellites the system uses and the American military would be blind in one eye. At the moment, the American system is the only one in existence and just about every aircraft and surface vessel relies on it for plotting its course from destination to destination. A second system will be in place by 2006 when the European Union launches its own GPS. It's not just the weaponry we need worry about, though, what about the early warning systems and attack assessment? All these depend on computers. And, going back to weapons, what if someone could get access to, and control of, the US nuclear missile system?

The type of person capable of hacking into military computer networks is already out there. Several have penetrated the American Department of Defence, as well as the CIA. True, these people have been tracked down and sentenced accordingly, but only after the event. In addition, we should not only look towards hacking as a method of Cyber Warfare.

In March 2001, Japan's Metropolitan Police Department disclosed that a software system they had acquired to track 150 police vehicles, including unmarked cars, had been developed by the Aum Shinryko cult. This is the same cult that gassed the Tokyo subway in 1995, killing twelve people and injuring six thousand more. At the time of the discovery, the cult had received classified tracking data on 115 vehicles. Furthermore, the cult had developed software for at least eighty Japanese firms and ten government agencies. They had worked as subcontractors to other firms, making it almost impossible for the organisations to know who was developing the software. As subcontractors, the cult could have installed 'Trojan horses' to launch or facilitate cyber-terrorist attacks at a later date.

A year or so ago, the American Government realised that 150 of its embassies were using software developed and written by citizens of the former Soviet Union. It was quickly removed. If we can send a virus into a system, surely we can develop software that will detect it entering the system and annul it at source? The computer networks need to be hardened with some form of alert protocol and automated response.

Then there is Electrical Magnetic Pulse, EMP. This involves the 'frying' of all electronic equipment within a given radius, depending on the size of the device used. America has designed a bomb for just this purpose and we are reliably informed that several hundred have been shipped off to the Gulf in anticipation of a war against Iraq. If American arms manufacturers can make an EMP bomb, then so can others. It's simply a matter of time.

The response to the threat of cyber terrorism has been to isolate those systems that are critical to the survival of our military, economic and political organisations. In essence, this means installing networks with no external connection other than for authorised users. Secondly, the manufacturers of computer software for such systems should provide full security clearance for all those writing the software. Software and computer networks should be installed so that in the event of a cyber attack they are able to route the problem away from the critical structure. An in-depth check and search for anomalies should be made before any critical software is installed. Securing both these measures should greatly reduce the ability of any outsider to enter a computer infrastructure. Additionally, all critical network systems should be duplicated, allowing the closure of the infested network, while continuing on the backup system. Where defence weaponry is controlled, there should be a simple 'pull the plug' attachment built into the system to prevent unauthorised firing. The satellites should be capable of being taken off line if the risk of cyber terrorism is high.

The Internet

The establishment of the internet and e-mail has taken communications around the world one huge step forward. Information and basic knowledge on just about any subject is available on the internet. Simply booking your holiday or sending your girlfriend flowers can now be done with a few strokes of the keyboard. Billions of e-mails a week speed up conversation, save telephone charges and enable us to communicate rapidly around the world. This is what the internet and e-mail was designed for. Unfortunately, the price we must pay for this service is high, not in monetary cost but in abuse and misuse.

Arms can be found for sale on the internet as well as the knowledge to make home-made explosives, or construct a bomb. Researching information on a vulnerable target and finding out who lives where, all serve to make the internet a major hit with the terrorist organisations. E-mail can be encrypted in such a way that no government agency can crack the code, therefore allowing terrorist organisations secure communications on a worldwide basis. The same system allows them to contact other groups and prepare joint operations. Business and bank accounts can be established over the internet which provide money for weaponry and operations; almost all these activities are untraceable, if done properly.

Stopping Terrorist Attacks

Put simply, stopping terrorist attacks is impossible. The Bali bombing and the siege in Moscow, coming so soon after 11 September, are proof of this. The very nature of a terrorist attack lies in its ability to strike anywhere and at any time. And, while the intensity and size of the attacks are on the increase, this only strengthens the resolve of nations to take some reactive counter-measure. For example, the reaction to the attacks on America served to rally, under the unity of world condemnation, an attack on Afghanistan. This unity, however, was short-lived. True, many Western nations have stayed the course, but there are those countries that openly oppose the USA. Within hours of the 11 September attacks, pictures of Middle Eastern men, women and children celebrating the attack, dancing joyfully in the streets, were transmitted over the television channels. In retaliation, many Muslims living in the West were subjected to assault, some people were even refused permission to board passenger aircraft because they simply looked Muslim. Most Muslim nations, of course, and the vast majority of Muslims were as appalled by the attacks as the rest of us. Although they may have different values to those of us in the West, Muslims are really no different to people in the West, with the same aspirations, the same ambitions in life.

For the Muslim nations, social tolerance is governed mainly by religion. You steal; they cut off your hand. You commit adultery; you are stoned to death. Such laws are something the Western nations see as barbaric. In turn, many Muslim believers see Christian nations as decadent, openly exhibiting sex, drugs and rock and roll. What matters most is how much tolerance we allow each other and how we share the belief that terrorism must be eradicated.

Combating future terrorism depends on recognising that the terrorist principles and tactics have changed. In the past, they had always used a hijacked aircraft, bartering the lives of the passengers and crew for a list of demands. Now they have hijacked several aircraft and transformed them into flying bombs. The flying bombs really had no use for the passengers other than as a deterrent to stop the authorities shooting down the aircraft. While we may not be able to anticipate every terrorist attack, we can predict what might happen.

We must also recognise that, while the terrorist organisations are free to inflict any atrocity they wish upon society, governments must act, at least overtly, within the confines of law. To wage war, a government needs the backing and support of its people. Even when the conflict is in full swing, soldiers are forbidden to commit crimes such as shooting innocent civilians. These same confines are not imposed on the terrorist organisation and this makes them incredibly difficult to deal with, but the people of the civilised world require their governments to act in a civilised manner. This is not, of course, always what happens. It is interesting to note that France took a solid stance against war in Iraq. France even blocked the proposed deployment of protective NATO troops and equipment to Turkey, the one NATO ally that borders Iraq. In doing so, France claims to represent the very essence of democracy and freedom, believing in peaceful methods of persuasion rather than war.

On 7 July 1985 this same nation sent its special forces to destroy the *Rainbow Warrior*, the flagship of the Greenpeace Organisation. Greenpeace is recognised internationally for its committed concerns on conservation and environmental issues, and for the most part the organisation has the backing of the world's nations. Although we might not always approve of Greenpeace's methods, they have rarely committed acts that could be interpreted as violent.

On the evening of 10 July 1985 *Rainbow Warrior* had arrived in Auckland and tied up at Marsden Wharf. Greenpeace had planned to sail the *Rainbow Warrior* into French territorial waters to disrupt a forthcoming French nuclear test. The French had other ideas and just before midnight divers attached two high explosive devices to the hull. Once the divers were clear of the ship, the explosives were detonated, blowing a large hole below the waterline near the engine room. *Rainbow Warrior* sank within minutes. One man, Fernando Pereira, a photographer, tried to recover some of his photographs from his cabin and was drowned in the process.

The discovery of a rubber boat that had been abandoned and the earlier sighting of a camper van that had been in the same area led the New Zealand police to interview two French tourists during their inquiries. The link between the destruction of *Rainbow Warrior* and the intended French nuclear tests demanded further inquires into the identity of the French tourists, who claimed to be man and wife. It was not long before their real identities became known. They were Major Alain Mafart, aged 35, and Captain Dominique Prieur, aged 36. Both were members of the French military, and were serving in a Special Underwater Warfare unit. It was later revealed that they were the action arm of a French Intelligence Service operation. While the bomb had prevented Greenpeace from interfering with the French nuclear test, the international condemnation proved far worse.

Shipping

To prevent future terrorist attacks, we must look at the options available to the terrorist organisations. One such option would be to translate the flying bomb attacks on America into the maritime scenario. Almost every major city in the world is based on the shores of a river or seaboard. The centre of London, for example, can be accessed directly from the River Thames.

Oil tankers and container ships continually link cities, nations and continents. Many of these ships are crewed by workers from the Philippines, (the world's biggest crew supplier) which incidentally is also home to the Abu Sayyaf militant group. Indonesia (the world's second biggest crew supplier) is home to numerous radical Muslim groups. A mere two per cent of shipping containers entering America are inspected and a container can hold a lot of explosives.

On the other hand, what if several small motor-powered launches or light aircraft packed with high explosive were to attack the shipping lanes (remember the Kamikaze pilots of World War II?). If the target were a holiday cruise liner, it would cause thousands of deaths. If they attacked oil tankers then the revenue lost and the ecological damage would be horrendous. If several vessels where hit in an organised attack, the death toll would equal that of 11 September. So how do you detect and stop a small launch attacking a larger commercial vessel? It's almost impossible. Although attacks on pleasure cruises would involve a great loss of life, it would have little economic impact – but consider what would happen if several oil tankers or rigs were destroyed at sea. The knock-on effect could be catastrophic to the industrial nations.

Vigilance is the key word and many Western countries have greatly improved their awareness of a seaborne terrorist attack. In January 2002 the MV *Nisha*, a cargo ship inbound for London docks, was seized off the south coast of England. In a dramatic dawn raid by Royal Navy units, including the Special Boat Service (SBS) together with Customs & Excise officers, the ship was stopped and boarded. The ship, flying the flag of St Vincent and the Grenadines in the West Indies, was then escorted to Sandown Bay in the Isle of Wight.

Once in dock, customs officers started their extensive search but no explosives or ammunition were found. In fact, the vessel was carrying raw sugar to a Tate and Lyle refinery on the Thames. The seizure was due to an intelligence tip-off that warned the British authorities such a ship could be carrying 'terrorist material'. In addition, the ship in question had disappeared off the satellite system for several weeks. It had also called in at Djibouti on its voyage, so it was entirely possible that Al-Qaida were involved. The British Government played down the incident, claiming the search was part of the nation's tighter security measures.

It is rapidly becoming apparent that there is a need for real security on the high seas – a security system that is not compromised by the quest for speed and economy while transporting goods over the world's oceans.

Intelligence Agencies

The answers to many of our questions with regard to terrorism sit firmly with our intelligence agencies, and the list of questions we should be asking them grows ever longer. Firstly, how come our intelligence services missed the warning signals for the 11 September attacks? Where were our listening posts, our agents and our monitoring stations? What were the CIA, MI5, NSA, GCHQ, NRO and JARIC doing wrong? If we are to believe the attacks on America were carried out by Osama bin Laden who, for the past few years, has been hiding in Afghanistan, how did he communicate to the operational units in America? Telephone and courier traffic would be fairly obvious, so how come no one spotted either? He has been on the American hit list for years – yet intelligence picked up nothing. If I were the President of the United States, I think I would be asking the heads of departments like the CIA a few serious questions. If, on the other hand, we accept that our security services were operating as normal, does it indicate that the terrorists' security is getting much better?

The question now is what lies ahead in the way of terrorist threats and what responses must the intelligence agencies prepare in order to foil or at least minimise these threats. There is no doubt that terrorism will continue to be a serious threat for the predictable future but are the intelligence services up to the challenge? It is true that many countries have had some minor success in apprehending terrorist individuals but most of those taken into custody are wanted for terrorist crimes going back many years. The French arrested the infamous 'Carlos' after they had arranged his extradition from Sudan. America managed to arrest Ramzi Youssef, thought to be responsible for the bombing of the World Trade Centre. The Germans even managed to extradite Soraya Ansari from Norway and made her stand trial in Hamburg. While these arrests are laudable, and go a long way to showing that governments never forget, they do nothing to prevent future terrorist attacks.

Many governments will claim that they have had successes in fighting terrorism, and that many incidents have been averted. Due to the protective nature of the intelligence agencies involved, they also decline to say how or when the information was attained. In many Western countries the intelligence agencies have been allocated more funds and more people. Is simply throwing money at the problem the answer, or does the intelligence world need to totally rethink its methods? Until recently most of the Western intelligence agencies were concerned only with the Russians and the Warsaw Pact countries. Terrorism was left mainly to the police. With the collapse of communism in the early 1990s came the opportunity for the intelligence agencies to change their methods of operation, but the process was not a swift one. The Cold War had instilled a policy within most agencies that remained intact, and the system catered for the larger established enemy, all but ignoring the puny terrorist organisation.

The dinner-jacketed agent socialising at the Russian Embassy played a game of cat and mouse with his counterpart. Intelligence on the enemy's latest weaponry was acquired through a network of sub-agents and spies, motivated by money, sex and greed. As terrorism replaced the more traditional enemy, the intelligence agencies found it difficult, if not almost impossible, to gain any real information. With the exception of the Israelis, entering a terrorist organisation required skills and personnel the intelligence agencies did not have. Moreover, it would take many years to train new agents capable of infiltrating a terrorist organisation. This new breed of agent needed to look like and be able to act like those members of the organisation he was trying to penetrate. The agent would have to talk the same language and have the same religion as any other member of the terrorist organisation. Finally, they would need a reason and a means to attach themselves to the group. Any cover story would have to be totally watertight. Additionally the agent would probably need to 'prove' himself by actually carrying out some form of terrorist activity.

Even when an agent has successfully entered the terrorist organisation, his background, cover story and general habits must constantly be adhered to; one slip could result in an agonising death. Recruiting, training and selecting men and women for such tasks is not easy. Hence, the number of undercover agents currently inside terrorist organisations is minimal by comparison to those sent to spy within the former Soviet Union.

One would think that government listening stations, such as GCHQ in Britain, need only to concentrate their efforts in a different direction to refocus on the terrorist threat. Monitoring the airwaves of the Soviet forces was a major task, as every government and army relies heavily on its communications system. This is not the case with terrorist groups, who have a tendency to use mobile phones or the internet to communicate. This means that the sender and recipient need to be identified amid the billions of messages sent every day – not an easy task. Still, new equipment and software does allow intelligence agencies to pinpoint a particular mobile phone number and listen in to the conversation. Internet traffic can also be intercepted and its origins located. In addition, new methods of electronically tracking an individual are now available. This, when coupled with the latest satellite technology, offers a clearer picture of those involved in terrorist activities.

Among the intelligence community, regrouping to take on the fight against terrorism raises the problem of interagency mistrust, jealousy and competition. This often happens between rival agencies of the same country, or between the intelligence agencies of various nations. It is commonly known that intelligence agencies are very loath to part with information, especially if it is at the expense of losing a field agent. Warnings about a minor terrorist incident may well be suppressed in order to protect the identity of the undercover agent.

> Author's Note: During my time working undercover in Northern Ireland I witnessed several cases where intelligence was withheld, sometimes at the cost of human life. The same cry would come up every time, 'We must protect our source.' Intelligence was also withheld from senior officers in order to prevent that same information being disclosed. For example, if a Brigadier was informed of a special SAS operation, he in turn would warn his duty intelligence officer. When this officer went to sleep for the night, he would pass on the information to the night intelligence sergeant, and so down the line goes the information either to be ignored or forgotten (in which case regular troops could end up blundering into the SAS operation), or to be misinterpreted as some kind of tip-off (in which case regular troops could also end up blundering into the SAS operation).

There is a new need for interdepartmental co-operation on intelligence and the exchange of intelligence on an international scale. Nevertheless, the balance between security and prevention must be weighed carefully against that of losing an agent. As intelligence agencies evolve in the future, one thing is certain, their agents will need to be tougher, and their electronic surveillance smarter. Fighting terrorism starts with good, accurate intelligence and its correct interpretation. It is our first line of defence.

Diplomacy

As this book nears completion, we stand once more on the brink of war and once more the target country is Iraq. At present, we have the United Nations (UN) weapons inspectors in Iraq searching for weapons of mass destruction. So far, none have been found. This leads both America and Britain to believe that Iraq is hiding something and both want to attack. The UN, on the other hand, feels the weapons inspectors should be given more time. Thousands of American and British troops have already been dispatched in preparation for war, with both countries seeking active support. Equally, many countries are seeking to prevent the war, with Germany and France joining forces in the anti-war campaign.

This struggle between old allies is music to the ears of Saddam Hussein. Despite their differences, every nation in the West thinks his removal is long overdue; the political manoeuvring centres around how he is removed, who undertakes such an action and what happens once he is gone. This difference of opinion threatens to undermine the very fabric of NATO, a united entity that has successfully defended Europe for so many years.

This diplomatic struggle between the nations causes friction on both sides, leaving the UN looking weak. The problem is complicated by the fact that most of the world wants only to see the removal of Saddam Hussein and his regime, without the destruction of the country and its people. Various options have been put forward, such as asylum for Saddam in nearby Saudi Arabia. This is not likely to happen.

America sees itself as the world's police force and actively seeks to confront those nations who are likely to pose a major threat. Although seeking the sanction of the UN, America has the might to do pretty much as she pleases and the UN could do little to stop her. Fortunately, America is a law-abiding nation, and while she is strong-willed, she realises the problems any independent action would cause. If the French, Germans and Russians have their way, as members of the UN security council, they will block any new resolution to invade Iraq. This leaves America and Britain to go it alone. If on the other hand America declined to invade, this would leave Saddam Hussein as the clear winner. The political damage caused by disunity among the Western nations would be little short of catastrophic. It could open up a vacuum in which terrorism would flourish.

Author's Note: It is an interesting fact that under President Clinton, the world appeared to be a much safer place. Peace talks between the Palestinians and Israelis where started, and America's intervention between Britain and the IRA also helped to bring about a peaceful settlement. These two events had a dramatic effect on many of the terrorist organisations, some of which decided to capitulate and seek a peaceful settlement. Interestingly, the American economy during this peaceful phase achieved new heights. Then came a change in administration, and the 11 September attacks, and most of President Clinton's work was undone, including the economy.

Assassination

When diplomacy fails, we can always turn to disposing of our enemies in a more traditional way. If we are to believe what we read in the newspapers, America has once again sanctioned the use of selective assassination in an effort to quell the terrorist threat. It is a subject that provokes all manner of debate.

Some would claim that we should not stoop to the level of the terrorist, while others argue that taking a life by assassination smacks too much of the 'Big Brother' government. Terrorist organisations rely on this irresolution among the general populace as it ties the hands of governments, seriously restricting their ability to counter the problem.

There is also the argument that, while assassination removes certain individuals, it does not guarantee the removal of the organisation. Finally, assassination has the ability to bite back, i.e. you kill our leaders and we will kill yours.

One nation that has continued to refine the skills of the assassin is Israel. They systematically hunted down all those responsible for the Munich Olympic massacre and assassinated them. Israeli policy on assassination continues to this day and many, including America and Britain, are requesting copies of the Israeli handbook on assassination. Israel has used a variety of assassination methods, including helicopter gunships. This type of killing takes place when inserting a ground crew is hazardous or simply not possible. The problem is, the target area is usually large and it is often the case that many innocent people are killed. This serves only to encourage further terrorist acts by the Palestinians. Killing innocent civilians, while claiming they are simply protecting the state of Israel, has only helped to alienate international opinion, and gain support for the Palestinians.

The former Soviet Union also used assassination as a means to rid themselves of their enemy. Although several foreign spies were selected for assassination, for the most part the Soviets killed their own dissidents. Leon Trotsky, the communist leader, was assassinated in Mexico City in 1940, while at the start of the Russian invasion of Afghanistan, President Hafizullah Amin was also targeted for assassination.

The question that should really be asked is, 'Is assassination an effective strategy? Does it really make any difference?' Many American Presidents have been assassinated, but these deaths have had little effect on the running of the country. So what, if any, would be the benefit of assassinating Saddam Hussein or Osama bin Laden . . . revenge? Better they are captured and held for trial. This then makes them vulnerable, and the people can see they are vulnerable. If, in the end, the death sentence is required, then so be it.

Sometimes it is difficult to differentiate between assassination and suicide. If the government version says suicide, and there is not proof to say otherwise, then suicide it is. All the same, circumstances can be interpreted in several different ways.

On Tuesday 18 October 1977, at 9.00 a.m. in the morning, Chancellor Helmut Schmidt was at home, still celebrating the success of Germany's anti-terrorist team at Mogadishu. They had successfully assaulted (see Chapter 5) the hijacked aircraft and rescued all passengers and crew save the pilot. The main terrorist demand had been for the release of the Baader-Meinhof member held in Stammheim prison near Stuttgart. Schmidt's good mood was short-lived as he was informed that all four members of the Baader-Meinhof gang had committed suicide. Coming within days of the hijack, their deaths immediately aroused suspicion that the German Government had somehow prearranged their 'suicides'.

Stammheim prison is no ordinary penal complex. It is a new maximum-security detention centre, specially built to house such criminals as the Baader-Meinhof. The seventh floor, where the suicides occurred, is the top floor. The roof above is designed and protected not only to prevent escape, but also to prevent any possible rescue by helicopter. The seventh floor is divided by a wide corridor, with five cells on one side and three on the other; at the end of the corridor is a guard room which is permanently manned by prison officers. This room controls the only access to the floor and provides an uninterrupted view of the corridor, allowing the prison officers to see every cell door. On the left, the side with three cells, Andreas Baader and Jan-Carl Raspe were housed, with Raspe closest to the guard room. There was an empty cell separating the two. On the opposite side Gudrun Ensslin and Irmgard Möller were housed, with Möller being closest to the guard room. Once again, the prison officers had deliberately left an empty cell, separating the two women.

A month before the aircraft hijacking a German industrialist, Hans-Martin Schleyer, had been kidnapped by Baader-Meinhof members in an effort to secure the release of their leaders from Stammheim. Immediately after the kidnapping, the cell doors had been padded with mattresses in an effort to prevent verbal or visual contact between the terrorists. The windows, all of which were on the outside wall, did allow the inmates to shout from the top floor and be heard at street level. This fact has been verified by several newspaper reporters who clearly heard them while waiting outside Stammheim.

Discovery of the suicides came at seven in the morning. The prison officers' routine involved passing keys to each other and waking the prisoners in preparation for breakfast. Before the occupants of each cell could be released, the padding that covered the doors had to be removed. By the time this had been carried out, it was close to 7.30 a.m. The members of staff had released the central locking system to the cells and were expecting to be greeted on their breakfast round by the prisoners standing at their cell doors. Raspe was in the nearest cell, but there was no movement. One of the prison officers took a few steps to investigate. The cell was in disarray, with Raspe's body lying across the bed, his head turned away from the door. His head had fallen forward on his chest and there was blood on the wall next to him. One of the officers went forward to check on Raspe. At this stage he was still breathing. Immediately the cell door was closed and locked. The officers rushed to the phone to ring the doctor and call for medical orderlies. This was all done in a manner intended not to alert the other prisoners.

When the officers and the medics returned to the cell they found Raspe still alive. It was at this stage that they noticed a pistol in the cell. Evidence taken from reports made afterwards cannot ascertain where the pistol was actually found. The gun had been picked up and wrapped in a piece of cloth. An ambulance arrived at 8.00 a.m., just twenty minutes after the opening of the cell door, and Raspe was taken to hospital. Although he received emergency treatment, and was prepared for theatre, Jan-Carl Raspe died at 9.40 a.m.

Meanwhile, the prison officers returned to their normal routine of taking breakfast to the other prisoners. At 8.10 a.m., the door of Baader's cell was opened after they removed the soundproof padding. On opening the door, the officers were confronted by a second mattress blocking their view. They pushed this out of the way and went into the cell, which was in semidarkness as the curtains had been closed. A medical orderly, who had stayed to help the officers, stepped into the dim light. Baader was lying on the floor, with his head in a pool of blood. The medic immediately felt for signs of life; there were none. A gun lay beside the body and this was noticed by one of the prison officers. The routine was repeated, they closed and locked the cell door.

Since there was no life-saving action needed for Baader, the officers anxiously went to the other prisoners' cells and started to unlock them. Again a medical orderly went in first. The next room to be entered housed Gudrun Ensslin, and once again they had to remove a screen and go into a room with poor light. They were met by the sight of two feet hanging from the cell window. The prison doctor entered the cell and confirmed that the prisoner was cold and dead. She had apparently hanged herself.

The final cell to be opened was that of Irmgard Möller. They found her lying on her bed covered by a blanket. The medical orderly turned her over, expecting to find yet another corpse, but as he removed the blanket, Möller moved and groaned. Her chest was covered in blood, resulting from the fact that she had stabbed herself repeatedly in the heart with a bread knife. Unlike the others, Möller's vital signs appeared strong and she also appeared to be conscious. The prison doctor was once more called forward, whereupon he examined Möller. A second ambulance was called for as the doctor treated Möller for heart failure and severe chest wounds. Shortly after, she was removed to hospital (not the same one they had taken Jan-Carl Raspe to). The knife wounds had caused the tissue around the heart sac to be punctured, nonetheless doctors were able to rectify the damage and put her in a stable condition.

An inquiry into the deaths of Raspe, Baader and Ensslin returned a verdict of suicide, but there remained many unanswered questions. Other inmates, on the floor below, said they heard Baader and the others walking about or going to the toilet, but no one heard any sound of gunfire. Why not? How did the terrorists, locked in separate cells in a maximum security prison, simultaneously learn of the German Government's success in Mogadishu, 3,500 miles away – and this within a very few hours of its occurrence? Jan-Carl Raspe was supposed to have used a 9mm Heckler and Koch pistol that he had hidden in the skirting board of his cell. He had put the gun to the right side of his head and fired. No shot was heard.

Andreas Baader had hidden his 7.65mm FEG gun in his record player in his cell. The gun had been previously hidden in his other cell wall. He had shot himself through the back of the neck after shooting two rounds into the wall, to make it look as if a struggle had taken place. Reports also say that he used a mattress to deaden the noise of the gun shots. Difficult to believe that he could have knelt on the floor, put a mattress between him and the back of his head, then put the pistol to the back of his head and pulled the trigger.

Gudrun Ensslin had hanged herself with a piece of towelling. She had tied the cloth to the grating of her window and stood on a chair then kicked it away. This was a carbon copy of her old friend Ulrike Meinhof's death. Meinhof had even died in the same cell.

Irmgard Möller had taken one of the prison cutlery knives and stabbed herself unsuccessfully in the chest. She is still alive and refuses to talk about the incident. The public wanted the bodies thrown on the garbage heap, but the mayor of Stuttgart, (Irwin Rommel's son) had the bodies buried together in a common grave.

SUMMARY

I write this summary as a kind of personal postscript to emphasise I am a British citizen living in the West. Had the author of this book been a Muslim living in the Middle East, the whole approach to terrorism would have been different and would have provided a different understanding of the problem. We all recognise that terrorism exists, but its existence is subject to different interpretations. While all terrorist organisations exist to create terror, some are simply doing so to overthrow a corrupt regime. In many cases, we in the West recognise this and support their struggle, providing covert training and weapons. It is true to say, however, that the majority of terrorist organisations are simply at odds with their own society, and wish to establish territorial, political, or religious changes.

We must also recognise that acts of terrorism are escalating at an alarming rate. To some degree we are countering this threat by increasing our campaign against the terrorist organisations. Vigilance has been given a much higher priority with arrests of many suspected terrorists being made on a weekly basis. Our intelligence agencies are starting to come to terms with the new threat, and the flow of useable information is steadily on the increase. Rogue governments that sponsor and harbour terrorist organisations are being brought to task. Where they do not do so willingly, they run the risk of war by UN-backed forces.

The media shows every incident related to terrorism, and while they are newsworthy, reporting of these events also serves to encourage fear among the common people.

While the threat of nuclear and biological terrorism is a possibility, the likelihood of such an incident actually taking place in the near future is minimal. On the other hand, I am convinced that suicide bombing is on the increase and that the 11 September attacks on America are viewed by terrorists organisations as successes to which they aspire. In response, vigilance and retaliation will remain our answer to any new attacks. This policy will continue until we can find a peaceful solution to many of the world's problems.

As previously stated, I have travelled around most of the world and have been involved with counter-terrorism for over thirty years. In all that time, I have met and worked with people of many religions, in many countries, and can only conclude that most of mankind wishes only to live in peace. I am sure the world will survive and, in the end, peace will prevail.

POSTSCRIPT

Throughout this book, I have made several references to the possibility of a pending war aimed at removing Saddam Hussein from power in Iraq. That possibility became reality when, on Thursday 20 March 2003 at approximately 5.35 p.m., the first American missiles fell on Baghdad city – the war on Iraq had begun. It continues as I write.

How did this war materialise? After the Gulf War of 1991, Saddam Hussein agreed to destroy all his chemical, biological and nuclear weapons. The process was to be supervised by UN weapons inspectors. In late 1998 the Iraqis made life so difficult for the UN inspectors that they were forced to leave. Although America and Britain protested, Iraq refused to allow the inspectors to return, and the whole process of Iraqi disarmament fell into limbo. Trade sanctions were imposed denying Iraq food, medicine and other basic requirements in an attempt to pressurise Saddam Hussein's regime into accepting the will of the international community. The Iraqi people suffered because of the sanctions but neither the sanctions nor the suffering of his own people had any real effect on Saddam Hussein, cosseted in his luxurious palaces in the Iraqi capital, Baghdad.

Then, in 2001, the world witnessed the 11 September attacks on America. This led to a war in Afghanistan, a country that had previously provided sanctuary for many terrorist organisations – including that of Osama bin Laden. The success of the Afghan war emboldened the Americans, leading them to increase the pressure on Baghdad. While the Iraqis deny having retained any biological and chemical weapons, there has been no independent verification of the destruction of the chemical and biological agents Iraq was known to possess. On 12 September 2002, President Bush asked the UN Security Council to pass a new, tougher resolution insisting that Iraq disarm and Resolution 1441 was passed. This demanded that Iraq co-operate with the UN weapons inspectors. Teams of experts returned to Iraq under the direction of Hans Blix, a Swedish expert in international law, expert in disarmament and former head of the International Atomic Energy Agency. America, Britain and other allied nations had begun a build-up of military force in the Middle East, designed to demonstrate the military might of the Western powers to Saddam Hussein, in the hope that the apparent willingness to use force might persuade him to fully co-operate with Blix's weapons inspectors.

The initial report presented to the UN by Hans Blix was thin. On the one hand, Russia, France and China (all members of the Security Council), seized on the fact that Blix's team appeared to have made some progress, asserting that the inspections alone could peacefully disarm Saddam Hussein. America and Britain took a different view, maintaining that prolonging the inspections was pointless because the Iraqis would continue to confound Blix's team and continue to conceal their weapons of mass destruction. Both countries pushed for a final UN resolution that would present Saddam Hussein with an unavoidably brief deadline for co-operation in the decommissioning of his weapons of mass destruction. With an ever more powerful US and UK military force gathering around Iraq, moves to establish this resolution at the UN were abandoned when it became apparent that both France and Russia would veto any proposed resolution that imposed further pressure on Iraq.

President Bush then issued an ultimatum to Saddam Hussein – he had 48 hours to leave Iraq. Saddam had to choose to go into exile and allow a new regime to be established in Iraq or else America, along with those nations that supported its hardline policy, was ready to take independent action. The deadline expired and Iraq was plunged into war.

It was not the war the world had expected as, unlike in the Gulf War of 1991, the United Nations played no part in the conflict. Exasperated at the UN's inability to enforce its own resolutions and remove Saddam Hussein from power, America, Britain and their allies went in alone. This was not a popular decision and huge peace protests were staged around the world. Unprecedented opposition to the American and British action continues as I write, but the war goes on.

In fairness, despite the amount of bombs which have rained down on Baghdad, the allies have tried hard to ensure that only military targets were hit, leaving the vast majority of civilians unharmed. The initial pounding of the city was designed to catch Saddam Hussein and his senior Ba'ath party members unawares. A 'shock and awe' tactic was employed, aimed at forcing the enemy into submission by destroying its leadership. This failed and the bombing continued; by the end of the first week, thousands of Tomahawk missiles and smart bombs had crashed into their targets in and around Baghdad. This devastation was made even more dramatic as television channels showed a continuous display of orange flames leaping into the night sky. Then, in direct contrast, as daylight appeared, a calm descended on the streets of Baghdad, and people went about their daily business.

In the first week, the British took the oil fields in the south, saving them from destruction and claiming that the wealth of the oil would be used to rebuild a new and better Iraq. The port of Umm Qasr was secured, allowing the first ships laden with humanitarian aid to be brought in. As I write, the southern city of Basra has also been taken, although isolated skirmishes continue to bog down the British troops around Iraq's second city.

From the onset, the Americans pushed directly to Baghdad and within a few days were just one hundred miles short of their destination – then they became bogged down. The military claimed they were not halted by the enemy, but were simply waiting for their lengthy supply column to catch up. From the point of view of an objective observer, even if this is true, it looks likely that American troops will have to clear Baghdad street by street.

Iraqi resistance has been varied. The Iraqi military commanders continue to appear on TV boasting about how they have halted the invasion; at the same time, they show how missiles have killed hundreds of innocent Iraqi civilians. They seem more intent on fighting a propaganda war than actually engaging the enemy. Iraqi resistance on the ground has been wide ranging. While thousands of Iraqi soldiers have surrendered, others have sought to fight to the end. Unlike the Gulf war in 1991, where the Iraqis were simply removed from Kuwait, this time they are fighting for their home country.

The media war on both sides has been unremitting. The media caravan has followed this war from the very start, almost every military unit having its own 'embedded' reporter or television crew attached to it. Anchor news teams at home press their field reporters for ever more information, while the tabloids use any and all dramatic stories to sell newspapers. In part, this has led the general public to believe the war is not going well. Press coverage of American and British dead being shipped back home for burial or hospital treatment has raised concern, yet compared to other wars these numbers are small.

What will be the outcome of this war? Despite the lack of backing from the UN, America has gone ahead with the war, thereby showing itself to be the most powerful nation on earth. It has the power and might to stand alone and by its actions has shown that it no longer considers the views voiced by the UN to be of paramount importance. We have yet to see if America will be satisfied with winning the war against Saddam Hussein. Will it then seek to invade North Korea? Or Syria? Or Iran?

The loser in all this is the UN, for it has shown that it is unwilling to enforce its own resolutions. It is true to say that if the United Nations had had its way, the only winner from the situation would have been Saddam Hussein. Almost everyone agreed that he should be removed from power, but few nations were keen to take direct action. The UN weapons inspectors would have hunted around Iraq for several more months, found nothing of significance, and been withdrawn. This would have left Saddam Hussein free to continue his despotic treatment of his own people. If the UN is to regain any ground in the future then it must become fully involved in the humanitarian effort that will be required after the war.

The other loser in this is the European Union (EU) and the NATO alliance. Countries America thought she could count on, such as France and Germany, have also isolated themselves, not just politically but also economically. How can the EU survive when there are such deep divisions between four of its leading nations? NATO has also faulted. When it was proposed that Turkey should supply bases and air cover for any invading forces, a huge international debate ensued, eventually resolved by Turkey itself where the parliament voted not to allow any invasion of Iraq via Turkey.

As I write this final episode, American forces are about to enter Baghdad. There is the threat that in a final fit of desperation, Iraq will use chemical weapons. American and coalition forces are well prepared for such an attack, but I fear the people of Baghdad are not. In such a case, a simple shift in the wind direction could cause innumerable casualties. While I have no doubt that America and her allies will win this war, at least territorially, whether they succeed in winning the hearts and minds of the Iraqi people is another matter. What happens if the people of Iraq don't want to be liberated? Will America simply enforce its will? It is hard to envisage an American-style Iraq being allowed to develop in the midst of so many Arab nations. While some neighbouring nations may complain, few have the power to resist American military might.

Perhaps most important of all, the war and its resolution will do little to improve Muslim–Christians relations. Arab governments may be unable to confront America militarily, but terrorist retaliation tactics will be inevitable. The war against Iraq has provided yet another excuse for the terrorist organisations to attack the west. In doing so, I fear that America, Britain and Israel will bear the brunt. Whatever the outcome, terrorism is certain to increase.

APPENDIX A: TERRORIST ORGANISATIONS

Most of the terrorist organisations and revolutionary groups listed below are still very active today. Some, such as HAMAS, are extremely active while others may only carry out an attack every six months. All achieve the same end result – they kill. For the most part, those that die as a result of terrorism are innocent.

To give some perspective, the total number of members for all those organisations listed below is around 30,000 worldwide. That's roughly the same number of people killed every year as a result of terrorist actions.

1. Abu Nidal Organisation (ANO) – worldwide
2. Abu Sayyaf Group (ASG) – Philippines
3. Breton Liberation Army (ARB) – France
4. Armed Islamic Group (GIA)
5. Armed Forces of National Liberation (FALN)
6. Armenian Secret Army for the Liberation of Armenia (ASALA)
7. Army of National Liberation (ELN)
8. Aum Supreme Truth (Aum) – Japan
9. Basque Fatherland and Liberty (ETA) – Spain
10. Devrimci Sol (Revolutionary Left)
11. Democratic Front for the Liberation of Palestine (DFLP)
12. Front de la Liberation de la Bretagne (FLB)
13. Front de la Liberation de la Cote de Somalie (FLCS)
14. National Front for the Liberation of Corsica (FNLC)
15. Al-Gamaa't al-Islamiyya (Islamic Group, IG)
16. HAMAS (Islamic Resistance Movement)
17. Harakat ul-Mujaheddin (HUM)
18. Hizballah (Party of God)
19. Islamic Resistance Movement
20. Jaish-e-Mohammed – India
21. Japanese Red Army (JRA)

22. Kach and Kahane Chai – Israel
23. Kurdistan Workers' Party (PKK)
24. Liberation Tigers of Tamil Eelam (LTTE)
25. The Lord's Resistance Army (LRA) – Uganda
26. Mujaheddin-e Khalq Organisation (MEK or MKO)
27. The Palestine Islamic Jihad (PIJ)
28. Palestine Liberation Front (PLF)
29. Popular Front for the Liberation of Palestine (PFLP)
30. Popular Front for the Liberation of Palestine-General Command (PFLP-GC)
31. Al-Qaida – Worldwide network
32. Revolutionary Armed Forces of Colombia (FARC)
33. Revolutionary Organisation 17 November (17 November)
34. Revolutionary People's Liberation Party/Front (DHKP/C)
35. Revolutionary People's Struggle (ELA)
36. Revolutionary United Front (RUF) – Sierra Leone
37. Sendero Luminoso (Shining Path, SL)
38. Tupac Amaru Revolutionary Movement (MRTA)
39. Alex Boncayao Brigade (ABB)
40. Continuity Irish Republican Army (CIRA)
41. Irish Republican Army (IRA)
42. Islamic Movement of Uzbekistan (IMU)
43. Loyalist Volunteer Force (LVF)
44. New People's Army (NPA)
45. Orange Volunteers (OV)
46. The Party of Democratic Kampuchea (Khmer Rouge)
47. Provisional Irish Republican Army (PIRA)
48. Qibla and People Against Gangsterism and Drugs (PAGAD)
49. Real Irish Republican Army (rIRA)
50. Red Hand Defenders (RHD)
51. Sikh Terrorism
52. Sudanese People's Liberation Army (SPLA)
53. Ulster Freedom Fighters (UFF)
54. Ulster Volunteer Force (UVF)
55. Zviadists – Russia

APPENDIX B: MAJOR TERRORIST INCIDENTS, 1970–2002

6 September 1970 Members of the PFLP hijack three aircraft and fly them to a desert airstrip known as Dawson's Field in Jordan. Although all the hostages are released unarmed, all three aircraft are blown up on 12 September. The event triggers a massive backlash from the Jordanian authorities and many hundreds of Palestinians died. The Palestinians retaliate with the formation of the group known as 'Black September'.

21 July 1972 An IRA bomb kills 11 people and injured 130 in Belfast, Northern Ireland. Ten days later, three more IRA car bombs leave six dead in the village of Claudy.

5 September 1972 Munich Olympic Massacre – eight terrorists from the Palestinian 'Black September' group seize eleven Israeli athletes in the Olympic Village. A bungled rescue attempt by West German authorities ends with nine of the hostages and five terrorists being killed.

3 February 1976 A school bus containing 30 children is hijacked by four members of the FLCS (Front de la Cote des Somalis) close to Djibouti. The rebels force the driver to take them towards the Somali border, a distance of 180 k.m., where the terrorists wait to negotiate. On the afternoon of the following day, snipers from the French GIGN fire on the terrorists, killing four out of five of them. The remaining terrorist manages to kill one of the children before he is killed.

27 June 1976 A combined group of members of the German Baader-Meinhof Group and the Popular Front for the Liberation of Palestine (PFLP) seizes an Air France airliner and its 258 passengers. They force the plane to land in Uganda, where on 3 July Israeli commandos successfully rescue the passengers.

23 May 1977 A train travelling between Assen and Groningen in Holland is hijacked by nine Moluccan terrorists, who seize 51 hostages. At the same time 110 hostages, mostly children, are seized at an elementary school at Bovensmilde. The stand-off lasts for three weeks until Dutch marines assault the train, killing six of the terrorists while the other three surrender. Two hostages, who panicked when the firing began, are killed.

13 October 1977 Lufthansa flight LH181 is hijacked by four members of the PFLP, while flying from Palma Majorca to Frankfurt. The aircraft flies around the Middle East until it finally touches down in Mogadishu. The pilot has been murdered in Aden, which forces the West Germans into action. A team of German GSG9 accompanied by two British SAS storm the aircraft killing three of the terrorists and seriously wounding the fourth.

16 March 1978 The Italian Prime Minister, Aldo Moro, is seized by the Red Brigade and assassinated 55 days later.

4 November 1979 Iranian extremists seize the U.S. embassy in Tehran and take 66 American diplomats hostage. An American rescue attempt ends in disaster and the loss of many American servicemen. Most of the hostages are not released until 20 January 1981.

20 November 1979 200 Islamic terrorists seize the Grand Mosque in Mecca, Saudi Arabia, taking thousands of pilgrims hostage. An assault by Saudi and French security forces eventually retakes the shrine, but only after some 250 people are killed and 600 wounded.

30 April 1980 Six armed gunmen from the organisation Liberation of Khuzestan from Iran enter the Iranian Embassy in London taking 26 people hostage. After several days of negotiations, in which five hostages are released, the embassy is assaulted by the SAS. Two of the hostages die at the hands of the terrorists but the remain nineteen are released unarmed. Of the six terrorists, only one survives.

6 October 1981   Egyptian President Anwar Sadat is assassinated while reviewing troops. Members of the Takfir Wal-Hajira sect are held to be responsible.

18 April 1983   63 people, including the CIA's Middle East director, are killed, and 120 injured when Islamic Jihad rams a 400-pound suicide truck-bomb into the U.S. Embassy in Beirut, Lebanon.

23 October 1983   Islamic Jihad carries out a second suicide bombing of Marine Barracks in Beirut. The truck, packed with 12,000 pounds of high explosive, kills 242 Americans. A simultaneous suicide attack on a French barracks results in a further 58 French soldiers being killed.

12 April 1984   18 American servicemen are killed and 83 civilians are injured in a bomb attack on a restaurant near a U.S. Air Force Base in Torrejon, Spain. Hizballah claim responsibility.

5 June 1984   More than 100 people die when Indian security forces assault the Golden Temple in Amritsar, which had been seized by Sikh terrorists.

31 October 1984   The Indian Prime Minister Indira Gandhi is shot and killed by members of her security force.

23 June 1985   An Air India Boeing 747 is destroyed over the Atlantic when a bomb on board detonates. The 329 people aboard are all killed. Kashmiri terrorists are blamed for the attack.

30 September 1985   Four Soviet diplomats are kidnapped in Beirut by Sunni terrorists. After one diplomat is killed, the Russians retaliate by kidnapping relatives of the terrorists and mutilating them. The three remaining diplomats are later released.

7 October 1985   The cruise ship *Achille Lauro* is seized by Palestinian terrorists while sailing in the Mediterranean. They hold the 700 passengers hostage. One American passenger is murdered before the terrorists make good their escape.

5 April 1986   Two American soldiers are killed, and a further 79 injured, when Libyan terrorists detonate a bomb in a nightclub in West Berlin.

21 December 1988   A bomb is detonated aboard Pan-Am flight 103 as it flies over Lockerbie, Scotland. All 259 passengers and crew are killed, as well as 11 people on the ground. Libyan terrorists are thought to be responsible.

17 March 1992   A huge bomb blast completely destroys the Israeli Embassy in Buenos Aires, Argentina. 29 are killed and a further 242 wounded. Hizballah claim responsibility.

26 February 1993   Followers of Umar Abd al-Rahman, an Egyptian cleric who preached in New York City, organise the bombing of the city's World Trade Center. A car bomb placed in an underground garage kills six and injures more than a thousand.

25 February 1994   Baruch Goldstein, a Jewish right-wing extremist and an American citizen, machine-guns Moslem worshippers at a mosque in the West Bank town of Hebron. Goldstein manages to kill 29 Palestinians and wounds another 150 before he is overpowered and beaten to death.

24 December 1994   Members of the Armed Islamic Group seize an Air France flight to Algeria. The aircraft then flies to Paris where members of the GIGN carry out a successful assault. Four terrorists are killed during the rescue.

20 March 1995   Twelve people are killed and several thousand injured when the Aum Shinri-kyu cult release Sarin nerve gas in a packed subway station in the centre of Tokyo. A second attack takes place in the Yokohama subway.

19 April 1995   The Federal Building in Oklahoma City is destroyed when right-wing extremists Timothy McVeigh and Terry Nichols detonate a massive truck bomb. The devastation costs the lives of 166 people and injures hundreds more.

31 January 1996   Members of the Liberation Tigers of Tamil Eelam (LTTE) ram a truck packed with explosives into the Central

Bank in downtown Colombo, Sri Lanka. The blast kills 90 civilians and injures more than 1,400 others.

26 February 1996   A Hamas suicide bomber detonates his bomb on a bus in Jerusalem, killing himself and 26 other people. 80 more are injured.

15 June 1996   The IRA detonates a large truck bomb in the centre of the main Manchester shopping precinct. Although no one is killed, 206 people are injured. The bomb causes widespread property damage which takes millions of pounds and three years to repair.

25 June 1996   A bomb hidden in a fuel truck is detonated outside the American services housing complex, Khobar Towers, in Dhahran, Saudi Arabia. 19 American military personnel are killed and 515 wounded.

20 July 1996   The Spanish terrorist group ETA continues its campaign against foreign tourists when a bomb explodes at Tarragona International Airport in Reus, Spain. No one is killed but 35 people are wounded.

17 December 1996   The Tupac Amaru Revolutionary Movement (MRTA) seizes the Japanese Ambassador's residence in Lima, Peru during a party. Many foreign diplomats are among the several hundred people taken hostage. After months of negotiations, the Peruvian government successfully assaults the embassy, killing all the rebels, one hostage and two police officers.

17 November 1997   Members of Al-Gama'at al-Islamiyya (IG) walk into the Hatshepsut Temple in the Valley of the Kings near Luxor and open fire with automatic weapons on the many tourists. 58 tourists and 4 Egyptians die, with many others wounded. The terrorists are pushed into the mountains nearby, where they eventually commit suicide.

7 August 1998   A bomb explodes at the rear entrance of the US embassy in Nairobi, Kenya, killing 12 American citizens, 32 Foreign Service Nationals (FSNs) and 247 Kenyan citizens. More than 5,000 are injured in the blast. A second bomb goes off at the US embassy in Dar es Salaam, Tanzania, just seconds later. This results in 10 dead and 80 injured. Supporters of Osama Bin Laden are thought to be responsible.

15 August 1998   The Real IRA explodes a 500-pound car bomb outside a local courthouse in the central shopping area of Omagh, Northern Ireland. 29 people are killed and a further 330 injured.

1 March 1999   About 150 armed Hutu rebels attack three tourist camps in Uganda, killing four Ugandans, and abducting sixteen tourists. Two of the three Americans taken are killed, along with six other hostages.

12 October 2000   The American warship *U.S.S. Cole* is attacked in Aden, Yemen, by a small dinghy packed with explosives. The dingy rams into the warship, killing 17 sailors and wounding 38 others. Supporters of Osama Bin Laden are suspected.

9 August 2001   Members of Hamas claim responsibility for planting a bomb in a Jerusalem pizza restaurant. The explosion results in 15 deaths and 90 injuries.

11 September 2001   Supporters of Osama Bin Laden's Al Qaeda organisation   hijack and crash two commercial aircraft into the twin towers of the World Trade Center in New York, destroying the complex. A third aircraft is hijacked and flown into the Pentagon, Washington D.C. A fourth hijacked aircraft crash lands in southern Pennsylvania; it is thought that its target was somewhere in Washington. More than 5,000 people die as a result of these acts.

12 October 2002   An hour before midnight, two huge explosions tear apart several bars and nightclubs situated in Kuta Beach, Bali, Indonesia. The two blasts kill more than 180 people and injure 300 more; many of the victims are young Australian tourists. It is suspected that the bombs were planted by a radical Islamic group, Jemaah Islamiyah.

23 October 2002   50 Chechen guerrillas – 32 men and 18 women – storm a Moscow Theatre, taking all 700 members of the audience hostage. 41 hostages, including children, Muslims, citizens of Georgia and a pregnant woman, are released within the first few hours, in exchange for a televised statement by the rebels. Although more hostages are released, the Russian authorities decide to assault the theatre using knock-out gas. The scheme misfires and 115 hostages die as a result of the rescue.

ACKNOWLEDGEMENTS

This book is not intended to be a judgment, in either the legal or historical sense; it is little more than a reconstruction of events. Help in preparing it has come from many sources, not least many Palestinians who do not wish to be named. My thanks also go to my research assistant Julie Pembridge, who has worked on the book for over a year. I would also like to express my gratitude to Andrew Howell, the CEO of BCB International Ltd, for use of their extensive archive material.

No one writes a book completely by himself – we all need a mentor, a critic and, in my case, someone to check my grammar. Rod Green made sure that no small detail was overlooked, and finally cut the book into shape.

Finally, my sincere thanks go to all at Virgin Books, especially Mark Wallace, who gave me the breathing space when I so desperately needed it.

PICTURE CREDITS

The photographs in this book are reproduced with kind permission from the following copyright holders:

Focus Magazine, Germany
Military Picture Library (Pentagon)
Arab World Press.
Kurdish Forum
Lebanese Wire
Progress Publishing – Moscow
Graham Lewis Pictures
Barry Davies

In sourcing the photographs for this book, where the originals were not held by the author, every reasonable effort was made to contact the original copyright holder and obtain permission in writing for the use of the photographs.

INDEX